FURNITURE PROJECTS WITH THE ROUTER

FURNITURE PROJECTS WITH THE ROUTER

Kevin Ley

GUILD OF MASTER CRAFTSMAN PUBLICATIONS LTD

This collection first published 2002 by
Guild of Master Craftsman Publications Ltd
Castle Place, 166 High Street,
Lewes, East Sussex BN7 1XU

Principal illustrations by Ian Hall and Simon Rodway

ISBN 1 86108 345 9

A catalogue record for this book is available from the British Library.

Cover photography by Kevin Ley

Colour origination by Universal Graphics (Singapore)
Printed and bound in Singapore by Stamford Press Pte Ltd

CONTENTS

NOTE

Though every effort has been made to ensure that the information in this book was accurate at the time of writing, it is inevitable that prices, specifications and availability of some of the products mentioned will change from time to time. Readers are therefore urged to contact manufacturers or suppliers for up-to-date information before ordering.

MEASUREMENTS

Although care has been taken to ensure that the metric measurements are true and accurate, they are only conversions from imperial; they have been rounded up or down to the nearest millimetre, or to the nearest convenient equivalent in cases where the imperial measurements themselves are only approximate. When following the projects, use either the metric or the imperial measurements; do not mix units.

Detailed conversion tables are provided on pages 114–15.

INTRODUCTION

It is not necessary to have a great talent in order to make beautiful pieces of furniture – just the desire to do it and the time and patience to learn the basic skills. The piece does not need to be complicated or technically difficult to make, in order to be good. The workshop can be a garage, converted on a permanent or even temporary basis. Portable power tools have never been cheaper or better, and remove much of the drudgery entailed. Routers make a huge number of previously skilled hand operations easy. Biscuit jointers and modern glues make for quick, accurate, strong joints, and belt and orbital sanders enable an excellent finish to be achieved. And there is nothing wrong with using these labour-saving devices – if the Georgian or Shaker makers had had them they would have used them, and made even more beautiful furniture. Indeed, the Shakers are credited with inventing the first circular saws.

The essence of the whole business is the wood: its strength and weakness, beauty and wilfulness. You must learn to work with it and not against it – not for nothing is the term 'going against the grain' a part of our language. Choose carefully the right species for the task, and use it economically and sympathetically to get the most out of it. Use your judgement to choose the best-figured pieces for the most prominent places, and let the natural beauty of the wood speak for itself.

Remember it has a mind of its own and will punish you if treated badly. If working on a piece intermittently, remember to leave the wood stacked flat and supported on sticks between sessions. This ensures that moisture loss or take-up is even over all faces and there is less risk of warping or twisting in your absence.

There is sometimes an assumption that all the furniture in a room should 'match' – why? Have different pieces in different woods for variety and interest. Avoid using stains – they mask the true beauty of the wood, hiding the figure and subtlety of the tonal range in every piece. Good, clear protective finishes like Danish oil, or the new water-based acrylics, enhance the natural beauty and increase practicality in use.

Try to use timber from certified managed sources, but remember that far more deforestation is caused by the slash-and-burn techniques used to create short-term pastures for beefburger production than by timber felled for productive use. A mature tree harvested at the right point in its growth lives on as a useful piece of furniture.

Fitness for purpose is paramount in these projects – what use is a drinks cabinet too short to hold a bottle of your favourite malt? There are no cutting lists given, so the dimensions can be changed to suit your exact purpose without fear of any 'knock-on' effect on the list measurements. Producing the cutting list is an important part of the making process in its own right, getting the maker right into the heart of the project.

When making these pieces I have made some mistakes, which I hope to help you avoid, and in the writing up I have sometimes seen a short cut, or a better way to go, so I give you the sanitised version – thereby justifying the expense of the book!

Use these projects for ideas – change anything to fit your own requirements. Above all, enjoy the making.

DEWALT POWER SHOP
CLAMPGUIDE
trend

Part One
PRACTICALITIES

The author in his present workshop

My workshop

Making the transition from fly-boy to furniture fabricator

During many postings in the Royal Air Force Regiment I never referred to the small building next to the married quarter as anything other than a workshop – then nobody would get any silly ideas about putting a car in it. When my son was young, we were at a neighbour's house when he saw that their garage was empty. 'How does he make things, Daddy?' he asked. 'He can't, son,' I replied sadly, 'He's a fighter pilot'. 'That's right,' said my neighbour, going along with the joking, 'I can't see too well.' He then walked straight into a door, later insisting that it was for effect and nothing at all to do with the drink, and the bleeding would soon stop.

Service life was great, but the need to put down roots and get some stability was strong. We took the plunge and bought a derelict farmhouse in a Yorkshire village, close to the RAF Regiment Depot at Catterick. Some pretty serious 'making things' had to happen then, to get it habitable. I used any room we weren't living in – which at first was most of them – as a workshop, moving on as the room was brought into service. Eventually the house was finished and a garage block was built, with one double garage designated as my workshop and another next to it for cars. At least at first...

Crate Expectations

Now I started to make some fashionable pine furniture for the house. I had access to plenty of reclaimed pine in the form of packing crates and was able to make a lot of functional stuff! I soon started using 'proper' wood and developed a real love for

"I started using 'proper' wood and developed a real love for it, almost for its own sake."

it, almost for its own sake. I still hate using any design that detracts from, or any finish which covers, its natural beauty. I soaked up furniture designs wherever I found them: books, magazines, museums, shop windows or catalogues. I was often more interested in the furniture used in the sets of films and plays than in the plot.

I also really enjoyed working out how to make things and stretching my abilities, or sometimes having to make design features – which is just a euphemism for alterations – to get a result with my limited experience. Other people liked some of my work and commissioned me to make pieces for them. I had the option to retire from the RAF at age 44 and decided, with the arrogance of ignorance, to be a professional woodworker. Like a good soldier I did what reconnaissance and preparation I could in the years before I left. Alan Peters's *Cabinetmaking: The Professional Approach* and Ernest Joyce's *The Technique of Furniture Making* figured high on my list of bedtime reading. Cometh the hour, cometh the man, so when de-mob finally arrived I had developed both my business and bench skills and a personal style of furniture which owed much to Shaker and Arts and Crafts – I even had a rudimentary customer base.

Porsche To Shove

The workshop had expanded into part of the garage next to it but by now I had acquired the standard-issue mid-life crisis Porsche, so that had to have a home as well. Military life leaves one cold and wet at various times and places and I didn't like it. Neither does wood – a perfect excuse for a namby-pamby warm and dry workshop. I also understood that tools need to be clean, dry and slightly oiled – again, the perfect cover. I realised I was going to enjoy my new career.

A sawdust burner, insulation, draught-proofing, a dehumidifier and plenty of lights were installed in the workshop to bring it up to standard. Much later on I decided to cover the concrete floor with flooring-grade chipboard, fixed with No Nails glue. It only took a couple of hours, cost practically nothing, and made an enormous difference to the function and comfort of the place. Neither furniture nor machines slide well on concrete and a wooden floor is much kinder to dropped items – especially edge tools! The business went well – I had decided that to be a self-employed furniture maker I needed competency at a range of skills, apart from woodwork. I learned to value my time; that an idyllic country

A man who understands tools need to be clean, dry and slightly oiled

The wood store, with dehumifier

My old garage workshop

workshop does not have a passing trade; that the hand that does the books runs the business and that half the money spent on advertising is wasted – but which half? All this, and many other truisms to boot.

Publicity Be Damned!

A lot of angles for free publicity were tried – successfully – but analysing the results was even more important. For example, I got far more business from a free display in a local building society window than from pictures and reviews of my furniture in national glossy magazines such as *Homes & Gardens*. A ten-minute slot on local TV news featuring, among other things, a bureau in French walnut with twelve secret compartments, netted two farmers trying to sell me fallen trees! But it was a photo of a lady's writing desk in one of the glossies that got me a nice order in sycamore and fumed oak for an Arab sheikh's London house. The local paper ran the story – the furniture was ideal for black-and-white photos – and the feature was seen by Len Markam, who is a freelance writer. He did an article about me for Issue 2 of the then new *Furniture and Cabinetmaking* magazine. Paul Richardson, then a mere mortal, liked some of my stuff and asked me to write an article. I initially resisted – I had left the RAF to avoid staff work, which is just about all that is on offer at a certain age and rank. However, his silver tongue and some portraits of the Queen eventually persuaded me. I soon found that much of the drudgery of writing is removed by a word processor and that I think at about the same speed I can two-finger type. The diversification and contact with like-minded people was welcome, so there I was writing on a regular basis for *Furniture & Cabinetmaking* and now for *The Router* as well!

Man Of Harlech

In 1997 my wife Yvonne and I were looking around the Welsh Marches, half-considering an eventual move to the area, when I spotted the perfect workshop right next door to a nice house. This was too good an opportunity to miss so the decision was made and we sold up and moved. I had learned my lesson the hard way – this time the workshop was set up first! That enabled me to fulfil my order-book commitments and do all the domestic DIY stuff as well. This workshop is on the first floor over a double photo-studio/garage. One half of the ground floor is soon to be converted to a painting studio for Yvonne. The steps up are inconvenient but there is plenty of natural light, it is well insulated and there is a good wood store in the loft above. The floor area is at a premium so I tried to use the space above and below as much as I could.

A central dust extractor was situated on the ground floor with the 100mm (4in) ducting running under the workshop floor to all the main machines. Even the large seventies-style hi-fi speakers have the grilles set into the ceiling over the workbenches and the cabinet bodies in the loft above! The assembly and working benches, both 2.4m (8ft) long, are either side of a radial-arm saw which enables long lengths to be cross cut easily. The planer-thicknesser and table saw are side by side, with tables of the same height, enabling them to augment each other. They are centrally placed to allow an 8ft sheet or board to go over them.

Sycamore and fumed oak chest

Ley's lines

- *Norwood 10in table saw*
- *Norwood 12in planer-thicknesser*
- *Electra Beckum BS 450 band-saw with 12in depth of cut*
- *DeWalt 1250 radial-arm saw*
- *APT WV 2000 dust extractor*
- *Microclene air filter*
- *Pulsafe respirator helmet*
- *Stihl chainsaw with selection of bars and chains*
- *Elu DB180 lathe*
- *Elu MOF 177 heavy-duty router*
- *Trend T5 router*
- *Nu-Tool CH10 drill press*
- *Makita biscuit jointer*
- *Leroy Somer wet-and-dry grindstone*
- *Ashley Iles chisel set*
- *Power drills and screwdrivers*
- *Selection of hand tools*

Dimension Discipline

Working discipline is essential in a small workshop. One piece is worked on at a time, with only in-use timber in the shop. I also have to be ruthless with off-cuts and keep everything tidy. The workshop is warm, light and cosy to work in and the stairs even remind me that furniture has to get in and out of clients' houses. If it won't come out of the workshop it probably wouldn't get into a house! I suppose I could always use more space – but then who couldn't? All in all I enjoy this workshop the most out of all those I have had. It is comfortable, convenient, secure, and working in it is a real pleasure.

What with new business, repeat orders from my existing clients, making stuff for our own use – Yvonne is getting involved with our own furniture designs now – and writing for GMC, I seem to have a nice balance between selling, making and writing. What more could a man want? ●

Modern routers have many excellent features, so how do they compare with the old favourites?

A CHANGE OF PARTNER

The last time my old Elu MOF 98 died on me, I thought it just needed another set of carbon brushes for the motor. Surely enough, a closer inspection revealed that they were worn right down. I went to my 'spares' drawer, which houses endless replacements of consumables such as drive belts and brushes, on the grounds that a machine only breaks when you are using it.

However, within a few weeks these new brushes that I had just installed also wore out, although this time I was lucky enough to be coming to an end of a heavy routing session. Unfortunately I hadn't found time to replace my stock, so I decided to pay a visit to a workshop that specialises in motor rewinds and other electrical renovations. I wanted to know why my brushes had worn out so quickly. After a brief look they established that one of the commutator segments (part of the armature) had broken off and the edges of the resultant slot were chewing the brushes up.

REPAIR

I used to get my Elu, Black & Decker and DeWalt spares from the service centre at the B&D factory at Spennymore, not too far from where I used to live in North Yorkshire. They no longer provide this service but it has been taken over by BMJ Power of Middlesbrough, who seem able to supply just about anything from stock, and by return of post. All it takes is a telephone call and a credit-card number.

Like many people who have been lucky enough to have owned an Elu router, I was very attached to mine as it had been the workhorse of my workshop for almost my entire professional career. I am not a tool collector, and if any of my apparatus should perish, I usually replace it with the same.

Several things needed to be replaced – the complete armature, brushes and while I was at it, the top and bottom bearings, which were several years old. The total cost was pretty hefty, so I asked about a replacement or a trade-in. To my utter dismay, I could not buy an Elu MOF 98 as, like all its siblings, it had been replaced by a brand-new DeWalt model.

I worked out that even if I rebuilt my old machine something else could go wrong, resulting in further expense and inconvenience. A new, younger machine would have several desirable features such as micro adjustment, soft start, and a warranty. So I took a closer look at a potential replacement.

I would have to assess the potential of any replacement before I could commit myself to a long-term relationship! I had a few questions that needed answers – would we be compatible, would I constantly be making comparisons with my old partner, would I call it 'Elu' in moments of stress or passion, or even in my sleep? More importantly, would it fit my router table and range of cutters?

REPLACE

I had never owned the ubiquitous Elu MOF 96 light router, as I used my MOF 98 for even the most delicate hand-held work. At the Axminster show a couple of years before, however, I had tried the Trend T5 and was so impressed by its ease of control, accuracy, and value for money that I got one. It provided me with solid back-up and meant that I wouldn't have to change any of the essential settings if I needed to use a router in the middle of a run. It also conveniently fitted my Elu table, although the maximum collet size was only 8mm, which suited its power.

As I was so satisfied with the T5, I contacted Trend to see if they had a suitable replacement for my heavy Elu. Surely enough, they did – the 1800W T9. It had all the modern features, fitted

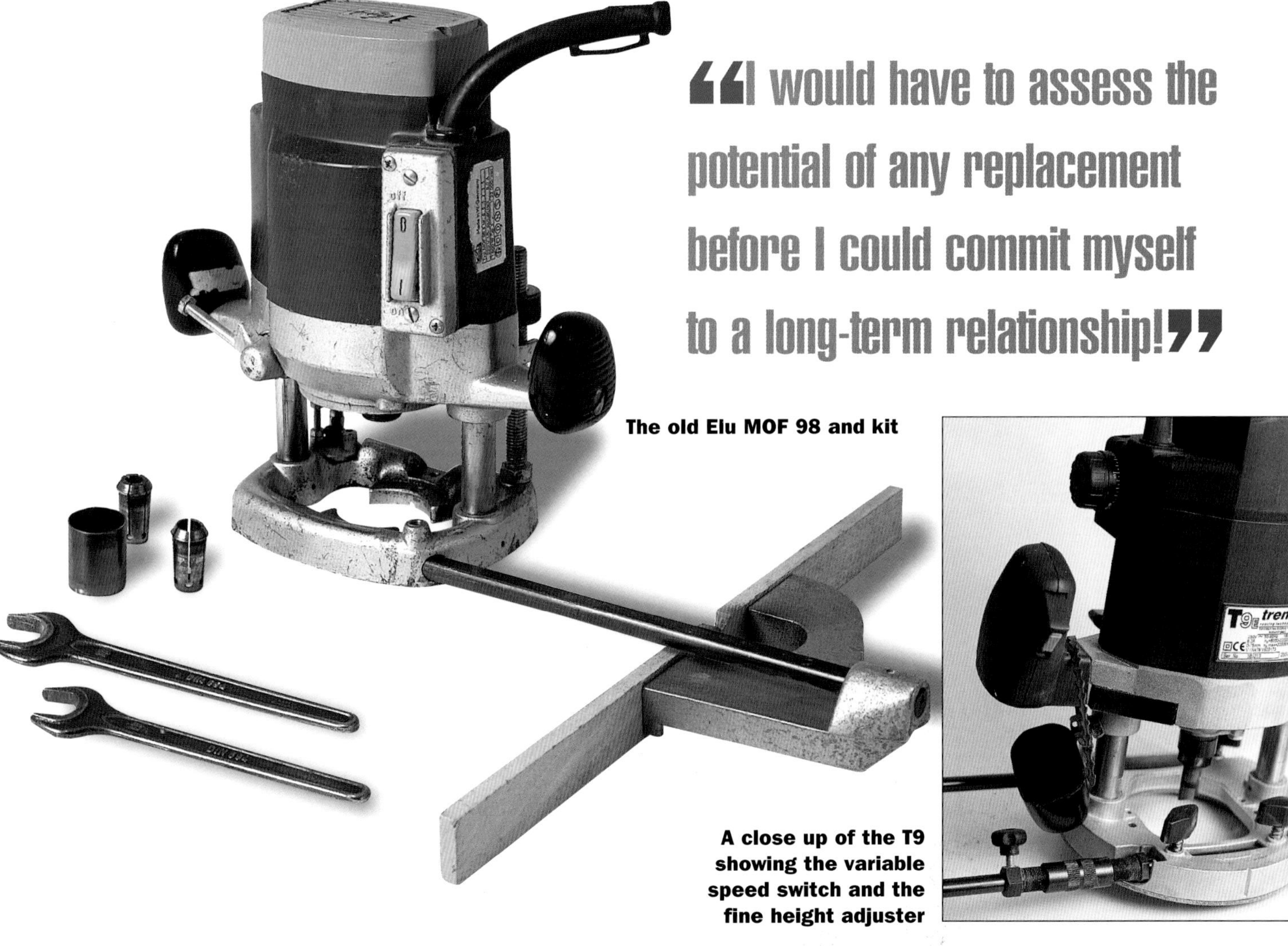

"I would have to assess the potential of any replacement before I could commit myself to a long-term relationship!"

The old Elu MOF 98 and kit

A close up of the T9 showing the variable speed switch and the fine height adjuster

my table, and its collets fitted my range of cutters, which had ½in, ⅜in, ¼in and 8mm shanks. The price was only twice as much as repairing the Elu. So, without hesitation, I ordered the Trend.

THE HONEYMOON

The new machine arrived during my summer break, which was ideal as the workshop was clean, tidy, and empty. All the benches were clear so I unpacked it, read the manual, and had a good play. Once I started to use it I realised how far things had improved over the last 15 years!

INSTRUCTION MANUAL

The instruction manual is clear, well written, and in English, without each page being translated into 10 other languages including Swahili! The diagrams are easy to understand and the purpose of all applications and provided accessories, is accurately described. The parts are clearly named and listed with reference numbers to assist with future identification. A catalogue of all the available cutters and accessories, as well as other Trend products, and a routing guide, which gives a huge amount of useful information, are included in the pack.

THE MOTOR

Whenever I had switched my old Elu on, I certainly knew it had started – there was a terrifying thud as it went from zero to 20,000 revs in a millisecond and, if hand-held, a firm grip with both hands was most definitely required. The T9 has a soft start which gently but swiftly accelerates to full speed within a couple of seconds and with hardly any vibration at all. It also has variable speed control, which is useful with some of my larger-diameter cutters.

The motor switch has a dead man's safety facility, so that the safety catch must be disengaged and the switch held on – if you let go it switches off. There is a trigger-locking cap, available as an optional extra for use in table mode. This should only be used in conjunction with a 'no volt release' safety switch.

The MOF 98 had a straight on/off rocker switch which could be left switched on, and it caught me out a couple of times when I plugged it into the mains!

SETTINGS

The T9 side fence has considerably more reach than the Elu, and a micro adjuster. Over the years I had got used to the 'hit and miss' method of side-fence adjustment and I could get the accuracy I required eventually – but the Trend is a quantum leap in convenience and speed. I also find the extra reach very useful.

There are extra-length side-fence rods available but they only give another 50mm (2in) of reach. I did check with Trend and I was assured that this is not a misprint – just an anomaly of production and manufacture. I can't really see the point in having both, although I would prefer a choice when initially buying.

The dial depth adjustment is another joy to use – the old method of a graduated scale with a pointer was OK as far as it went, but I did most of my setting using the different-diameter cutter shanks, between the depth stop rod and the three turret stops. The dial system allows initial setting down to a fraction of a millimetre, very fine adjustment and repeatable settings.

A fine height adjuster is provided as a standard extra with the router, which can be very helpful in table use. I have fitted mine permanently, even though it does make it awkward to stand the router upside down to change cutters. This machine is used mainly on the table, and it is possible to hold it upside down in a vice or change cutters with it on its side.

CUTTERS

Trend has a huge range of cutters and accessories to fit its own and many other makes of router. One of the most useful accessories I have is the quick-clamping guide batten, for use out of range of the side fence.

When I needed a deep-cutting 4mm straight cutter to use Tanselli wafers as

1

2

3

Photo 1 **Using an extra-long fence with a fine adjuster on the T9** Photo 2 **The Elu and an old home-made wooden batten guide** Photo 3 **Using the Elu to trim doors with a wooden batten guide**

loose tenons, I found a spiral 'up cutter' which also gives better chip clearance.

Two collets (a ¼in and ½in) come with the router and all the other sizes are available as extras, so I ordered an 8mm and a ⅜in. I also found that my old Elu collets will fit the Trend collet nut, but the Elu collet nut is difficult to tighten and loosen on the T9. I liked the spindle lock and one-spanner cutter-changing system, which is similar to the T5's.

DUST SPOUT

Trend has addressed the serious problem of dust extraction from the machine, by providing a bolt-on dust spout of clear plastic. This enables a vacuum hose to be attached and dust extracted without obscuring vision. The extraction point is close to the cutter, making the system very efficient.

TEMPLATE GUIDE

Included is a 30mm guide bush and centring pin for template use. This can be fitted easily, works well and a full range of different-diameter guide bushes are available as extras.

ACCESSORIES

Trend has a huge range of accessories covering all aspects of routing from humble DIY stuff to the highly professional CNC SMART machining centre, for computer-aided design to computer-aided manufacture applications. This is certainly a catalogue to keep in hand for reference – if you need it they have probably got it. Some of the tradesmen's time-saving jigs, such as the floor access system, lock and hinge jigs, and staircase housing templates, must be a godsend.

NIGGLES

I tried very hard but could only find a couple of minor flaws. The fine height adjuster was very difficult to fit, and needed to be internally de-burred with a fine emery cloth, and the captive nuts on the dust spout weren't – but that was sorted with a spot of superglue.

ALL'S WELL THAT ENDS WELL

There has been a vast improvement in routers over the last 15 years. I only tested the Trend, but I'm sure other machines have some or all of the features I have found so useful. As you can tell, I'm more than happy with my new partner and don't see any affairs on the horizon!

Its user-friendly nature, improved accuracy and health and safety improvements are all to be unreservedly welcomed. Another advantage is that Trend, who stock a full range of accessories and spares, are based here in the UK so if I do have a problem it can be dealt with.

I do miss my Elu – gone is the white-knuckle grip and tensed muscles before switch-on, the shock of discovering the rocker switch is in the 'on' position when you plug into the mains, the clouds of dust covering the visor of the protective helmet, and the anguish of adjusting one of the settings and finding one more piece which should have been done! If this whole affair has taught me anything, it is to keep an open mind about new products and make sure I don't miss genuine improvements!

Using the T9 against a shiny new Trend guide

The T9 mounted under an old Elu table

> "...I'm more than happy with my new partner and don't see any affairs on the horizon!"

RECOMMENDED READING

Kevin Ley's Furniture Projects
Kevin Ley
GMC Publications Ltd

Mastering the Router
Ron Fox
GMC Publications Ltd

Routing for Beginners
Anthony Bailey
GMC Publications Ltd

Woodworking with the Router
Bill Hylton & Fred Matlack
GMC Publications Ltd

● All the above titles are available from:

GMC Publications Ltd
166 High Street
Lewes
East Sussex BN7 1XU
Tel: 01273 488005

The sandman cometh

A close look at belt sanding techniques

I don't have any hang-ups about using belt sanders. They are dismissed by some 'serious' makers as instruments of the devil and only suited to wood butchery. I, too, can be serious, if absolutely necessary, and I find that used safely and skilfully these machines can save hours of boring, repetitive work preparing a surface for final finishing.

Like any tools, particularly power tools, belt sanders must be respected and used properly. Remember, you can do as much damage to a table top with a badly set and used hand plane, as with a belt sander – it's just that the belt sander can do it quicker.
Be warned: practice is required and technique must be developed.

Machines

A belt sander has a removable sanding belt which runs under tension between two rollers. A slipper plate, slightly proud of the base, brings the sanding area of the belt into contact with the work. The rear roller is powered by the motor and the free-wheeling front roller is spring-loaded to give tension in the belt. An adjustment is provided to enable the angle of attack of the front roller to be altered, enabling the belt to run centrally over the rollers. A fan on the motor causes a flow of air which is used to carry the dust into the collection system.

With skill gained from practice, furniture makers find belt sanders are valuable assets

Safety

Apart from the usual general safety rules for power tools there are some specifics for this one:

- Use both hands to operate the sander.
- Make sure the work being sanded is anchored properly.
- Be aware the sander will try and run forward when it comes into contact with the work.
- Wear eye and ear protection.
- Ensure adequate dust removal, or protection from dust.
- When using the sander upside down, take care not to touch the belt, particularly the edge. It will give a nasty, ragged, tear cut which is painful and takes a long time to heal... I know!

"I don't have any hang-ups about using belt sanders"

Accessories:

Sanding frame

A sanding frame, or shoe, is a metal frame which surrounds the base of the sander, beyond the sanding area. It can be raised or lowered to control the amount of stock taken off by the belt in one pass, rather like adjusting the blade height on a plane. It gives the sander a larger 'footprint', stabilising the base to help prevent 'dig-ins', and gives a more even surface.

Inversion frames

An inversion frame enables the sander to be used safely upside down, like the table for a router, so that suitable work can be taken to it. It's useful for shaping and finishing end grain, and rounding over ends. A parallel guide, or fence, allows edge sanding, and a cross-belt fence, end sanding or shaping.

Variable speed

The variable-speed facility is useful to enable slower speeds to be used for delicate work, or when removing paint so it does not melt and clog the belt.

Dust

The design of the belt sander makes it relatively easy to collect most of the dust produced before it gets into the workshop environment. All have more or less efficient dust-collection systems ending up in a dust bag. However, these 'dust bags', by their very nature, only collect the big bits. The really fine stuff, which is the serious health hazard, goes right through. I would always recommend a vacuum dust extractor connected to the sander in place of the dust bag.

The 'suck' of the dust extractor is added to the 'blow' of the sander to ensure even more efficient collection, and the dust extractor has far better filters.

Micro-filter system

Bosch recently produced a 'micro-filter system', which is a rigid plastic container with a paper bellows filter to replace the fabric dust bag. This works on the same principle as workshop dust extractors and domestic vacuum cleaners, filtering out even the finest dust and compressing it to enable safe, easy disposal.

I've tried one which was designed for orbital sanders and was not really big enough for the belt sanders, with their much higher output of dust. It worked well and appeared to be very efficient at filtering all the dust but, predictably, filled up quite quickly. I understand larger ones are being developed to fit the belt sanders. Bosch have promised to send me one of their new random orbital sanders to test the micro-filter system.

Belt changing

When the belt you're using starts to leave as fine a surface as the next belt up, causing you to work hard with extra pressure and sand an area several times, or leaves shiny roller marks

Using a sanding plate over an edge and level to the work

Using a DeWalt 431 in a sanding frame, essential for keeping a surface flat

instead of removing stock, change it! Keep it, though: old belts have a second life for cleaning up, making into one-off shaped sanders or for use on the lathe.

A lever releases the tension on the front roller to enable the belt to be removed and replaced. This is a good time to clean the underside – shavings can easily block the dust-collecting system. Tracking adjustment may be necessary after a belt change.

Technique

Electrical leads and vacuum hoses should be hooked up to the ceiling, with something like a rubber bungee, clear of the work area. All glue ooze should be removed with a scraper; if left it will quickly be melted onto the belt and clog it. Test that the sander can be moved freely to all extremities before starting.

Use the sander like a plane. Keep a firm two-handed grip, applying light pressure evenly to the back and front. Start it just above the work, let it get up to speed, and gently lower it down, tilted slightly to the front to allow the power take-up to bring it level as the whole slipper plate is brought into contact. Move it along the work in the direction of the grain, in long, steady, even strokes, overlapping each pass.

Run off all edges to about a third of the slipper length where possible. Keep the sander level, be careful not to let it dip and taper the edge. Make sure you have good footing and can easily move along with the sander, so that it is held centrally between your arms, your head is always over it, and you can keep full control. Dig-ins occur when the sander is at arm's length and even pressure is not applied at the back and front. Do not apply heavy pressure, use the correct grit grade, and let the weight of the machine do the work.

For maximum stock removal, hold the sander at about 10° to the line of the grain. This will leave sanding scratches across the grain, so always finish with the sander running parallel to the grain. Lift the sander carefully off the work, without tilting it, before switching off, and remember to put it on its side, or let it stop before putting it down! It's sad to watch a sander ploughing its way along the bench doing untold damage as the motor winds down.

"The belt sander can be used very effectively to sand edges, following easily round external curves"

Sanding belts

The best belts to use are cloth-backed, and coated with aluminium oxide grit. Paper belts are cheaper but tear quickly, and other grit coatings don't last as long. All the manufacturers produce a range of cloth-backed aluminium oxide belts from 40 to 150 grit. The coarser grades: 40, 50, 60 are best used for resurfacing old floors and stripping paint. However, don't be frightened to use the coarse grits, they certainly remove some stock! The penalty is the extra time with the finer grits to remove the scratches left. A single, light pass-over with a new belt of the correct grit grade, removing the right amount of stock, is likely to achieve a level, even surface. Progressively finer grit grades remove any scratches.

Scrubbing away with a worn or too fine belt gives an uneven surface with the likelihood of dig-ins, burns, and unreasonable wear on the machine. It can be compared to hacking away with a blunt plane or chisel. I keep 40 grit for levelling, use on wild grain, and badly torn or chipped surfaces, but the majority of my work is with 80 and 120 grit to remove planer ripples or lines from chipped blades. This leaves a surface suitable for final finishing – usually with a random orbital sander – starting with the same grit grade.

Edge sanding using Makita 9903 with fence

Using a steel scraper plane to remove glue ooze will minimise wear and tear on your abrasives

Sanding a mitre with a DeWalt 431, inverted, with fence

Levelling

Use a straightedge to chalk-mark the bumps, and remove them freehand with a coarse grit. Taper the removal into the surrounding area. Keep re-marking and removing until the surface is flat, then go over the whole surface with the same grit, preferably with the sander in a frame.

Smoothing areas

The surface is assumed to be already flat, so to retain the flatness remove an even amount over the whole surface. This requires even downward pressure, constant speed of travel and even grit wear. You can achieve even pressure by allowing the weight of the machine to do the work. The constant speed of travel of the sander is achieved by experience and ensuring clear lines of travel. The even grit wear is achieved by starting at the front edge, right-hand side and working progressively to the back edge, left-hand side; then working backwards to the front right-hand side again. The whole process is aided considerably by a sanding frame.

Keep with the coarsest grit until all the marks and blemishes are removed. Do not 'spot treat' tears or marks; you must work over the whole area until they've gone. Then change to the next fineness of grit and go over the whole surface, working up to finishing with 120 or 150 grit. Finer grits than this tend to burn the work, so at this point the belt sander has done its work and we are in finishing-sander territory. With fine grits, a sanding frame and care, you can even use this technique on veneered surfaces!

Frames

As the grain on the rails runs at right angles to the grain on the stiles, the rails should be sanded first. Only take the slipper far enough on to the stiles to level the joint. Then sand the stiles. Adjust the belt to run to the edge of the slipper, so it can be taken right to the edge of the rails, but not over, to scratch across the grain.

Edges and ends

The belt sander can be used very effectively to sand edges, following easily round external curves. A parallel guide is very useful in keeping the belt at right angles to the top, otherwise frequent checks with a set square are necessary. In an inversion stand with a parallel guide small pieces can be taken to the sander for edge sanding. If the guide runs across the belt, the sander can be used on end grain.

"The belt sander does not replace the plane – imagine edge jointing with a sander!"

Nose sanding

Use the nose of the front roller to sand internal curves and, with a coarse grit and a bit of practice, to sculpt hollows in a chair seat.

Sanding metal

Sand metal with aluminium oxide grits, but remember sparks will fly! Don't use a dust bag or dust extraction system for this – or they will catch fire. Make sure the sparks coming out of the extractor port are caught in a non-flammable container. I never like the idea of sparks and wood dust or shavings mixing!

Conclusion

The belt sander does not replace the plane – imagine edge jointing with a sander! It does have limitations, but with skill and practice can do an enormous amount of work quickly and effectively.

We could all spend *hours* surfacing and thicknessing boards with a hand plane, and I bet the end result would not be as good as a few minutes with a planer-thicknesser.

The result is what matters, rather than how it is achieved. ■

Sanding an internal curve with the DeWalt 431

Using the nose of the Makita 9903 to shape a chair seat

INTO (RANDOM) ORBIT

Random orbital sanders have greatly improved machine sanding techniques for the individual craftsman

Taking the elbow-grease out of sanding: a survey of fine finishing with machines

At the end of the previous article I left the surface ready for final finishing. In this article I will cover the system I use to achieve this, with a combination of hand and machine techniques, using random orbital and palm sanders, and hand sanding blocks. There is a good selection of excellent different makes of these items available, but, as this is not intended as a review, I will just cover the ones I use in my own workshop. There are also other techniques, but I will simply outline those I have found to work.

Safety

These machines are relatively safe and apart from the usual general safety rules for power tools there are few extras. Both hands should be used, where possible, to operate the random orbital sander. Make sure the work being sanded is anchored properly, and ensure adequate dust removal, or protection. Keep hoses and cable hooked up out of the way. Eye and ear protection is a matter of personal choice – I don't see any great danger, but ear protection is probably a good idea for prolonged periods of use.

The Bosch micro-filter system

Using the random on a frame

Palm sanders can be used tight up against an edge

'The newer random orbital sanders have a circular base, which revolves slowly at the same time as the semicircular movement, preventing the scratches characteristic of older models'

Random orbital sanders

The old half- or third-sheet orbital sanders had a rectangular base, with a constant semicircular vibrating movement which could leave small comma-shaped scratches in the surface.

The newer random orbital sanders have a circular base, which revolves slowly at the same time as the semicircular movement, preventing the scratches characteristic of older models. A fan on the motor sucks up the dust, through holes in the base plate and sanding disk, into the collection system. The sanding discs are fixed to the base with a Velcro-style system. The more powerful examples have a variable speed facility, which is useful to enable slower speeds to be used for delicate work, or when removing paint, so that it does not burn or melt, and clog the disc.

In the case of my Bosch system a soft plastic skirt or suction hood is available – essential to improve dust extraction. There are also various fittings to enable vacuum hoses, and the micro-filter system to be attached.

Palm sanders

These are small, light, rectangular-based sanders, again with holes in the base for dust extraction. They have the advantages of accessibility and one-handed operation. The higher the orbit rate, the finer the finish. They do not have a random movement, so must be used with care, though given the likely areas of use this is usually not a problem. Sanding sheets can be attached with clamps or the Velcro system.

Paper punches are usually available to perforate sanding sheets for through-base dust extraction, and there are also fittings to attach vacuum hoses. For my palm sander I also have the fittings to attach the micro-filter system.

Micro-filter system

The Bosch micro-filter system is a rigid plastic container with a paper bellows filter. The bellows shape presents a large surface area, allowing good throughput of air as well as very fine filtering. It is a far better filter, and much more robust than fabric or paper bags. The dust is also compressed to hold more in the container and enable easy, safe disposal.

I find it excellent for short periods of use and if out of range of the extractor system. The filtering level is as fine as a vacuum extractor, but of course it does not have the power of suction. The plastic skirt accessory is essential to keep the dust in range. Efficiency is seriously reduced if the filter becomes clogged, so the container must be emptied frequently.

Sanding blocks

These can be of wood, cork, plastic, or foam. There are all sorts of methods of fixing the sanding sheets, from just wrapping them around, to self-adhesive backing, various clamping systems or Velcro. There are also washable sponges with permanent abrasive faces, more suitable for rubbing down paint.

I prefer the Siafast system with a hard

Typical set-up for a random orbital sander

Siafast hand-sanding block and sheets

Sanding sheets

A lot of makers seem to be very stingy with abrasive paper. It is a false economy – worn sheets don't remove any stock and, with the extra pressure one is tempted to use, can mark and spoil the surface. The way to save money on these sheets is to buy in boxes of 50 or 100 – much cheaper than packs of 10!

I am also a great believer in the Velcro-backed stick and peel system. Quite apart from the convenience, the efficiency of the power transfer between the pad and the sheet is hugely increased. No movement is lost with the sheet slipping between the driven pad or block, and the surface being sanded. The Velcro backing also increases the strength of the sheet, helping to reduce tears and, therefore, tears.

Also, pre-cut ready-punched sheets save a lot of faffing about. The pre-punched holes are much cleaner and more efficient for dust extraction, than doing it yourself, even with the punching tool accessory.

Aluminium oxide grit is the most suitable and longest-lasting for our purposes, and I keep a range of grits from 60 to 320. Most of my work is from 120 to 240 on the machines and to 320 on the blocks, but the coarser grades are useful for shaping, or pieces straight from the planer or saw.

Remember that sanding sheets are useless if damp: they – like you and the whole of your workshop – must be kept warm and dry.

face for flat areas, and a soft face to follow profiles and curves, both with the Velcro system for attaching sheets. I have several blocks, clearly marked, with different grit grades, to save time.

Dust

Dust is a health, fire, and explosion hazard – the finer, the more so, in all cases. For effective sanding, and prolonging the life of the abrasive and the maker, dust must be removed quickly and efficiently from the sanded area. Any which is trapped between the base and the surface will clog the abrasive. The dust may also contain loose pieces of the abrasive grit, which can leave unsightly marks.

On the random orbital and palm sanders it is extracted, by a fan on the motor, through holes in the base plate; this system is infinitely improved by attaching a vacuum dust extractor to boost the air flow, and a skirt or suction hood helps to keep the dust in the right place to be picked up.

Even then some dust – especially the finer and more hazardous – will get into the workshop environment, and hand sanding adds even more. A workshop air filter to clean the ambient air should be used while sanding is in progress.

Changing sheets

When the sheet you are using starts to leave the same finish as the next grade up, when there is less resistance causing you to use extra pressure, or it leaves marks, shiny areas, or scratches, it is time for a change to a new one of the same grit.

When the surface is uniform and the friction against the pad is constant, it is time to change to a finer grit. Each grit removes the scratches of the previous, coarser grit.

Techniques

Sanding is precision work and should be undertaken with a sensitive touch. Abrasives are cutting tools – examination of sanding dust under a microscope reveals that it is, in fact, small shavings, like those from a chisel or scraper. Sand at a steady rate to allow the time for the myriad cutting edges of the grits to do their work.

Make sure the area around the piece is clear, and hoses and leads are out of the way, to enable easy, safe access. Keep the pressure even at all parts of the stroke with machine or hand.

Rounding over or 'fluffing' sharp edges or angles should be avoided or the work will look woolly. Remember too that blemishes invisible to the eye are only too apparent to the touch – run your finger tips over the whole surface, because someone will!

Random orbital sanding

The beauty of the random element of this type of sander is that it can be used in any direction – even across the grain – without leaving scratches. This makes it ideal for sanding frames, where it is necessary to sand across the grain at the junction of a rail and stile. It is also ideal on flat surfaces provided it can go over the edges. In the case of surfaces which have been belt-sanded, start with a disc of the same grit grade as the last belt

‘In extreme cases the pad remains stationary and the body of the sander moves – until there is a flash and a puff of blue smoke – and you are buying a new one!’

Using the palm sander on an edge

used. In the case of unprepared surfaces choose as coarse a grade as is necessary.

Hold the sander in both hands and move it smoothly and evenly over the whole surface; don’t allow it to tip over edges, and use no more downward pressure than the weight of the machine.

Pressure reduces or cancels the random effect and the result is scratches. In extreme cases the pad remains stationary and the body of the sander moves – until there is a flash and a puff of blue smoke – and you are buying a new one!

Examine the surface carefully, bouncing light off it from several angles and running your hands over it, until you are satisfied that the previous grit scratches have been removed, then change to the next finer grit, and repeat the process, down to 240 grit.

This type of sander is unsuitable where there is a raised edge, for instance on a fielded panel: the disk will keep bumping the edge and damage it. This is where we move on to the palm sander.

Palm sander

Essentially this should be used in exactly the same way as the random orbital, but because the base is rectangular, and the oscillations very small, it is possible to go right to an edge. It can also be used in one hand and is ideal for small areas, edges, stop chamfers, rounded nosings, edges, and fieldings.

The final sanding finish is still a hand operation

It can be particularly useful in renovation and refinishing where the finishing is light and takes place on an assembled piece.

Hand-sanding

The final sanding on any piece must be by hand. This is the closest inspection the piece will ever get, and now is the time to remove any blemishes and marks. Beware of using the abrasive sheet loose in the hand: it is easy to apply pressure too locally and cause problems.

Wherever possible, use the abrasive on a block, follow the line of the grain and figure, start at the grit you finished with on the power sander and go down to 240.

Make sure you have good light and you are able to view the piece from several different angles to check the surface. Light, even pressure on abrasive sheets, in good condition and of the correct grit, will pay dividends.

Any sanding between coats of finish should be light, and by hand rather than machine. Any blemishes revealed by the first coat must be removed before second-coating – it won’t get better!

My verdict

Though it does not replace the plane and/or the cabinet scraper, sanding is usually necessary at some point in the process of finishing. Your whole piece can initially be judged by its finish. Doing it properly can make or break the project; because having seen it, people want to touch – ask the judges of *F&C*’s Axminster competition! ■

Suppliers

Bosch: sanders, abrasive sheets, accessories.
01895 838743. www.bosch-pt.co.uk
Axminster power tools: sanders, abrasives, air filters.
0800 371822. www.axminster.co.uk

Part Two
THE PROJECTS

Braced

A nicely proportioned set of interior doors for a country cottage

WHEN we were considering a move to our new cottage my wife naturally said it was perfect; once we were in, however, there were inevitably some small alterations required... Apparently it just needed cutting off its foundations, moving six inches to the left and twisting a tad more towards the sun! Seriously though, one of the small alterations needed was to change all 16 of the internal doors. The pressed hardboard frame and panel doors that were already there were a masterpiece of clever use and processing of materials, but I had to agree – they did nothing for a 17th-century stone cottage with exposed oak beams and oak floors. Ho hum, replacement time – and I could tell I wasn't going to get away with softwood, either.

As one door opens...

The appropriate design was ledged and braced cottage doors, with tongue-and-grooved upright boards. I priced up this sort of door with my local builders' merchant and found that excellent-quality imported eastern European softwood doors were about £30 each. The same thing in oak, made locally, was closer to £300! We decided that oak was essential for the look, and that it might therefore be a good idea to make them myself. The braces made the doors look too heavy and agricultural for our purposes, so I decided to use three ledges, or cross pieces, and no braces. An essential design feature was that the boards would be of random widths to emphasise their handmade nature, which would also be more suitable for a cottage of this age.

A nice pair of handmade oak doors

...another closes

Having decided on oak I set off to ny local wood yard to try and find something suitable. Bearing in mind that the doors are approximately 2m ($6^1/2$ft) high, I was really looking for stock close to 7 or 14ft to minimise wastage. In the end I found a parcel of kiln-dried brown oak boards on special offer, mainly in 2.4m (8ft) lengths. The reason it was on offer was because the ends were split for some way into the stock, but I reckoned I could get my $6^1/2$ft lengths out so I snapped it up. I was even more pleased with this buy when I found it also contained sufficient tiger oak for a hanging corner cupboard (see pages 30–2) and the remainder of the brown oak made a free-standing corner cupboard. There was very

Beauties

Ledged but not braced

"my wife naturally said it was perfect; once we were in, however, there were inevitably some small alterations required..."

little wastage.

The wood was sticked and stacked in my timber store, where a dehumidifier helped to condition it thoroughly before use. I always keep my workshop as close as possible to the end-use conditions of the piece so that it continues to adjust during the production process. If you find the workshop too cold and damp for your own comfort, then so does the wood!

Scores on the doors

Time spent at this stage always pays dividends in the final result. I laid out all the boards and set about them with chalk, marking out as many 2.03m (6ft 8in) lengths (25mm (1in) oversize each end) as were there, being careful to turn them over and check the other side for faults and appearance. I then selected the best, to the total width of boards required, cut them to length on the radial-arm saw and to width on the table saw. All the boards were then faced, thicknessed and matched up to individual door widths, ripping wide boards down where necessary. Each board was finally edge-planed on the jointer. The cross pieces were cut from the remaining timber – faults could be allowed on one side, as only one face would be visible. They were also ripped, faced, and thicknessed to size.

You're not coming in

Given the size of the individual doors (approx. 1980 x 760mm (6ft 6in x 2ft 6in) – Fig 1) and the number required, the routing was going to be a very long and repetitive business. I carefully arranged everything so the timber had to be moved the minimum number of times and the least distance.

I used roller stands to support the lengths as they passed over the router table, gloves to protect my hands, and a filtered helmet for eye and lung protection. Dust extraction was used on the router but I've never found it totally satisfactory, so the Microclene ambient air filter really came into its own.

I felt that a slot in each board and a loose tongue was quicker and easier to achieve

Photo 1 **Loose tongue and slots with cutter**

than tongues and grooves, and would perform the same function. A circular TCT cutter designed for cutting slots for biscuits was ideal for the job, its extra diameter making for a quick, clean cut (see Photo 1).

The loose tongues were cut from best-quality 4mm birch-faced three-ply, stained to match the colour of the oak. They were cut so that the two outside ply faces had the grain running across the width of the tongue, with the grain of the inside ply running along the length. This gives the maximum strength where it is needed (see Fig 3). Once the slots had been finished the cutter was changed for a chamfer cutter, the table turned around and the boards passed back over to chamfer the edges of the boards on each side (Photo 2). The cross pieces were cut to length, ie. 6mm (1/4in) in from each edge of the door to allow for easy final adjustment of the door width. The front face edges were then rounded over with a 6mm (1/4in) radius rounding-over cutter.

Put wood in't hole

The top and bottom ledges on the doors would carry the hinges and, since the hinges had already been fitted into the door frames and the recesses cut, the top and bottom ledges on each door were sited to allow reuse of these recesses. The ledges were placed on the bench in the correct position and strips of ply tacked to the bench on each side to hold them in position. A batten was pinned to the bench edge to locate the first board at right angles to the ledges. The boards were secret dovetail-nailed to the ledges, through the tongues (Fig 2). When the next board is fitted to the tongue and butted up to the first one, the nail head is covered. The nails are not only angled to go into the ledge but are pointed inwards towards each other to achieve the dovetail effect. This makes for a good, strong nailed joint. A good-sized blob of glue was applied to the centre of the area where the board crossed the ledge to give extra strength and rigidity and to fix the centre of the board. This would ensure any future movement was equal on each side.

Knobs and knockers

I searched high and low for light, decorative strap hinges and Suffolk or sneck latches for the doors. There is any amount of heavy, cast-iron exterior door furniture available but it would not give the authentic effect we wanted. In the end I found just what I was looking for in a local shop which supplies period fittings. They were handmade in beaten iron but hideously expensive; remember I had sixteen doors to fit out! I decided that if I could get a metal-cutting blade for the bandsaw I could cut the hinges out of oversize lightweight exterior strap hinges, and modify mass-produced Suffolk latches. One phone call to Dure-Edge later and I had the necessary blade and some good advice about how to go about it. I bought oversize shiny black and standard strap hinges, and marked out the shape

Photo 2 **Cutting slots for loose tongues**

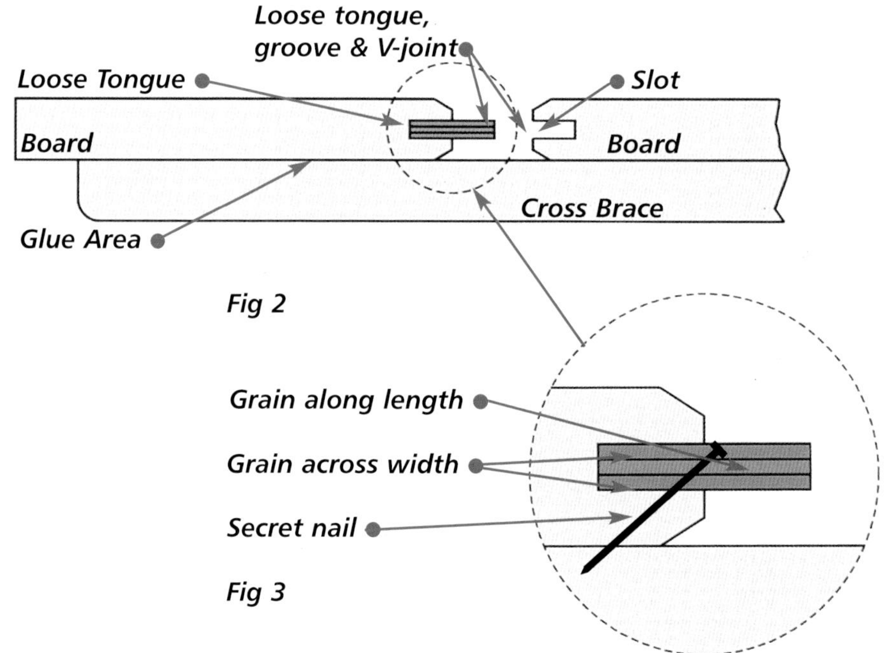

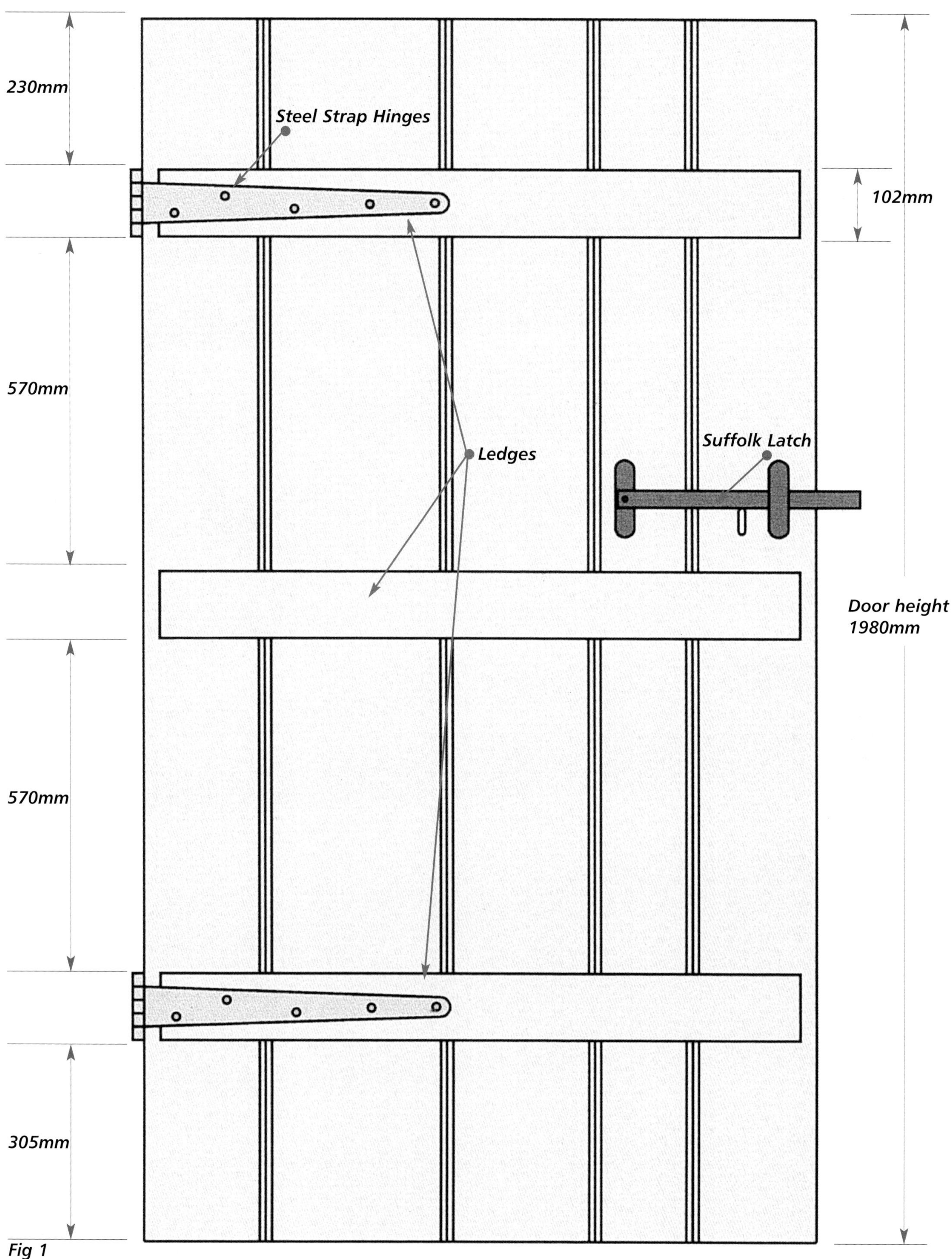
230mm
Steel Strap Hinges
102mm
570mm
Ledges
Suffolk Latch
Door height
1980mm
570mm
305mm
Fig 1

required using a template. This shape was cut out on the bandsaw, which I had fitted with the metal-cutting blade. I slowed down the cutting speed as far as I could and lubricated the blade by rubbing it with candle wax. The corners of the latch fittings were rounded over on the bench grinder. All were finished on the grinder and belt sander and painted with a satin-black metal-finish paint. All wood dust was thoroughly cleaned from the bandsaw to prevent fire from the sparks, and the dust bag was taken off the belt sander so the sparks did not set fire to it, or to the dust in it. Needless to say, hand and eye protection was worn throughout the process. The end result was excellent and a fraction of the cost of either cast iron or the handmade door furniture (see Photo 3).

Shut that door!

The doors were offered up to the frames and marked accurately to size. A clearance gap of 3mm (1/8in) was left to the top and sides and 6mm (1/4in) to the bottom. The door was taken back to the workshop and the router used with a 50mm (2in) deep, 13mm (1/2in) straight cutter, against a fence, to cut the door to size (see photo 4). The size of the doors made it much easier to use a router and bring it to the door, rather than attempting to take the door to a jointer or saw to trim it. When cutting across the grain at the top and bottom I scored the final edge to prevent break-out.

The doors

The doors were belt-sanded down to 150 grit before assembly and finally hand-sanded to 240 grit after trimming. Three coats of boiled linseed oil were applied at 24-hour intervals. I warmed the oil to reduce viscosity and to help penetration. The first coat was liberally applied and left to soak in and then refreshed every 15 to 20 minutes until no more could be absorbed. It was then vigorously rubbed off with an absorbent cloth, so that no oil built up on the surface. The first coat is the most important, since only a small amount of extra oil penetrates once it has dried. The surface was denibbed with 240 grit and two further light coats applied at 24-hour intervals. The advantage of an oiled finish is not that it is strong, but that it is renewable. Any scuffs or marks that accrue in the future can be removed or covered with a coat of teak oil.

Photo 3 ***Hinges & templates***

Photo 4 ***Trimming the door exactly to size using a 1/2in router with a 13mm deep straight cutter***

Men they couldn't hang

The strap hinges were fitted to the frames, the trimmed doors placed in position and fixed in place with tapered wedges. The hinges were then fixed to the doors using screws long enough to go through the ledges and into (but not through!) the front boards. This gives maximum support to the door. Once each door was hung it got a final coat of Danish oil in situ, to cover any slight handling marks. Danish oil contains a hardener which helps the linseed oil to cure. After a week or so each door was buffed with a soft cloth.

Slammed shut

It was a long and boring job. I split the task into two batches of eight doors, with a break of a couple of months in between. However, I was still very glad when the task was finished. But, despite all that, we're still very pleased with the end result. I just hope that the wife was winding me up when she said she thought that ash might have looked better... ●

Wonder wardrobe

A simple way to construct a space-saving wardrobe for the spare bedroom

We have a tiny room in our cottage which we laughingly refer to as a bedroom. It is just big enough for an exercise bike and some weights, and is used most of the time for workouts. Very occasionally it is converted into an overflow guest room by removing the gym kit and replacing it with a folding bed.

My wife and I worked out that a narrow wardrobe could just be fitted into the corner of the room, between the end of the bed and the wall. My plan was to make something that could hold a guest room conversion kit of sorts, consisting of a bedside table, bedding, a lamp and a radio, while the room was in gym mode, and then to provide clothes storage when converted to a bedroom for guests. I wanted something with a dual purpose.

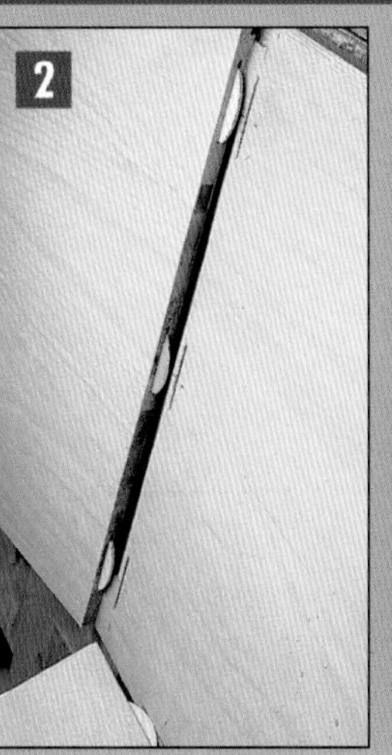

1 Both parts of the cupboard assembled
2 The biscuit joint between the back, base and sides
3 Biscuit-jointing the lipping onto a panel
4 The router set up with a wheel cutter for biscuits or Tanselli wafers

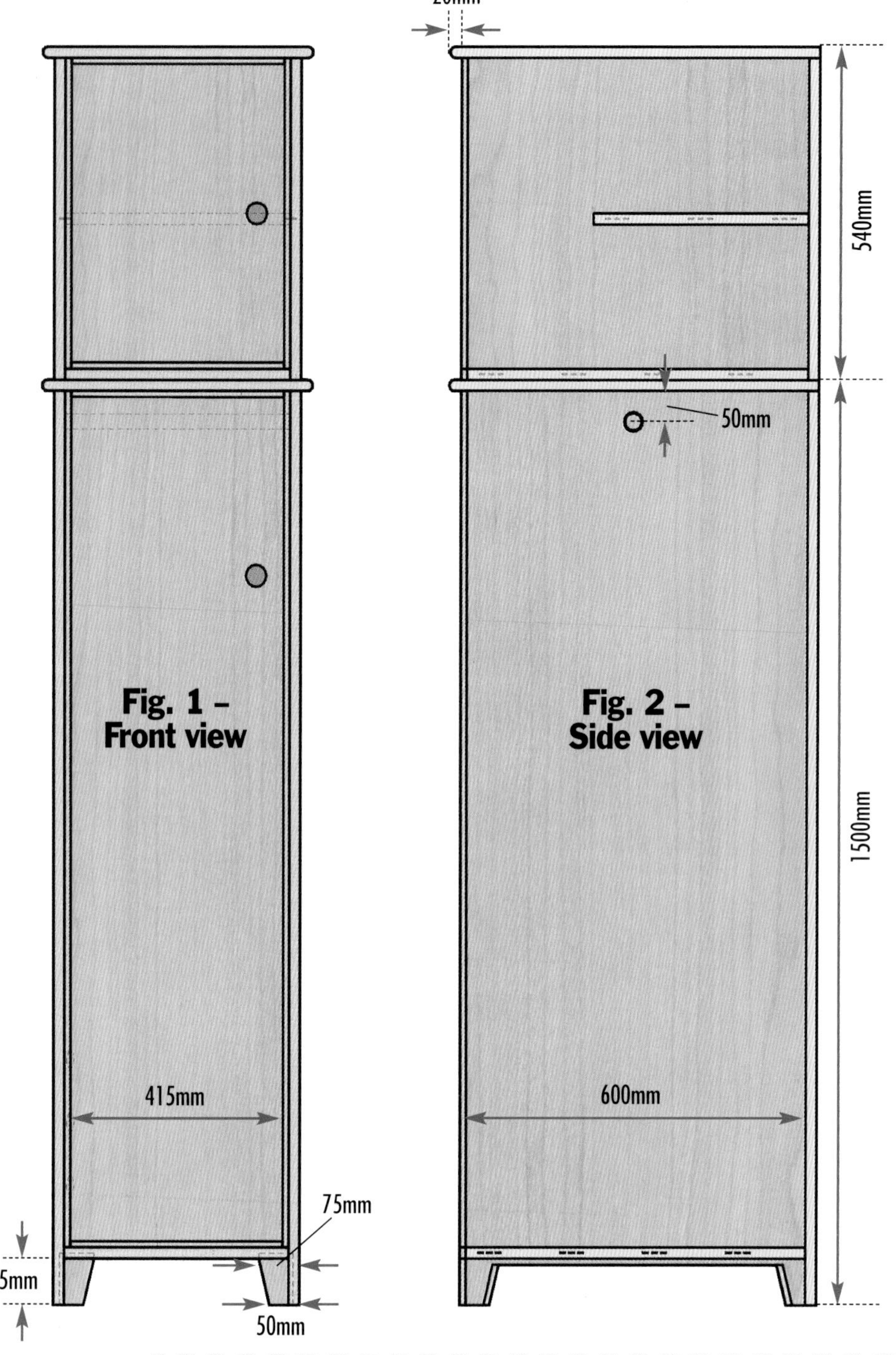

Design

I initially thought of making a built-in floor-to-ceiling cupboard but after careful consideration I felt that it might limit the options of a room that was already challenged for space.

A tall and narrow, free-standing cupboard would maximise the hanging and shelf space while minimising the loss of floor area. It was therefore the ideal solution. The top, that was to be short of the ceiling, could act as a useful place to store empty bags or cases.

A careful check with a mock-up revealed that the planned cupboard was too high to be able to go round one of the passage corners on the landing. My plans were therefore modified and I decided to make the unit as two stacking cupboards.

The width was determined by the length of the bed in the room, the depth by the 550mm (21½in) minimum required for a jacket on a hanger, the height of the bottom cupboard by the drop needed for a hanging dress or trousers, and the top cupboard by the ceiling height. Therefore not a great deal of design skill was required – provided, of course, I had an accurate tape measure! I decided on a nice pale wood to minimise the visual effect on the room.

Timber selection

Solid American ash (*Fraxinus americana*) was my initial choice of timber, but my local supplier mentioned that he had had some blockboard, delivered and priced as standard, which was in fact faced with a nice decorative American red oak (*Quercus rubra*) veneer. I ordered a couple of sheets on the spot, and a nice straight-grained, clean, even-coloured piece of solid red oak for the lipping.

What's this?

When the sheets arrived a brief glance told me that they were not faced with red oak at all, but ash. The solid lipping board was red oak, but my timber merchant had clearly got confused somewhere along the line - what was I saying about viewing prior to buying? However, after a quick check with the senior design consultant, my wife Yvonne, we thought the gentle contrast between the two woods was in fact very attractive and decided to stick with it.

Timber preparation

Though much more stable than solid wood in terms of shrinkage or expansion, blockboard will still twist, warp, bend, and bow, so care in storage and conditioning are essential. It is best stored flat with either sticks to allow

Blockboard & veneer

Blockboard is a type of plywood in which softwood strips are bonded together under pressure as a core, and sandwiched between two layers of thick veneer. The cupping grain direction of the core strips is alternated for stability, and the grain direction of the outer veneers runs at right-angles to the core, to minimise movement. The grain of the core strips runs the length of the sheet, while the outer veneer layers run across the width of the sheet.

Decorative veneers are bonded to the faces after the board has been manufactured, and run down its length as with the core strips. This type of timber is a sort of half-way point between solid wood and sheet material.

Red oak

Red oak looks similar to other oaks although, as its name implies, there is a reddish tinge running through its heartwood. It is cheaper, softer, and easier to work, although when doing so always ensure your tools are sharp to avoid tear-out. The texture is coarse, and the smaller rays give less figure. The fast-growing trees from the south can have a great deal of pale sapwood. As with most woods there can be variations, so it pays to have a brief inspection before buying.

TOP TIP
Ordering materials well in advance gives you the necessary time to condition them.

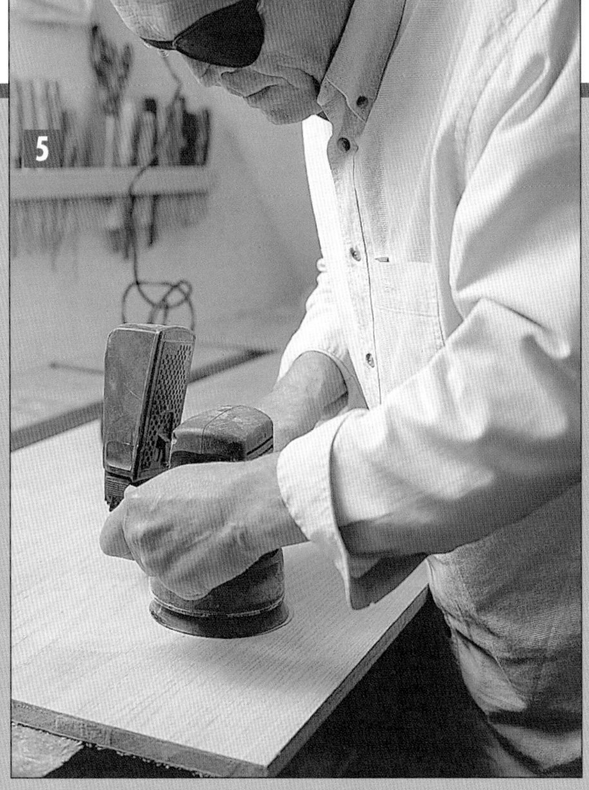

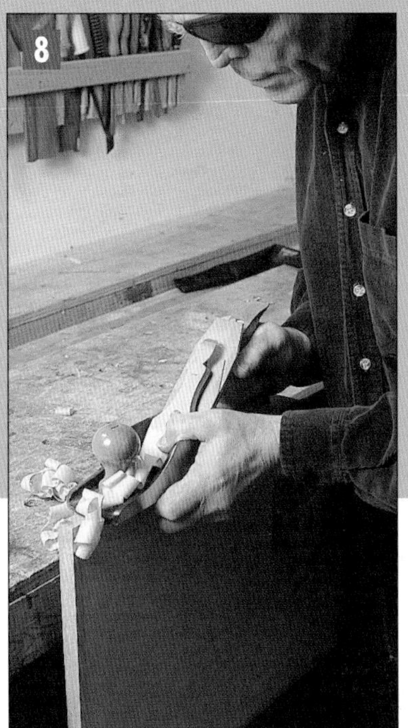

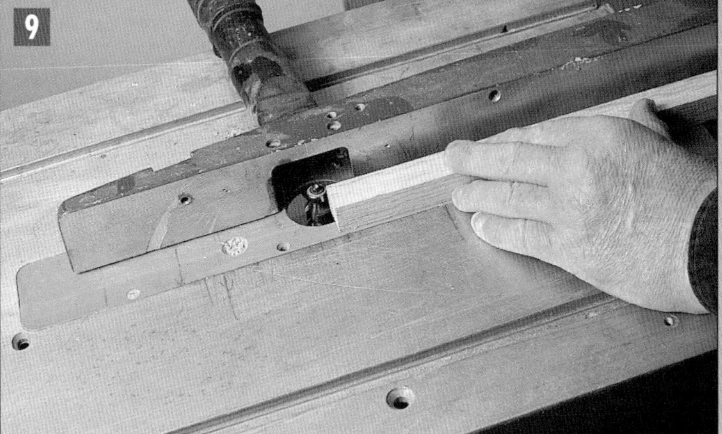

5 Using an orbital sander to clean up the panels

6 Clamping up the bottom unit

7 Clamping up the top unit

8 Planing the door edge to fit

9 Rounding over the edges of the lipping for the tops

the air to circulate, or several sheets of newspaper to absorb the moisture.

I did not have enough floor space available to lay my 2440 x 1220mm (8 x 4ft) sheets flat so I stood them upright against the wall with spacers between them. I placed these as near to vertical as I possibly could, to prevent any bending.

The solid piece of oak was laid flat on sticks. The workshop was, as usual, kept both warm and dry with my sawdust burner and dehumidifier. The materials were conditioned while I finished the other work in progress.

Ordering materials well in advance gives you the necessary time to condition them. Your workshop humidity should be as close to domestic levels as possible. If this isn't possible, cut the pieces down to manageable sizes and store them inside the house.

Construction

This sort of sheet material is best jointed with biscuits or the even stronger Tanselli wafers. A router with either a wheel slotter or straight cutter can be used, although a biscuit jointer is clearly the best option. While biscuits are easier and quicker than wafers for general work, the latter really come into their own when extra strength is required, or the widths are too narrow for biscuits to be used.

The edges of blockboard are difficult to clean up to an attractive finish, and need to be lipped with solid timber, especially if you are planning to use any edge mouldings.

Lipping

Strips of the solid red oak were prepared in suitable lengths for the component blockboard sheet parts. The strips were faced and thicknessed to a tad over 18mm (¾in) wide, and 10mm (⅜in) thick. They were then taped together in a block to keep them straight until required. The lipping for the tops was 20mm (25/32in) thick to allow for edge moulding. These lipping strips would be fixed along the cut edges of the blockboard with glue and biscuits. I used the smallest '0' size biscuits, to suit the lipping strip thickness, and prevent slot penetration.

It is very important that the sheet face is not proud of the lipping edge once it is glued on, as there is no room for adjustment in the thickness of the decorative veneer! The tad extra width was insurance to allow for the scraping and/or sanding of any inaccuracies in the lipping, down flush to the sheet surface.

USEFUL DEFINITION
Caul – a sheet of previously heated wood or metal plate used to press down a veneer or edging onto groundwork. Zinc plate is superior, but should be backed with wood.

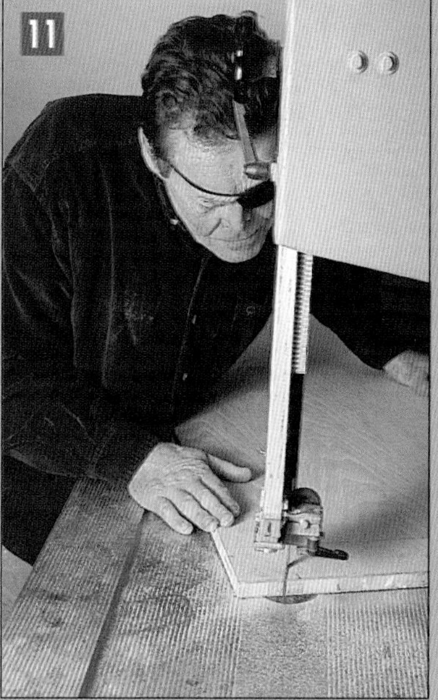

10 Turning a door pull on the lathe

11 Cutting out the foot shape on the bandsaw

12 Finishing the foot cut-out with a scraper and sanding blocks

13 The foot and lipping in detail

Biscuits

All the pieces of blockboard were cut to size, allowing for the addition of the lipping where appropriate. This must be done accurately, as there is little adjustment available once the lipping is fixed and any edge planing may expose the biscuit slot through the face.

The biscuit slots were marked at about 300mm (12in) centres on the sheets and transferred to the lipping strips. The jointer was adjusted to cut in the centre of the blockboard thickness with the correct penetration for the biscuits, and all the slots were cut in the blockboard.

I then re-adjusted the jointer again, this time by just half a tad, to cut the biscuit slots in the centre of the lipping strips.

PVA glue was applied to the edges, slots and biscuits, and the lipping was clamped up. 100 x 25mm (4 x 1in) strips of timber were placed between the clamps and the lipping to even out the pressure. Once it was clamped up, I used an extra clamp to squeeze up every couple of inches along the length to ensure any excess glue was pressed out.

The lipping was applied over several days as I did not have enough clamps to do it all in one go. All the pieces were left to set and any minor adjustments to the size were made.

TOP TIP
Biscuits are a godsend for this sort of application, and wafers are even better as they locate the lip to the board very accurately.

Base cupboard carcass assembly

The sides were drilled for the hanging rail, and the cutouts made to form the feet. The front edges of the feet were lipped without biscuits and held in place with sticky tape while they set. The underside of the front of the base and the inside face of the sides were slotted to take the front feet.

All joining edges were lightly planed dead square, removing any machining marks and adjusting to size where necessary. Diagonals were checked to make sure everything was square. The biscuit slots were marked and cut in the centre of the board, this time at the correct penetration for the larger biscuits (size 20), and the sides, back, and base were dry-fitted together. The inside faces were sanded to 150 grit with a random orbital sander, taking great care not to go through the top face.

Once the clamps and cauls were prepared and I was happy all was ready, I applied the PVA and clamped up, with the hanging rail in position.

Front feet

Once everything was set, the front feet, cut from red oak, were finished and glued into place. The outside faces of the carcass were also sanded down to 150 grit with an orbital sander.

The biscuit slots were cut in the top of the sides and back, followed by the slots in the underside of the top, set in by the 20mm ($^{25}/_{32}$in) overhang. The overhanging edges of the top, made of the thicker lipping, were rounded over with a 6mm radius cutter with a bearing guide on the T5. The rounded-over edge and the inside face were finished down to 150 grit. Glue was applied to the biscuits and the top was dropped on, clamped up, and left to set. Once the clamps had been removed, the outside face was sanded to 150 grit.

Door

The blockboard for the door was cut to allow 1mm ($^{3}/_{64}$in) clearance top and bottom and 1mm ($^{3}/_{64}$in) on the opening edge, after the lipping and piano hinge had been fitted. It was lipped in the same way and the hinge was fitted.

I used my self-centring hinge drill to get the holes spot on. For a couple of quid this is a brilliant time-saver. Before I

14 Drilling the screw holes to locate the top unit

15 Finishing the sides with a paint pad

16 Fitting the pull to the door with a double-ended screw dowel

stumbled across it in the Axminster catalogue, I had made a marker using the same principle with a ballpoint pen. The hollow outer case locates in the hinge countersink and the spring-loaded drill bit is pushed through its centre, exactly in the middle of the hole, every time! After the door had been hung, the clearances were adjusted to 2mm (5⁄64in) at the top, bottom, and opening edge; it had to be removed and refitted a couple of times to get it right.

Top cupboard

The top cupboard was made in the same way as the bottom cupboard, but with a half-shelf fitted halfway up, again with biscuits. The top cupboard was placed on top of the bottom cupboard and adjustments were made to sit it flush. Four screws, countersunk through the top of the bottom cupboard into the base of the top cupboard, located it into position.

Pulls

Pulls were turned from scraps of red oak and fitted with double-ended dowel screws, then removed for finishing.

Finishing

The units were separated and the doors and hinges removed for ease and convenience of finishing. All the power sanding had been done on the individual components during assembly, so all that remained was the final sanding by palm sander and hand blocks, which now took place.

As usual I used my favourite acrylic satin finish, Barford's Aqua Cote, to maintain the pale colour. It is a water-based floor varnish, which touch-dries quickly and reduces dust pick-up. It can be sanded and recoated in two hours, and hardens to a tough satin finish.

The first coat was applied with a paint pad before final hand-sanding, as the grain is raised considerably by the water base. This coat was sanded down with 240 grit on a Velcro sanding block with Velcro-backed sanding sheets, which provide a firm hold in use and are very convenient for quick changes of grit.

A further coat was applied with the paint pad and rubbed down with 320 grit on the same block. A third coat was applied and left for seven days in the warm, dry workshop to fully cure. It was then cut back with a Scotchbrite grey pad, to a nice satin lustre.

The doors were then re-hung, pulls attached, and the cupboards put in place.

Recommended reading

- ***Kevin Ley's Furniture Projects,*** **Kevin Ley, GMC**
- ***Space-Saving Furniture Projects for the Home,*** **Dave Mackenzie, GMC**
- ***Furniture-Mcking Projects for the Woodscraftsman,*** **Best of *Furniture & Cabinetmaking* Magazine, GMC**
- ***Beds and Bedroom Furniture,*** **Best of *Fine Woodworking* Magazine, Taunton**

All the above titles are available from GMC Publications Ltd, 166 High Street, Lewes, East Sussex BN7 1XU
Tel: 01273 488005

TOP TIP

I used my self-centring hinge drill to get the holes spot on. For a couple of quid this is a brilliant time saver.

Conclusion

This was my first substantial piece of furniture with blockboard, and I can see how its pre-finished, blemish-free stability would be an advantage in batch production and/or CAD/CAM applications.

However, I missed the surprises that you encounter with solid wood – knots, shakes, movement, interlocking grain, tear-out, colour changes – the things that drive you mad at the time! The blockboard felt soulless and dead, lacking in individuality or character. I also found the veneered top face thin, unforgiving and difficult to work with.

Despite all these misgivings it did the job well, senior management (my wife) was pleased with the end result – and in my case that's all that counts!

A different co

Utilise limited space effectively with this tiger-oak corner cupboard

EVEN though we had a good clear-out when we moved from our Yorkshire house to a smaller cottage in Shropshire, display space for my wife's china collection was at a premium. However, we decided that a corner of the new cottage's sitting room was ideally suited for a hanging display cupboard.

Generally corner cupboards don't provide as much space as they initially appear to, because the shape of the shelves restricts the display and storage possibilities. It would not be a problem in our case, though, as the china items were well suited to a small display area.

Design

As the cupboard was to display specific items we spent some time arranging each shelf's contents on an area marked out to represent the shelf size and shape, changing the area and the display until we arrived at the optimum sizes and spacings. I use the same method when making bookcases – avoiding making adjustable shelves, which are rarely moved after initially being filled, and which weaken the structure. Far better to line up all the items which are to go in it, and work out the shelf spacings beforehand, allowing much stronger, permanent, shelf fixing.

In this case, once we had worked out the number and sizes of the shelves, we measured the spacing required between them. The fronts of the cupboard were made quite narrow to give as large an opening as possible for the shelves. This resulted in a tall and slim design, making an elegant overall display, which fitted well into its corner of the room.

Timber

I had been making some cottage doors (described on pages 20–4) out of brown oak. While I was sorting through it to find evenly matched colour for the doors, I came across some attractive pieces of stripy or 'tiger' oak.

Brown oak is normal English oak that has been attacked by the beefsteak fungus (*Fistulina hepatica*). The fungus enters via an open wound or damaged area. Despite feeding off the tree it does little real damage, instead taking sustenance from the sap and excreting waste chemicals into the wood to cause an attractive colour change to a rich, dark, golden brown. Incidentally, though not poisonous, the fungus tastes revolting – not at all like steak!

Tiger or stripy oak is again normal English oak, which has been attacked by the same fungus, but the colour change has not taken place evenly, resulting in tiger-like stripes and streaks. The stripy effect is not even, and requires careful selection to obtain a pleasing effect. Both woods are relatively rare and very attractive.

After a lot of careful selection and marking out, there was just sufficient tiger oak to give a nice even effect to the most visible surfaces of the cupboard.

Marking out from template

Preparation

First I drew the outline of the top and base to real size on hardboard. The sides and fronts were housed directly into the top and base allowing a 13mm (½in) overhang; the sides fitted into the fronts in 6mm x 15mm (¼in x ⅝in) housings, while the left- and right-hand sides fitted together at the back in another 6mm x 15mm (¼in x ⅝in) housing. The shelves were also let into the sides and fronts in 6mm x 15mm (¼in x ⅝in) housings. Drawing this all to size on the hardboard allowed accurate measurements to be taken for all the component parts. I then cut a template for the top, base and shelves to make marking and cutting out easier. Next, all the carcass timber was faced and thicknessed to 15mm (⅝in), and where necessary jointed to width.

Biscuits were used to strengthen the joins and prevent any slippage when clamping up. I used a biscuit cutter on my small Trend router to cut the slots for the biscuits. The hardboard templates were used to mark out the triangular pieces most economically. The grain direction of the shelves, top and base should be parallel to the line of the front [see diagram] to allow for movement across the grain when jointed into the sides.

I chose the best faces of the sides, top, and base for the inside of the cupboard, as the other faces would not be seen in normal use.

Carcass construction

The sides and shelves were cut to size, the front edges of the shelves were rounded over and the shoulder cut in where they fit into the fronts (note the way that this shoulder is cut in). The inside edges of the fronts were finished square, and the tops shouldered.

The 15mm x 6mm (⅝in x ¼in) housings were cut in the fronts to take the sides, and in the right-hand side at the back, to take

Rounding edges on a router table

ner

Jointing side pieces with biscuits

the left side. Then the 15mm x 6mm (⅝in x ¼in) housings were cut in both sides and the fronts to take the shelves. All these pieces were sanded to a finish at this point, before assembly.

Next the top and base were cut to size and shape, and the housings for the fronts and sides cut 13mm (½in) in from the edge. The front edges were rounded over, and both pieces finished.

Assembly

The entire cabinet was now dry-assembled to check the fit of all joints, and any necessary adjustments made. Assembly was in two stages. First PVA glue was applied to the housings in the fronts and sides, and the fronts, sides, and shelves fitted together. To help keep the whole thing true I dry-fitted the top and base. Clamps were applied from front to back, everything was checked to ensure it was true and left to set.

After the glue had set I applied PVA to the top and base housings, fitted them to the sides and fronts, and clamped from top to base. Again I checked all was square and left it to set.

Decorative strip

I decided to add a small decorative strip to the top of the cupboard, and in order to support it, needed to add a crosspiece under the front of the top. This was cut to size, with a 45° butt joint at each end to fit to the inner edges of the fronts, and glued and clamped to the top.

A saw cut 3mm (⅛in) deep was made every 19mm (¾in) in a strip of oak 19mm x 6mm (¾in x ¼in) to leave a series of small raised pieces, which form the decorative strip. I marked the first cut and, using a register pencil mark on the fence of the radial-arm saw, made the remaining cuts. A similar result could be achieved, albeit more slowly, by marking each cut and making the cut by hand using a tenon saw with a wide set and a depth stop clamped to the blade. Alternatively a jig could be made and the cuts made with a router fitted with a 3mm (⅛in) straight cutter.

The best faces were chosen for the inside of the cabinet

The strip was sanded and finished and the centre piece cut to size, with a 22½° butt- join face at each end, and glued to the cross strip. The two side pieces were then cut, fitted, and glued to the fronts of the cupboard. The join between the sides and the front of the strip should be in the same position on the raised decorative square on each side, or it will look unbalanced.

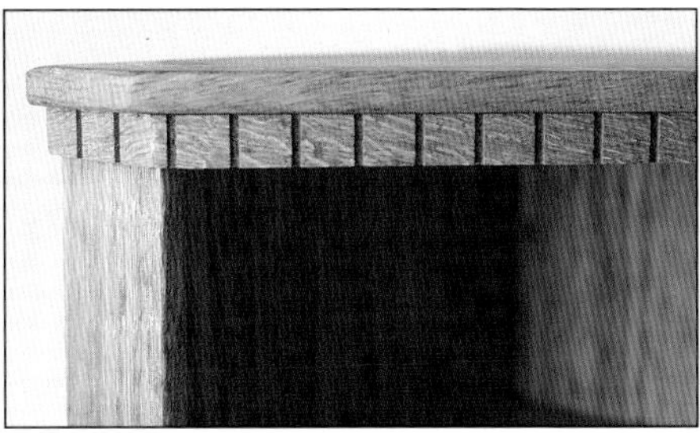

Close-up of decorative strip

Finish

I have always liked the look of old, oiled oak and when I tried boiled linseed oil on some scraps of this brown oak it looked fantastic. I hand-sanded the whole cupboard, checking carefully for glue ooze and marks, particular-ly on the visible inside faces. I then sanded down to 240 grit, wiped it all over with white spirit, and checked again. Once satisfied that the finish was good, I applied a liberal coat of warm, boiled linseed oil. Warming the oil reduces viscosity and helps penetration.

The old oiling adage of 'Once an hour for a day, once a day for a week, once a week for a month and once a year thereafter' is not far out. The first coat was liberally applied, left to soak in, and refreshed every 15 to 20 minutes until it would take no more (4–6 coats). It was then wiped off with a soft cloth. No oil must be allowed to build up

Cutting the decorative strip on the radial-arm saw

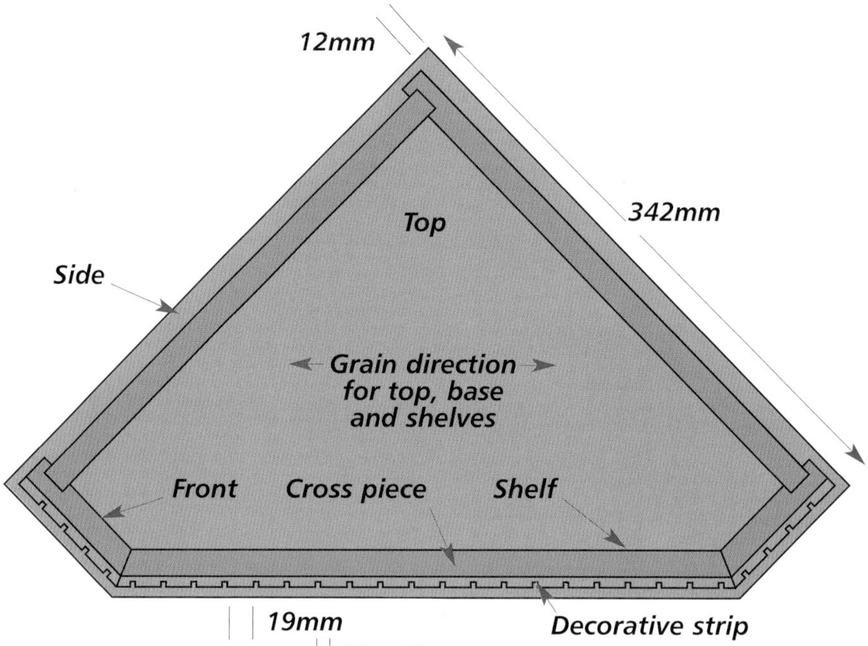

on the surface. The piece was then left to harden in a dry, warm place for 24 hours.

The surface was cut back with a Scotchbrite grey pad and further light coats applied every 24 hours. This too was cut back with the Scotchbrite pad, making sure that there was no build-up of oil on the surface. Once the desired effect was achieved I gave it a final coat of Danish oil to speed up the hardening process.

After a few days this last coat was cut back and buffed with a soft cloth to a nice soft sheen. Future care would be an annual light coat of teak oil.

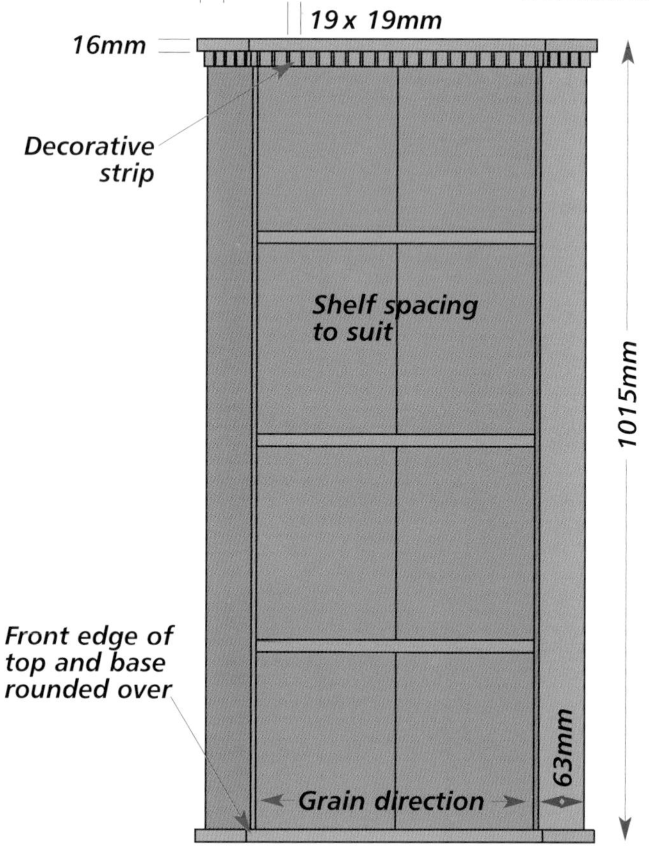

Cutting housings for shelves

Fully loaded

12mm
342mm
Top
Side
Grain direction for top, base and shelves
Front
Cross piece
Shelf
19mm
Decorative strip
19 x 19mm
16mm
Decorative strip
Shelf spacing to suit
1015mm
Front edge of top and base rounded over
63mm
Grain direction

The finished article

To hang the cupboard I drilled countersunk holes through the sides just behind the fronts at the base, and in the top back corner. These are all places where the screw heads would not be seen. These holes were marked through to the wall, which was drilled and plugged. It was then screwed through the sides, into the wall plugs, to hang firmly in position.

My wife was duly called for the seal of approval, and she completed the project by putting the china in place. Mind you, I think I prefer it empty – to show off that lovely wood! ●

Well oiled

Stand clear

Keeping abreast of technology with a unit to house a computer printer

The imminent arrival of my new computer forced me to address the rat's nest of cables and electrical sockets that had grown in the corner between my desk and computer station. My new system would also include a brand new printer, so some extra top area was required to re-site the printer.

The master plan

All that was needed was a very simple carcass with an open back to allow easy access for cables, somewhere to fix some multi-outlet sockets, and a shelf to allow storage on and under. The available floor space and the height of the existing station top dictated its size, and the height of the shelf was chosen to allow storage of specific items underneath.

Methods of construction

Speed and simplicity are the keynotes with this project – so wafer-reinforced butt joints are the order of the day. I had just acquired a brand new ¼in router and this seemed like the ideal opportunity to test it thoroughly. I decided to use it for the whole job, ignoring my trusty biscuit jointer.

Sides and shelf

Cut the sides out and clamp them together, giving a wider base for the plane to assist accuracy. Plane the edges to their exact size, and sand to a finish with an orbital sander. Cut the slots for the Tanselli wafers using the router with a spiral 4mm upcutter and a batten clamp. The slots for the back rails are cut using the side fence, and I decided to cut the joint at the top of the sides after the carcass had been assembled.

Cut the shelf and back rails to size, square the ends and cut the slots for the wafer joints, using a wheel cutter in the router.

Materials

This was to be a small, functional piece, so I started looking in the workshop for some offcuts of sheet material. I found sufficient 12mm (½in) MDF for the sides and further 18mm (¾in) pieces for the shelf, top, and back rails.

1 A rat's nest of cables

Carcass assembly

Cut the wafer strips to size to fit the rail and shelf joints, offer up the sides and make a dry run of the assembly to check that everything fits. Make any necessary adjustments, and go over all the pieces with an orbital sander down to 120 grit on the inside faces. Apply some PVA adhesive and clamp up the carcass.

Alternative construction

If you don't have a biscuit jointer, router or sash cramps, don't despair – this simple piece of MDF furniture can be fixed together by more traditional means, using screws and glue.

Tricky MDF

Because MDF can easily split when screws are wound in holes that are too tight, care is needed when using this method. After drilling the 3.5mm hole through the sheet and then countersinking its outside, use a screw to mark the hole position for the board edges.

- **Screws: 16 x 38mm (1½in) No. 10s**
- **Drill bits: 3.5mm twist or lip and spur bit**
- **Countersink: 8 or 12mm**

When drilling into the edges of MDF, make sure that the hole is no closer than 40mm (1⅝in) to the board end. This will help prevent splitting.

Assembly

Apply an even coat of PVA glue to the entire edge of the MDF, wiping off any excess immediately after assembly. Be careful not to over-tighten the screws, since they will only 'bite' just enough to give you a gluing pressure. It is worthwhile trying a practice hole on some scrap beforehand. Leave the glue to dry for 24 hours to ensure maximum strength. Fill the countersunk holes with a medium-tone, stainable wood filler.

Measure the diagonals to ensure the carcass is square, and stand it on a flat surface to cure.

Once cured, clamp pieces of scrap either side of the top of the sides to steady the router base, and cut the slots for the top joint with the spiral cutter using the side fence. Staying with this tool, cut corresponding slots in the underside of the top, allowing a 25mm (1in) overhang, and do another dry run to check the top fits. Make any adjustments, sand down the underside of the top and the outside faces of the sides down to 120 grit, apply glue and clamp the top on. Check the whole carcass to ensure it's square, and leave to set.

Staining

Carefully check the whole piece for any excess glue, and if present remove with a sharp chisel. If any marks or blemishes are present, get rid of them, firstly with a palm sander and then by hand. Once the surface is clean and smooth, start the staining. I decided to use an oil-based, dark-brown mahogany stain to match the other furniture as best I could. Dilute the first coat to a 50/50 consistency with white spirit, to avoid streaking on the absorbent surface of the MDF, and apply with a brush. Wipe all the surplus off with a soft cloth to ensure there is no surface build-up, and leave to dry for 24 hours. Rub the surface over thoroughly with a coarse cloth, add some white spirit and then apply another coat of the same stain the next day, leaving for 24 hours to cure. By now the colour should be about right, so apply three coats of Danish oil to the surface, leaving each coat to cure for 24 hours in a warm, dry area. Cut each coat back with a Scotchbrite grey pad before recoating.

Installation

After allowing it to harden fully for a few days, I fixed the multi-socket electrical outlets to the sides and made a cutout in the side to accommodate the wall-mounted telephone point. When the new computer and its peripherals finally arrived, the myriad of cables were routed to the power points and the whole area tidied up – which ironically took longer than making the stand!

Conclusion

This piece was made very quickly, at a minimum cost, and it serves its

2 Planing to size, with both sides cramped together

3 Routing the slots for the wafers using a router and straight cutter

4 Using a router to cut the shelf-supporting slots

5 Routing the slots for the wafers on the shelf sides

6 Sanding the sides with a random orbital sander

7 Cramping the shelf back and rails using sash cramps

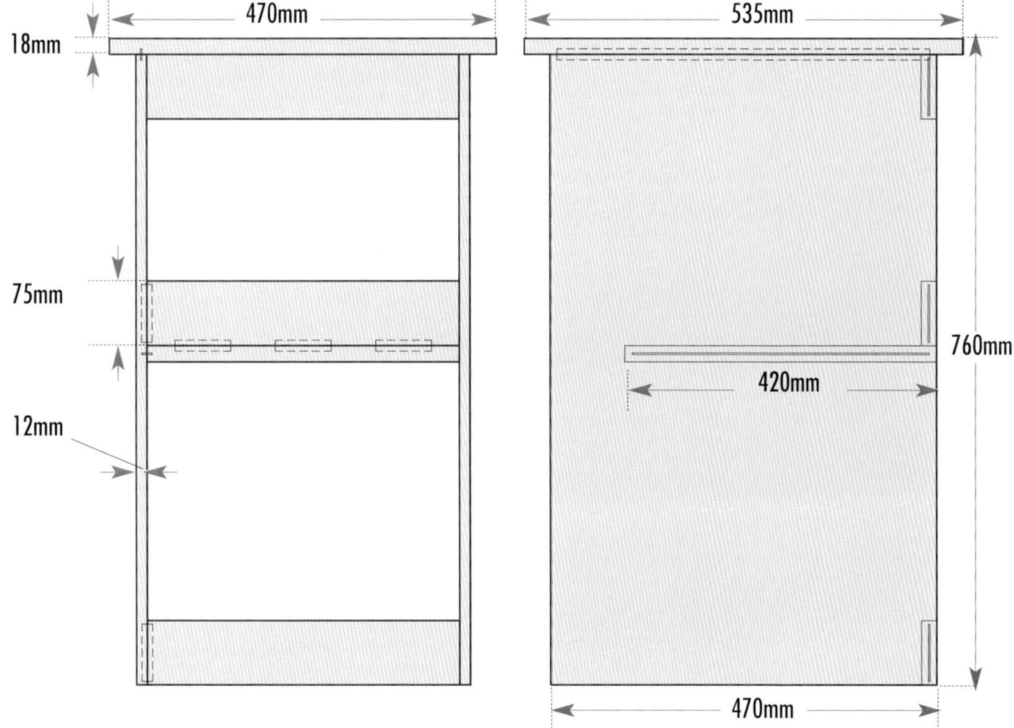

purpose excellently. I was surprised at how well the stained MDF blended with the existing solid wood pieces, although having said that, only a few square inches of it are visible!

I guess this is just one of those jobs where the satisfaction is not so much in looking at the final piece itself, but rather not looking at the mess that it has enabled to be cleared away!

And another thing...

While this is a very basic unit, its method of construction can be applied to any number of functional pieces, including workshop or kitchen units. At 12mm (½in), the sides are a little too thin – 18mm (¾in) would be better.

I usually put in a fixed back for the extra strength, but the cable access required meant that in this case this wasn't an option. The back rails were a compromise and fortunately they provide the unit with all the necessary rigidity.

A solid base is another feature that would improve the strength of the unit.

Using a biscuit jointer and a board of the same thickness throughout would make the whole job even quicker.

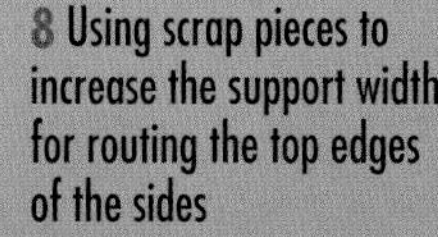
8 Using scrap pieces to increase the support width for routing the top edges of the sides

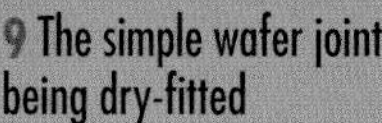
9 The simple wafer joint being dry-fitted

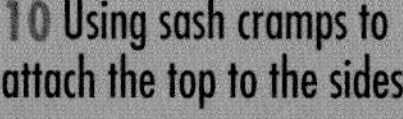
10 Using sash cramps to attach the top to the sides

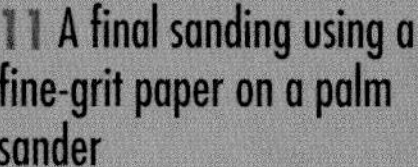
11 A final sanding using a fine-grit paper on a palm sander

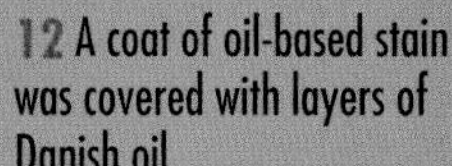
12 A coat of oil-based stain was covered with layers of Danish oil

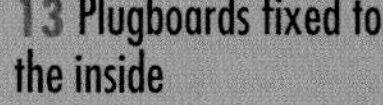
13 Plugboards fixed to the inside

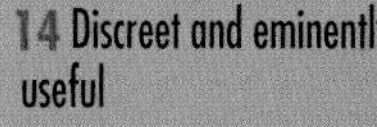
14 Discreet and eminently useful

Man in the Mirror

Some reflections on seven years' good luck, and three mirrors

Mirrors are wonderful – people (especially journalists) always see their favourite things in them! Mirrors can create an impression of space in a room and bring light into dark corners, as well as their more obvious practical function. The frame is as important to a mirror as to a picture, and over the years I have made quite a few for various clients. I aim to show three very differently framed mirrors in this article, each design using a different method of construction.

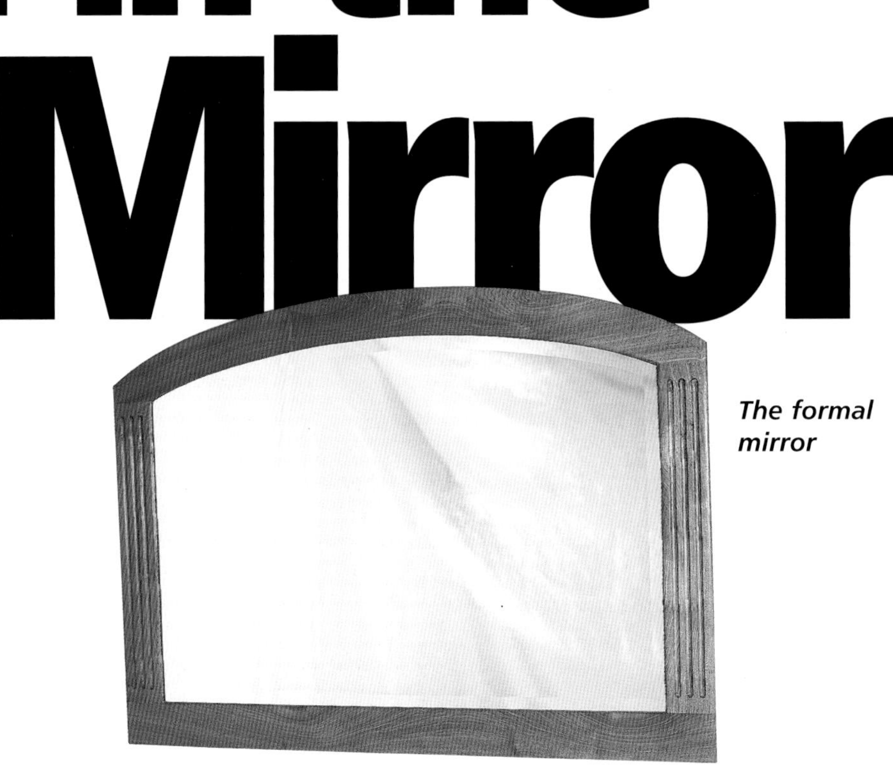

The formal mirror

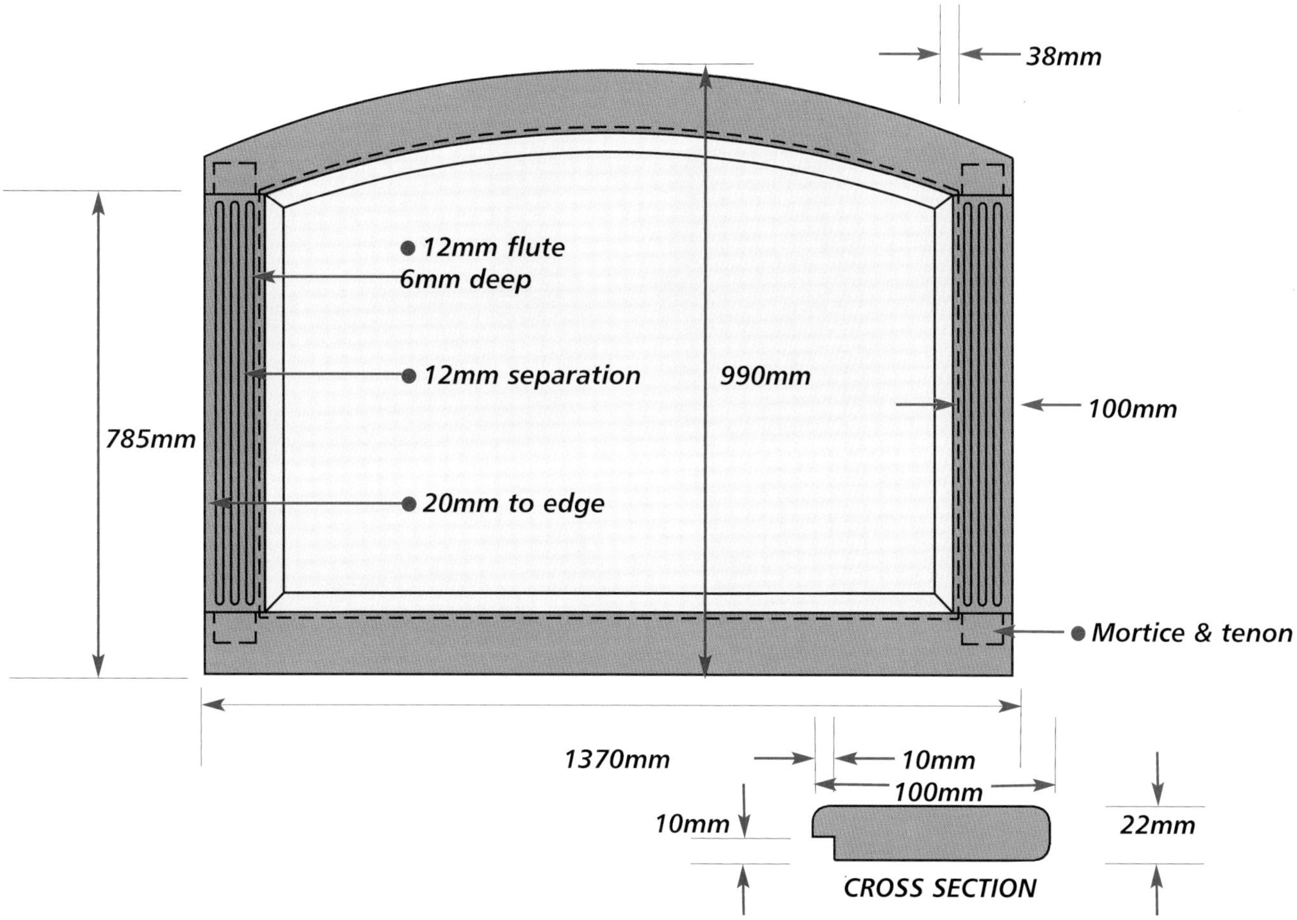

38mm

12mm flute
6mm deep

12mm separation

990mm

100mm

785mm

20mm to edge

Mortice & tenon

1370mm

10mm

100mm

10mm

22mm

CROSS SECTION

The formal mirror

Timber selection – This mirror was designed to go over an existing oak mantel shelf in a big traditional fireplace. The mantel shelf was very old, dark brown oak, with an oiled finish. New oak, even of the brown variety, did not look quite right but a nice piece of English walnut left over from a previous job was perfect – and I had exactly the right amount!

Native walnut is a lovely light, strong wood that works easily and cuts cleanly, giving off a nice scent. It's stable, moving very little with changes in humidity, carves well and polishes to a high finish. Its properties make it ideal for furniture making, and, incidentally, for stocks for good-quality guns. Unfortunately it is also fairly hard to find and expensive, but ideally suited to this sort of piece where a small amount of wood is used, all of it is on display, and the item is of relatively high value.

The overall size was decided by trying hardboard cutouts in the place where the mirror would go until it looked right. We decided that a fairly wide frame was required to keep it in proportion with the mantel shelf and the area of the mirror glass – 100mm (4in) seemed OK. The frame top would be curved, the sides fluted, and the edges rounded over to provide the finishing touches. We also decided on a 38mm (1 1/2in) bevel on the edge of the mirror glass to make it look even more formal and expensive. Finding someone who would bevel a curved glass edge at a reasonable price was not easy – there was a huge discrepancy in the quotes I got. This piece cost £100, over half of which was for the bevelling – but well worth it for the final effect.

Construction – Bearing in mind that this frame would end up over a fireplace containing a wood-burning stove, it was important to carefully condition the walnut before making it up. The four frame pieces were cut oversize, sticks put between them, the whole lot clamped together, and left in the room close to the fireplace to condition for a couple of weeks. Once I was happy that the wood was stable to the room conditions I took the cut pieces to the workshop. Here all the pieces were faced and thicknessed to 22mm (7/8in) and cut to exact width and length. The sides and bottom rail were cut to 100 x 22mm (4 x 7/8in) and the top rail to 230 x 22mm

Fluting on formal mirror

(9 x 7/8in) to allow the curve to be cut out. Mortices were cut at the ends of the inside edges of the top and bottom rails, and tenons to fit them cut in the ends of the side rails. The curve on the top rail was marked, cut on the bandsaw and finished with a plane and spokeshave. A rebate 10 x 10mm (3/8 x 3/8in) was cut with the router on the inside edge of the sides to take the 4mm thick mirror, and a 3mm (1/8in) thick

Organic frame ideas marked on rough-sawn burr

Final burr frame shape

hardboard back. A similar, but stopped, rebate was cut in the bottom rail. To form the rebate in the curved top I used a finger fence on the router table to follow the shape of the curve, and cut carefully, keeping the point of cut directly opposite the fence.

Edge fluting on formal mirror

Flutes

The flutes in the two side pieces were now cut 6mm (1/4in) deep with a 13mm (1/2in) core-box cutter. The side fence was used to cut the two edge flutes 19mm (3/4in) in from each side using the same setting, cutting to a marked end-stop line. The side fence was reset carefully and the centre flutes cut. All the flute cuts were set up and tested on a piece of scrap the same width as the side pieces.

Assembly – Having checked that the mortice and tenon joints fitted, I applied Titebond glue to the top inside edges of the mortices, brushed some onto the cheeks of the tenons and assembled the frame. The diagonals were measured to ensure everything was square and then it was left to set. Once this was complete the rebate corners were cleaned up and squared with a sharp chisel, and the front face and side edges were finished with plane and scraper, then sanded to 120 grit. The inside and outside edges were then rounded over to 6mm (1/4in) radius using a rounding-over cutter with a bearing guide. This prevented the cutter getting right into the corner of the inside edges, so these were finished with a chisel and careful sanding. The hardboard back was marked using the inside edge of the frame as a template. Adjustments were made to leave 1.5mm (1/16in) clearance all round the edges of the back when it sat in the frame recess, and it was taken to the glazier as the template for the mirror.

Finish – An oiled finish, which particularly suits walnut, was decided on. The frame was finally sanded down to 320 grit, and given a generous coat of oil which was renewed until no more would soak in. After 15 minutes it was wiped off with a soft cloth to ensure no oil was left on the surface. The first coat of oil is the most important, since once it has cured it forms a barrier to much more being absorbed. After 24 hours in my warm, dry workshop the surface was cut back with a Scotchbright grey pad, a thin second and third coat applied, and buffed with a soft cloth. Walnut is not very absorbent so any more coats might cause a build-up of oil on the surface with the resultant undesirable 'syrupy' effect. The mirror glass was then placed carefully in the recess and the back pinned into the frame to hold it in position. The finished mirror was delivered to the client, hung over the fireplace, approved of, and then drink was taken!

Organic mirror

This mirror was to go into an unheated washroom decorated in an ethnic style in earth colours. I suggested an organic shape in burr elm to suit the room style and colours.

"The finished effect really brought out the beautiful figure and colour."

Organic-shape mirror

Timber selection & preparation – Several years ago I collected and planked some burr elm, and it had been drying ever since in my humidity-controlled timber store. The main problems encountered with burr elm are wild grain, many live and dead knots of all sizes, ingrowing bark, cracks and blemishes. It can be very hard and quite soft all in the same board. Humidity has a serious effect since it takes in and gives up water relatively easily, causing movement. In my opinion all these disadvantages are far outweighed by the stunning visual impact of this beautifully figured, rich, warm, brown native timber. When I explain that it was harvested from hedgerow trees that would otherwise have ended up as logs it gains a conversational and conservational appeal to customers. I experimented with some different organic shapes on various pieces, chose the ones I liked best and brought them into the workshop for a couple of weeks to finish conditioning.

305mm

Biscuits

430mm

Construction – After facing and thicknessing to 22mm (7/8in) the shape was re-marked in chalk, the inside edges were cut and planed true, and the pieces cut to size. I decided on biscuit joints at the corners – I feel they are more trustworthy in this timber, where tenons can snap if the unpredictable grain direction is unkind. The positions of the biscuits were marked, taking care to ensure that when the final shape was cut out they would not be exposed. A 10 x 10mm (3/8 x 3/8in) rebate was cut with the router to take the mirror and hardboard back on the inside edge of the sides. A stopped rebate was cut in the top and bottom rails for the same purpose. The biscuit joints were glued and the frame assembled. Once the glue had cured, the final shape was cut out on the bandsaw. It was finished with a spokeshave, scrapers and various belt and drum sanders. The edges were rounded over with a 6mm (1/4in) rounding-over cutter on the router table to further soften the organic shape. The corners of the rebate were tidied up with a sharp chisel, and the back cut from hardboard. Again this back was taken to the glazier as a template for the mirror glass, which was cut while I waited.

Finish – I decided on a wax over Danish oil finish. Burr elm can be very porous and oil penetrates well into the wood, helping to stabilise it by slowing down moisture take-up and loss. The wax gives a pleasant sheen and smell. Any pits, cracks and blemishes were filled and then the frame was finished down to 320 grit. The first coat of oil was then liberally applied. It was left to soak in and then refreshed every 15 to 20 minutes until it would take no more (4–6 coats). This was then wiped off with a soft cloth to prevent any oil build-up on the surface and left to harden for 24 hours in a warm, dry place. The surface was cut back with a Scotchbrite grey pad and three further light coats applied at 24-hour intervals. The last coat was cut back with the Scotchbright grey pad, two coats of wax applied and buffed off with a soft cloth. The finished effect really brought out the beautiful figure and colour.

Final assembly – Once the finish was complete, the frame was laid face down on a thick piece of blanket on the bench, the mirror glass inserted into the rebate, and the back pinned into position. The mirror was hung in position and looked just right in its surroundings, the colours in the wood really enhancing the earth colours in the room.

Country-style mirror

This mirror was to go into a traditional-style kitchen in an old country cottage with a heavily beamed ceiling in dark old oak. A simple design was appropriate and I decided on the crossover, half-lapped corners used on some old frames.

Timber selection & preparation – I had some brown oak which was quite dark, and

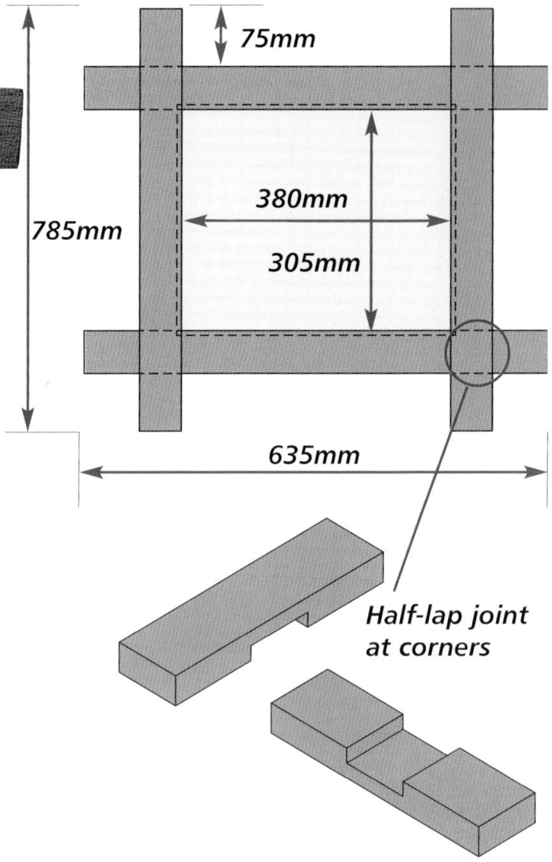

75mm
785mm
380mm
305mm
635mm
Half-lap joint at corners

with a suitable finish would do nicely. This was kiln-dried timber, and with its small dimensions I felt it would have time enough to condition in the workshop during the making.

Construction – The frame pieces were dimensioned to 56 x 22mm (2¹/4 x 7/8in) and cut to length. The four frame pieces were clamped in position with the correct faces uppermost and the half-lap corner joints cut on all four at the same time. I used a two-flute straight cutter, set to the correct depth, and a suitable straight-edged fence to set the width. The pieces were stop-rebated for the mirror and back, the joints glued and the frame assembled, checked for square, and left to set. Next, all

Routing half-laps

> **"These small projects can have big effects – and are also useful in using up some of those precious off-cuts"**

the edges were softened using a 3mm (1/8in) rounding–over cutter with a bearing guide. The frame was sanded to 240 grit, the rebate corners chiselled square, the back cut to size, and again used as the template for the mirror.

Finish – I wanted to darken the wood a bit, and the client wanted a 'wipe-clean' surface – just the job for a satin polyurethane finish. Four thin coats were applied with a pad, leaving for 24 hours between coats and cutting back all but the last coat with a piece of worn 320-grit aluminium oxide paper. The back and mirror were pinned into position. The completed mirror was delivered, where it was well received and hung in position.

Though simple in construction, these mirrors use a variety of timbers, construction and finishes – it doesn't have to be complicated to be good. These small projects can have big effects – and are also useful in using up some of those precious off-cuts! ●

Pinning back, showing pin-pusher

Perfect Partnership

A partners' desk in fumed mahogany and cherry

This commission came from a client for whom I had previously made six desks. I opted for two styles, both of which are the same size. The first, which his female staff are particularly keen on, has a front closed by a cupboard which doubles as a modesty panel, while the second, which he prefers, is open-fronted with a false drawer between the pedestals, leaving him plenty of room to strech his legs. I used American walnut (Juglans nigra) with burr elm (Ulmus spp.) panels for the latter style, and fumed oak (Quercus spp.) and sycamore (Acer pseudoplatanus) for the former.

Timber selection

I use our cottage as a showroom and display a range of styles of furniture in different woods, which enables my clients to see more possibilities. Fortunately my wife and I have eclectic taste in both furniture and style so this arrangement suits us both. Having said that, I have been known to sell the odd piece that she had considered to be 'ours' in her absence!

Over the years the client who commissioned this project has visited our cottage frequently and has thus become familiar with different timbers and treatments. He has always admired our fumed mahogany (*Swietenia macrophylla*) and burr elm longcase clock, and decided to have this desk in fumed mahogany, but with cherry (*Prunus* spp.) as a contrasting timber for the door panels and false drawer front.

Design

The requirement was for a large top on two pedestals with drawers, one of which has rails and is deep enough for suspension files. The depth of the top meant that drawers running the full depth of the pedestal would be too long for convenience, so cupboards were built into the front, giving access to the potential storage space from both front and back. The top is removable so that the desk breaks down into two separate pedestals, linked by the false drawer front and the top, for ease of movement.

Timber preparation

The timber had been kiln-dried when I purchased it and it was conditioned in my wood store for several weeks before I got started. It is critical to get the timber as close as possible to the likely moisture content of its final destination before you start working on it. I have a special wood store with a dehumidifier, and also keep my workshop close to domestic humidity

1 The rear view, showing the drawers

2 Detail showing the dovetailed drawers

3 Conditioning timber ensures good results

4 Belt-sanding the side panels

5 The desk top, showing the join using Tanselli wafers

6 A Tanselli wafer on the side frame tested to destruction

7 Using a random orbital sander on the side frames

8 Clamping one of the pedestals

9 Cutting the drawer dovetails on the bandsaw

10 Marking an escutcheon for a keyhole

11 Marking out for a drawer lock

12 Chopping out the lock recess in the drawer front

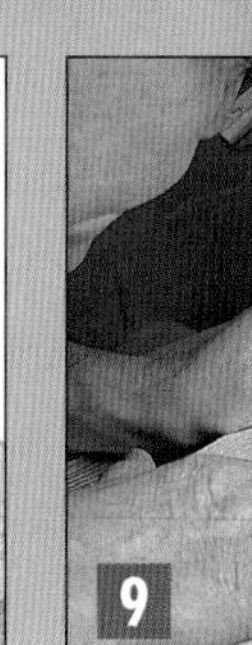

USEFUL DEFINITION
Partners' desk – a large flat-topped pedestal desk with space for two people to sit opposite each other.

levels with heating and another dehumidifier.

Timber that has been cut a little oversize can also be stacked on sticks in a spare bedroom for a few weeks to condition it to ambient humidity and temperature. During production always ensure that wood not being worked on is stacked and sticked to hold it flat and allow even drying on all faces.

Batch production

I made maximum use of rods and jigs with this project, ensuring that all repeat cuts were done at the same time and that I finished up with the correct number of pieces. The measurements of the first ones off were double-checked to ensure I didn't make multiple mistakes.

Cutting out

Both the mahogany for the drawer casings and the cherry for the door panels were marked out, cut, and dimensioned first. They were then stacked and sticked with a weight on top to get maximum conditioning time in the warm, dry workshop while I was doing the main construction.

I selected the pieces with the best figuring for the top, cut a little oversize and stacked. The selection progressed down in size and visual importance until I was left with the trimmings to make some of the internal pieces such as drawer frames and shelves, minimising waste. All this timber was now faced, thicknessed, and dimensioned to the exact size.

TOP TIP
I made maximum use of rods and jigs to ensure that all repeat cuts were done at the same time and I finished up with the correct number of pieces.

Construction

Top

The top was made up first, the boards edge-matched to disguise the joint and get the best figure. The edges were machine-planed and finished by hand to take out the planer ripples and leave the join slightly hollow at the centre. This puts slight pressure on the ends and allows for any extra shrinkage of the end grain. Tanselli wafers were used to strengthen and locate the joins and the top was clamped and left to set, then finished down to 150 grit with power sanders. It was stored flat on sticks with the top face protected by a hardboard sheet.

Sides

All four frame and panel pedestal sides were made next. The bottom rail was deep enough to take the moulded plinth, and show the same depth as the top rail above it. An insert was fitted to the inside to house the back, the ends of the drawer frames and shelves.

The inside edges of the frame were grooved to take the panels, and the corners joined using double Tanselli wafers, with slots cut with the Trend T5 and a spiral 4mm straight cutter. I had tested the strength of this joint to destruction and was very impressed.

The panels were made up of solid wood 10mm (⅜in) thick, and edge-jointed to size, with biscuit reinforcing. The faces were finished with belt and random orbital sanders, the sides assembled, checked for square and wind, and left to set.

The stopped housings to take the shelves and drawer frames were then cut with a router. The sides were clearly marked as right- and left-handed, and all the cuts were made using the T9 router and fence. A clamp guide was used for the cuts outside the range of the fence. Finally the frames were finished using a random orbital sander, particularly on the corners where the grain ran at right angles.

Drawer frames and shelves

The drawer frames were made up with a biscuit joint at each corner and a ply lip glued and pinned along the outside edge, for the drawers to run against. The shelves were cut to size, finished, and with the drawer frames, shouldered to fit the stopped housings in the side frames. The cupboard backs were cut to size from 5mm (³⁄₁₆in) mahogany-faced MDF.

Assembly of pedestals

Extramite™, with its long open time, was used to glue up the pedestals, which were then clamped, checked for square, and left to set.

The backs, which had been glued all round into the slot, were then pinned to the drawer frames and the shelves using a hardboard jig which held the pin in place for the hammer – a simple and effective aid.

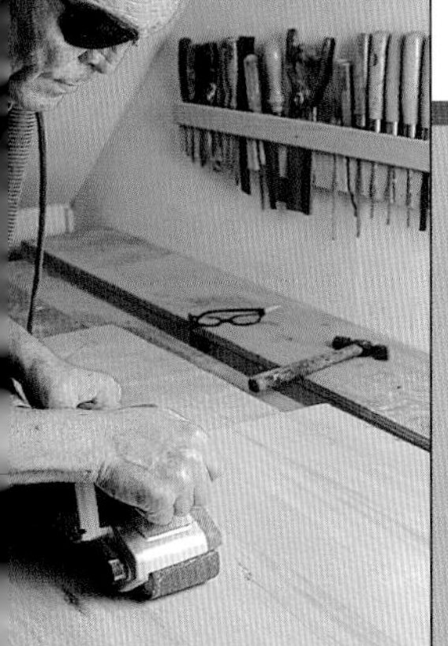

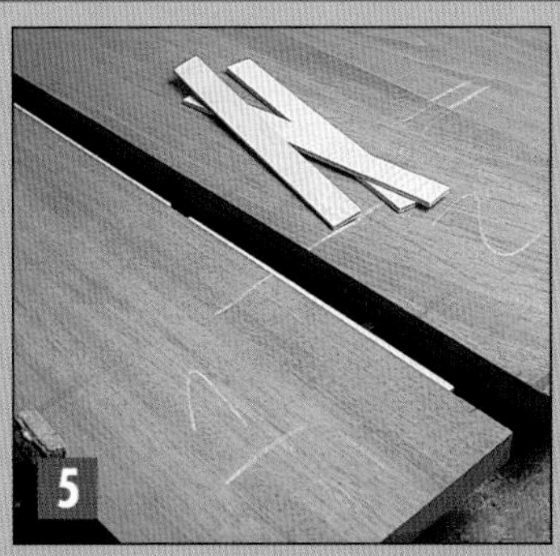

5

6

7

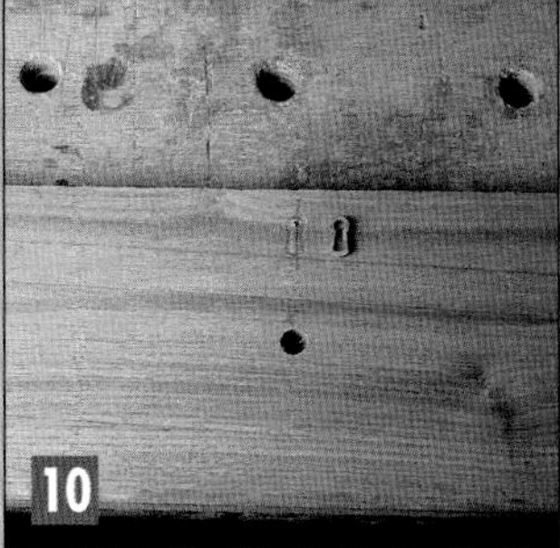

10

11

12

Plinths

The top edges of the plinth pieces were shaped with an ogee moulding cutter on the T9. The pieces were cut to length and mitred on the radial-arm saw, and hand-finished on a shooting board; the mitres were reinforced with biscuits. The plinth was glued and screwed to the pedestal sides, and a backing rail screwed between the sides at the front. I used a strap clamp with blocks, and G-clamps, and then screwed through from the inside. The mitres were tapped over and sanded to a finish when dry.

False drawer front

The false drawer front was made of a frame of mahogany with a floating flush panel of cherry, let into another rebate in the frame and held in place with beading, to look like a drawer.

This complete assembly would be screwed to the sides and top between the pedestals, from the inside rear.

Doors

The frames were made first – all the stiles and rails were dimensioned and the mortices and tenons cut.

A rebate was cut on the inside edges to take the fielded cherry panels, and beading was made to hold them in place. The panels were made up to size and fielded using a vertical profile cutter, then hand-planed and sanded to a finish. The panel faces were also power-sanded to a finish. The door frames were assembled, glued and clamped, checked for square and wind, and left to set.

Fitting the doors

Once set, the door frame faces were finished, again with a random orbital sander. The frames themselves were then fitted, leaving about 1mm ($\frac{3}{64}$in) clearance all round. This would be finally adjusted to 2mm ($\frac{5}{64}$in) on final fitting.

The hinges were recessed into the door frame only and not the carcass side, which leaves a neater line. They were positioned and scribed round with a scalpel. The T5 router fence and depth were set to take out the majority of the waste, and the recesses squared off with a chisel.

Brass butt hinges were screwed into the recess, using my wonderful, self-centring hinge pilot drill (which only cost me a couple of quid) and a power screwdriver.

A cutting gauge was used to scribe the screw line on the inside face of the side. The doors were wedged at the correct height, the screw line centred in the hinge screw hole, and the self-centring pilot drill used to make one hole in each hinge. The two screws were driven home, the door was checked to make sure it fitted, adjustments were made and the remaining holes and the screws were drilled and driven respectively.

Brass double ball catches were fitted – this was easy while the pedestals had no tops – and the spring-loading on the balls was adjusted to get a satisfying 'clunk'.

Door and drawer pulls

I turned the pulls on my lathe, making full use of sizing tools and a profile, which was cut from hardboard with notches for a pencil point to mark the relevant cuts.

Drawers

All the pieces for the drawers were cut to size, fitted and marked. The sides were slotted for the bases, taped together in double pairs with the top one marked, and the tails were cut on the bandsaw.

The fronts and backs were marked one at a time from the tails, and the majority of the waste removed with the T5. Each joint was then individually finished with a chisel and the drawer assembled, with the oak-faced MDF

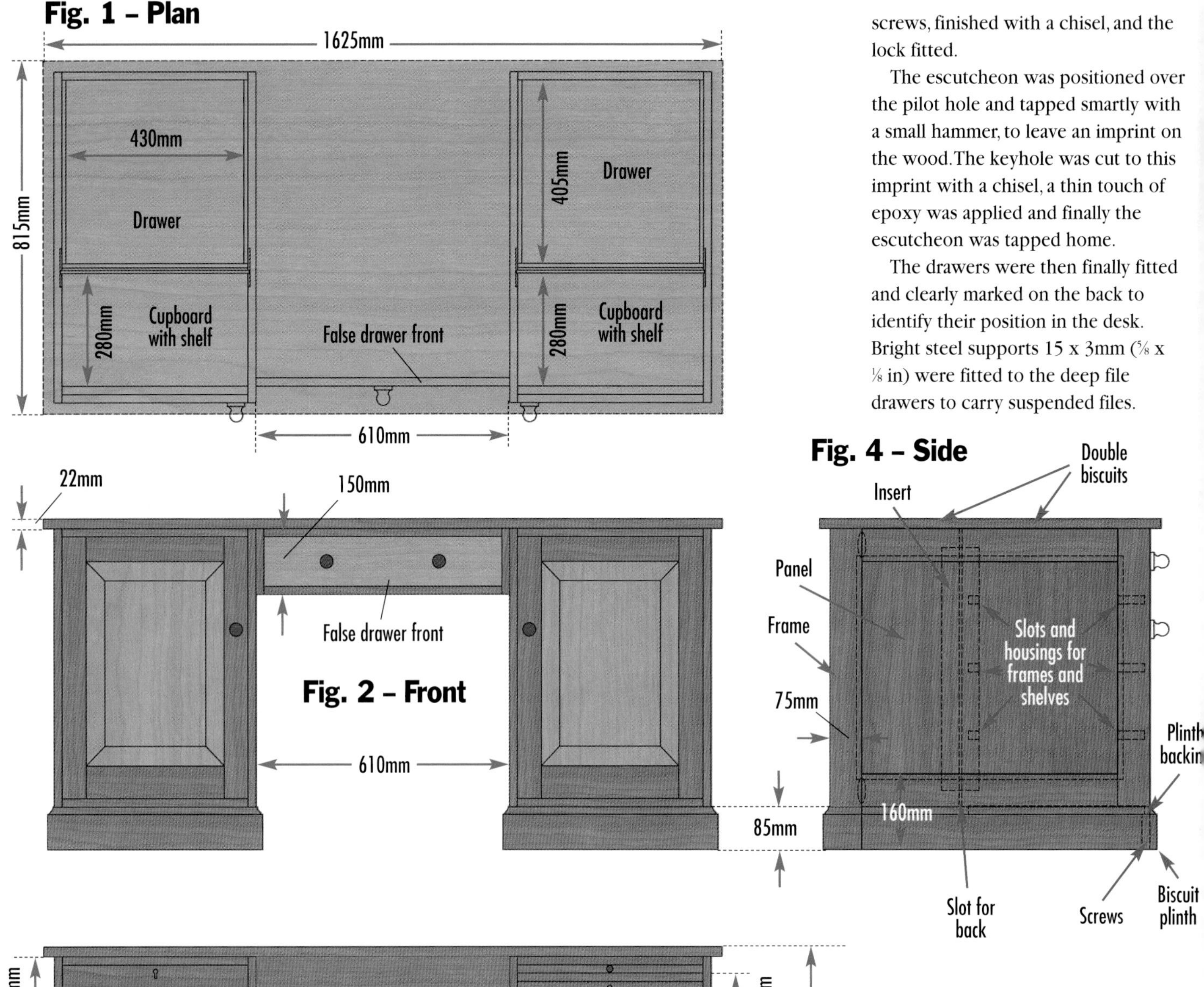

Paper rest

The paper rest was made from MDF, flush-faced with mahogany-faced MDF, and edge-lipped. 25mm (1in) holes had been drilled in the frame under the paper rest, before assembly, to give access for the screws fixing the top. The paper rest was fitted and a pull was attached. Stops, to prevent the rest being pulled out too far, were fitted from underneath once it was in position

base glued in all round and pinned at the back. It was then checked for square and wind, and left to set.

Before assembling the top drawers the locks were fitted to the fronts. They were positioned and the hole for the key pin was marked in the centre of the drawer at the correct height and drilled through. The recess was routed out, leaving a shallow shoulder for the screws, finished with a chisel, and the lock fitted.

The escutcheon was positioned over the pilot hole and tapped smartly with a small hammer, to leave an imprint on the wood. The keyhole was cut to this imprint with a chisel, a thin touch of epoxy was applied and finally the escutcheon was tapped home.

The drawers were then finally fitted and clearly marked on the back to identify their position in the desk. Bright steel supports 15 x 3mm (⅝ x ⅛ in) were fitted to the deep file drawers to carry suspended files.

Assembly

The desk was assembled on my level platform on the floor of the workshop, and all final tests and adjustments were made. The top was attached using screws through slots in the top rails of the pedestals. The false drawer front was screwed through from the inside to the pedestal side frames and the top.

Fuming

I carefully checked for glue marks and finished all the surfaces, hand-sanding down to 320 grit. Then I made a tent using 20mm (¾in) plastic overflow pipe and fittings bought from a builders' merchant for the frame, which was covered in a thin polythene sheet. The pipe comes in 3m (10ft) lengths with a range of push fittings, and is a cheap and convenient way of making a large temporary chamber. This can also be used in conjunction with a dehumidifier as a temporary conditioning tent.

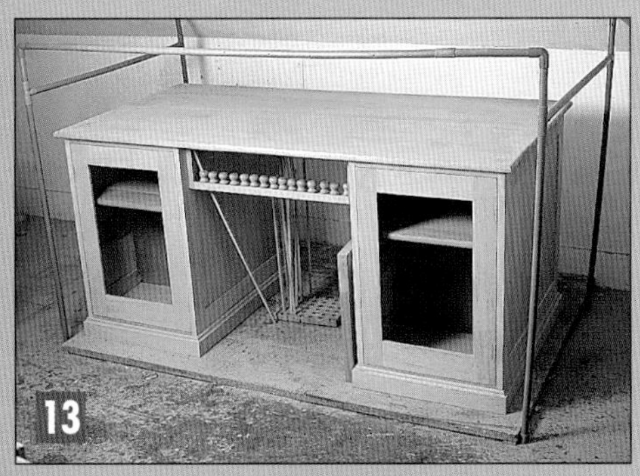

13 All of the pieces assembled for fuming

14 Tubs of ammonia were placed in the tent

15 Nailing the backs with a hardboard jig

16 Suspension file rails fitted to the deep drawer

17 Danish oil was chosen for the mahogany

18 The completed components ready for assembly

Plastic tubs of ammonia 890 were placed in the tent and the edges of the sheet were weighted down to the floor with strips of wood to make it airtight. Gloves and eye protection are an absolute must when using concentrated ammonia.

The cherry panels were not fitted while the desk was in the tent, as a test had established that it turns a deep golden brown if fumed. They were finished instead with three coats of acrylic satin varnish to keep their lighter, contrasting colour.

Finish

A Danish oil finish was chosen for the mahogany to really enhance its deep red-brown colour. I liberally applied a first coat of oil and renewed it every hour or so for a day, until the wood would really take no more. At that point I removed all surplus oil, to prevent any build-up on the surface, and left it to dry and harden in my warm, dry workshop for 24 hours.

This surface was cut back by hand with 320 grit, followed by a light coat of oil every 24 hours for a week, cut back between coats with a Scotchbright grey pad. I then allowed 10 days for final hardening.

Delivery and final assembly

My client arranged for one of his vans to collect this piece and I went up to Durham to assemble it and make any adjustments required. All went well – so well that I left with a new order for a floor-to-ceiling glazed-front bookcase, in the same timbers, for his new study! ❑

TOP TIP

It is critical to get the timber as close as possible to the likely moisture content of its final destination before you start working on it.

FUMING

A distinctive desk made in fumed mahogany and burr elm

The last order I was able to make in my old workshop was for a tall, tapered chest and companion desk with a single, tapered, three-drawer pedestal. The client had seen my burr elm apothecary's chest in an exhibition in the Bowes Museum. When he came to buy it, he enquired about having a small desk and chest of drawers made. Fortunately, I had an oak tapered-pedestal desk in the house which I had just completed for another client. When he saw it he was taken with the idea of the tapering pedestal, and decided to have one for his desk. He then saw a tall Shaker-style chest I had made some time ago, and, drawing it up on the computer to get a sense of the proportions, he decided, albeit a bit nervously, to use the taper for the companion chest of drawers in order to have two matching pieces.

wild, wild wood

My client was very keen on the burr elm, not only because of its beautiful figure, but because it was gathered locally from the hedgerows where elms have all but disappeared. However, we quickly realised that to make the whole piece from burr would be highly impractical. Firstly, I did not have enough burr or the sizes required, and secondly it was unsuitable for most parts of the construction. Although wild grain gives the piece its stunning figure, it has the drawback of lacking stability and strength, and is prone to being somewhat 'unpredictable' when worked.

The final decision was to use a relatively small amount of burr but to maximise its impact by using it for the drawer fronts. The remainder of the carcass construction was to be made from fumed, oiled Brazilian mahogany to provide a contrast of colour and figure while also emphasising the burr and giving a richness to the finished piece. Fuming immediately brings out the deep red colour of the mahogany, usually only reached after some time. As the chest was to be used for clothes storage, we opted for cedar of Lebanon, with its distinctive pleasant smell and insect-repellent properties, for the drawer casings.

The Brazilian mahogany, with its relative lack of figure, consistent grain and absence of faults, was easily selected, cut and dressed oversize and then stacked with separating sticks and placed in the conditioning cabinet. The cedar of Lebanon

Photo 1 The beauty of burr elm **Photo 2** The tapering design calls for excellent joinery **Photo 3** MOF 98 with block being set **Photo 4** Setting out the drawer-side pins **Photo 5** Dovetails in action **Photo 6** Finished drawers

for the drawer casings was treated likewise, with this stack weighted on the top.

Selecting the burr was much more demanding. The surfaces had to be examined carefully for figure, colour and faults. Then the provisionally chosen pieces were marked with chalk and put together to gain an idea of the overall effect. Next they were cut oversize, faced, thicknessed, checked again, then wiped with white spirit to show an approximation of the finished colour. After a final examination in detail, the pieces were clearly marked, stacked, sticked, weighted on top, and placed in the conditioning cabinet for a few days. The mahogany was removed to begin the project while the drawer material was left in for as long as possible.

carcass construction

The carcass construction was fairly standard with the sides housed directly into the top, and the drawer frames housed into the sides. The complication was in the taper. To make the measurement of distances and angles easier, it was essential to draw the front of the chest, full size, onto a piece of hardboard. Next, I transferred the angle of the sides from the vertical, as accurately as possible, onto a suitable piece of plastic (although hardboard will do) about 100mm (4in) square, and then cut it and used it as a reference for all machine settings and angle cuts for the piece.

taking sides

First the sides were made up, using two widths of mahogany for each one. The figure was matched carefully and the joint strengthened with a ply loose tongue. A 9.5 mm (3/8in) deep x 5mm (3/16in) wide slot was cut in the sides and top for the back, taking care to stop the slot in the top short of the overhang.

Next the housings for the drawer frames were cut. With the exception of the top and bottom, these housings were 19mm (3/4in) wide x 9.5mm (3/8in) deep (at the shallowest side) to take the full thickness of the frames. The top frame housing was 9.5mm (3/8in) wide and offset down to avoid the tenon for the top. The bottom housing was also 9.5mm (3/8in) and offset up, to leave room for the cut-out to form the side feet (**Figs 1&2**).

All the housings were cut at the required angle

Photo 7 Using base block while cutting housing **Photo 8** Cramping to ensure even pressure

7

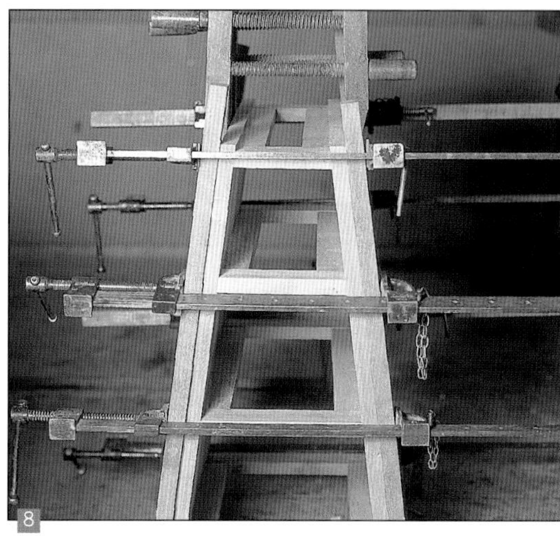

8

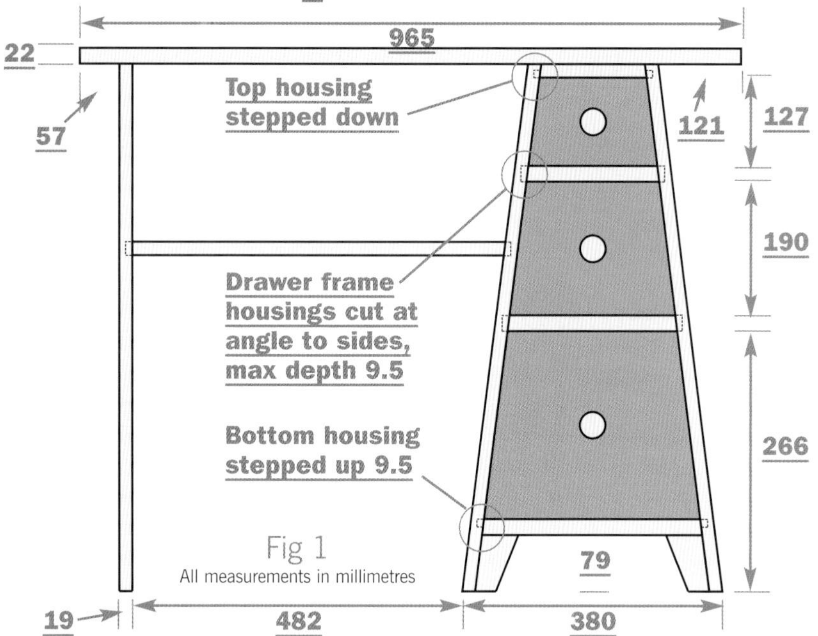

Fig 1
All measurements in millimetres

Fig 2
All measurements in millimetres

by fixing a block onto the router base to raise one side. The ends were then chiselled square and the housings cleaned out carefully.

in the frame

The drawer frames were now made up from 50mm (2in) x 19mm (3/4in) mahogany, with the sides tenoned into mortices in the front and back rails. The back rails were made 1mm (1/32in) longer than those on the front to make for easier drawer fitting and running. The front joint was glued, the rear joint dry-fitted, with an expansion gap left to allow for any subsequent movement (**Fig 3**).

The shoulders of the frames were marked on the front and back with the angle marker, 9.5mm (3/8in) in on the bottom edge, and cut 9.5mm (3/8in) deep with a tenon saw. The top and bottom frames were also rebated to 9.5mm (3/8in) and all of them were individually dry-fitted and finished.

Assembly had to be approached with even more care than usual

Housings for the front feet were cut 6mm (1/4in) deep on the front of the sides and the bottom frame. The feet were cut to size, dry-fitted and finished. Cut-outs for the feet on the sides were made and the edges finished. The angled shoulders on the top of the sides (where they fit into the top) were cut at the front and back and then finished.

top and back

The top was made up from three widths of 19mm (3/4in) mahogany. As with the sides, the figure was carefully matched and the joints were strengthened with a loose tongue of plywood. Care was taken to stop the slot for this tongue well short of the edge, so that it was not exposed when the edge was trimmed.

Next the angled housings in the top, to take the sides, were cut. This was done in the same way as the angled housings in the sides, and the top and sides were dry-fitted together to check for a good joint. The housings in the top were made 1mm (1/32in) further apart at the back, to correspond with the extra length of the back rails of the drawer frames.

The back was made from 5mm (3/16in) mahogany-faced MDF. I intended to use it as a brace during the assembly and gluing up, to help keep the shape of the carcass. It was cut accurately using the full-size drawing on hardboard, finished and test-fitted.

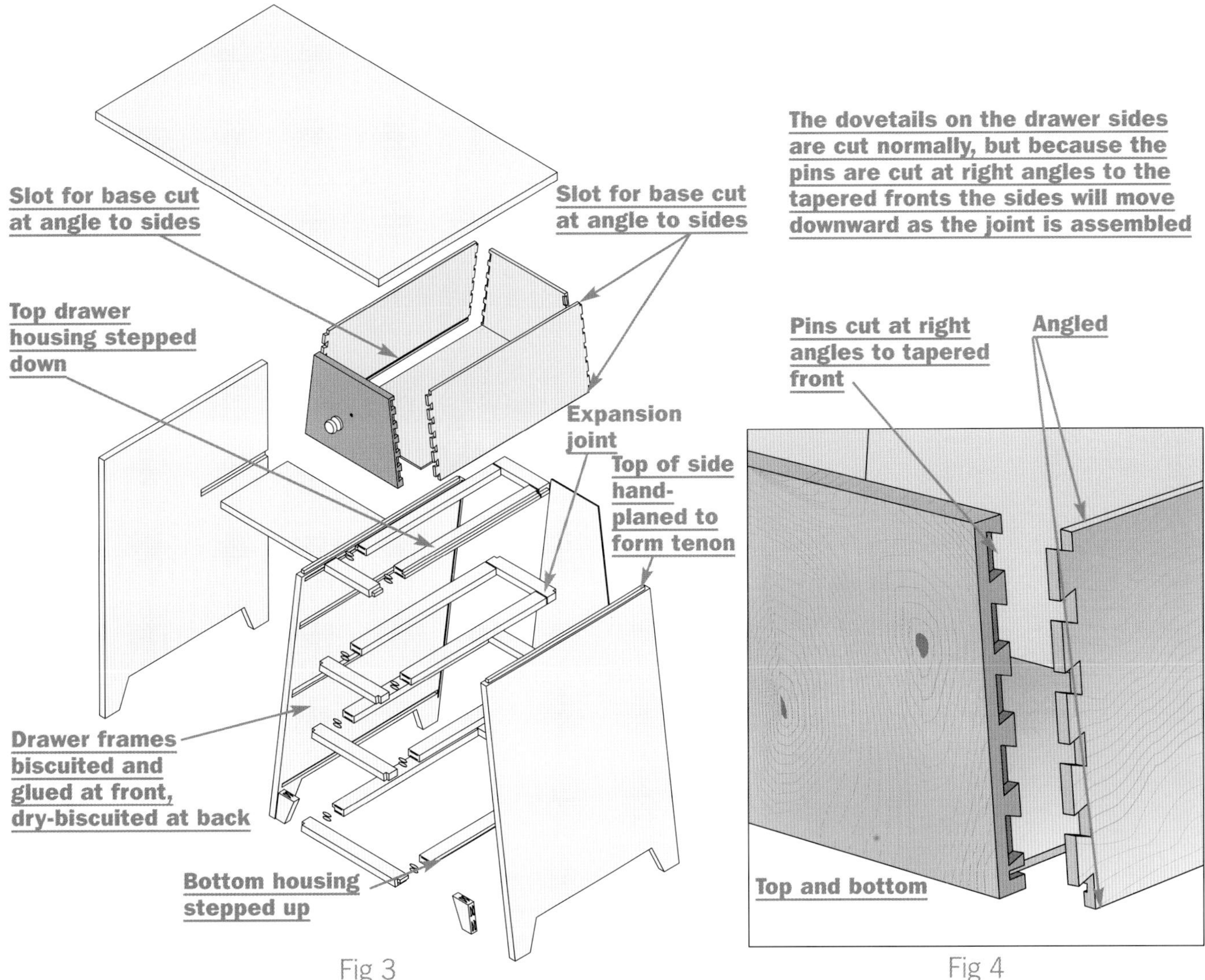

Fig 3

Fig 4

getting it together

Assembly had to be approached with even more care than usual. The top could not be fitted after the frames, because of the angled housings, so the first stage of the gluing up would be the sides, frames, and top, all in one go. I prepared everything, carefully finishing all the pieces I could, and dry-fitted the whole thing. I used battens with shallow notches cut into them to hold the sash clamps level and to stop them from slipping.

Cascamite was made up and applied to the front and back of the frame housings (**Fig 3**), leaving the sides of the frames a dry running fit to allow for future movement. As the grain of the top and sides was running in the same direction, glue was applied all along the housings and to the top of the front and back rails of the top frame.

The back was dry-fitted to help keep the taper even. The frames and top were positioned and the sash clamps were placed across the front and back. The eveness of the taper was checked by measuring the diagonals, which should be equal, as with a square construction. A further check was done with the plastic angle setter on each drawer frame, and all seemed to be well. The top was held to the top rail using G-clamps, and left overnight to set.

The next day the back was carefully slid out and glue was applied to the slot and the backs of the back rails. The back was replaced and pinned to the rails, glue was then applied to the foot housings and the feet were fitted.

drawing to a close...

Now that the carcass was complete, I fitted the drawer components. The top and bottom of the sides needed to be cut at an angle (**Fig 4**), so I set the table-saw blade and the planer fence to the correct angle using my trusty angle setter. I also cut the slots for the drawer bases on the table saw while the angle was set. Next, I cut and fitted the drawer fronts, remembering that because of the taper anything taken off the bottom edge would also reduce the width. To reduce the height without altering the width, I planed the top edge, then cut the slots in the fronts to take the drawer bases. Using the fronts as a pattern, I cut the backs, which were 5mm (3/16in) lower than the sides. They fitted on top of the base and, because of the taper, need to be lined up in exactly the

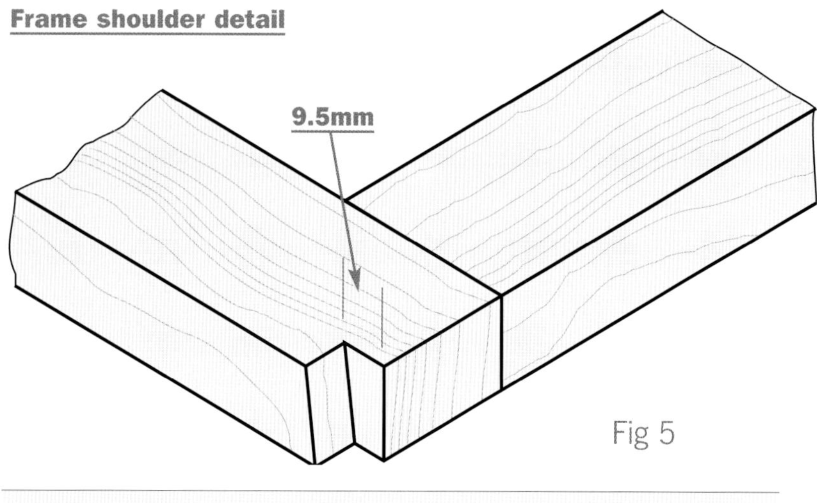

Fig 5

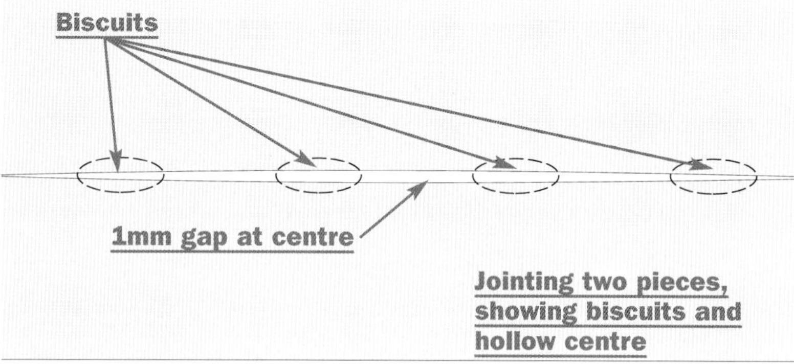

Fig 6

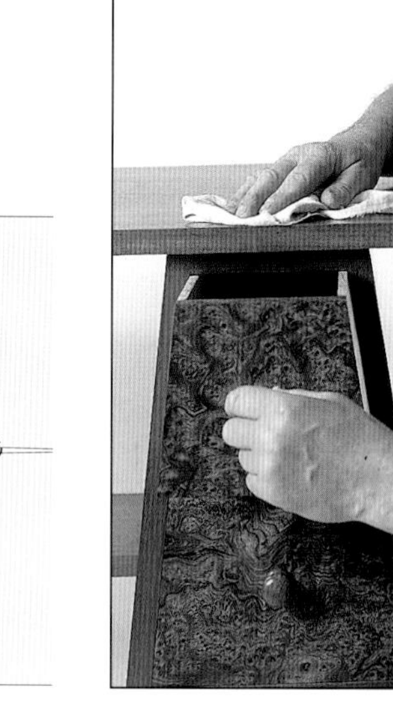

I was pleased with the unusual look of this tapered piece and so was my client

right place.

I cut strips of 5mm (3/16in) ply 13mm (1/2in) wide, and fitted them in the base slot cut in the drawer fronts. The backs were cut to the correct height, put on the edge of the bench, and the fronts offered up to them until the backs registered onto the protruding ply. They were then marked with a knife and cut and checked for fit. After the backs had been cut, I oiled the backs of the drawer fronts to help stabilise the burr, applying several coats prior to assembly.

drawer dovetails

The dovetails were marked on the sides, cut just short of the line on the bandsaw, and finished with a chisel. The positioning of the pins was critical, as they would be cut at right angles to the tapered front. Consequently the sides would move down the front as the joint was assembled. I marked the horizontal and used a set square to measure the amount of offset.

Allowing for it, I marked the pins on the edges of the drawer fronts. I marked the backs with a set square from the edge of the front, and removed the waste with a router, dovetail saw, and chisel. The joints were glued up and the drawers assembled, with the cedar of Lebanon-faced MDF bases glued in all round for extra strength.

Drawer pulls were made from off-cuts of burr, and then pegged, glued, and screwed into the fronts. The drawers and stops were fitted, keeping in mind that due to the taper any adjustment to the height from the bases would result in a corresponding reduction in the width of the drawer.

fuming to the finish

The carcass was wiped over with white spirit to remove any glue marks and left to dry before being hand-sanded to 320 grit. All surplus glue was removed and the whole piece double-checked for marks, blemishes and raised grain. It was then placed in a polythene tent, with about 140ml (5fl oz) of 890 ammonia in saucers, and left for 24 hours. This process must be undertaken with care, and eye protection should always be worn, as ammonia has a particularly adverse effect on the eyes and contact causes permanent damage.

To finish, I used Danish oil, as it brings out the deep richness of the figure and colour of the burr while also giving a silky finish to the mahogany. The burr was quite porous and the oil penetrated well into the wood, helping to stabilise it. The first coat was liberally applied and refreshed every 15 to 20 minutes until no more would soak in. The burr took considerably more coats of oil than the less porous mahogany. The chest was wiped off with a soft cloth between coats to prevent oil building up on the surface, and then left to harden for 24 hours in a warm, dry place.

Finally, the surface was cut back with a Scotchbrite grey pad, after which further light coats were applied every 24 hours and then cut back again until the desired effect had been achieved.

EIGHTH WONDER

A many-sided table by our multi-faceted author

An old elm in the bottom field of our Yorkshire cottage had been killed by Dutch elm disease, and had to come down. I managed to save the main trunk and had it cut into through-and-through boards, which were then air-dried for several years. I eventually wanted to make this wood into furniture to compensate for losing the tree from our view.

This table was going to sit in the centre of an octagonal Persian rug, so I felt that making it octagonal as well would reinforce the visual effect. What's more, there was a square table made from the same tree's wood sitting on a square rug at the other end of the large living room. The room had rough stone walls, a heavy beamed ceiling, soft furnishings in earth shades, and white walls. A robust but not too agricultural design in the warm-coloured elm would complement the room colours and construction nicely. The table would also get fairly heavy use – cups, drinks, footrest – and the top would be hinged to make use of the storage space in the pedestal. I decided on frame and panel construction to give plenty of allowance for movement and make use of some of the relatively small pieces of elm left after cutting out the insect-damaged areas.

Elm can vary considerably in colour, texture, figure and stability depending on which of the subspecies it is. English is the darkest, with the wildest grain, most ornate

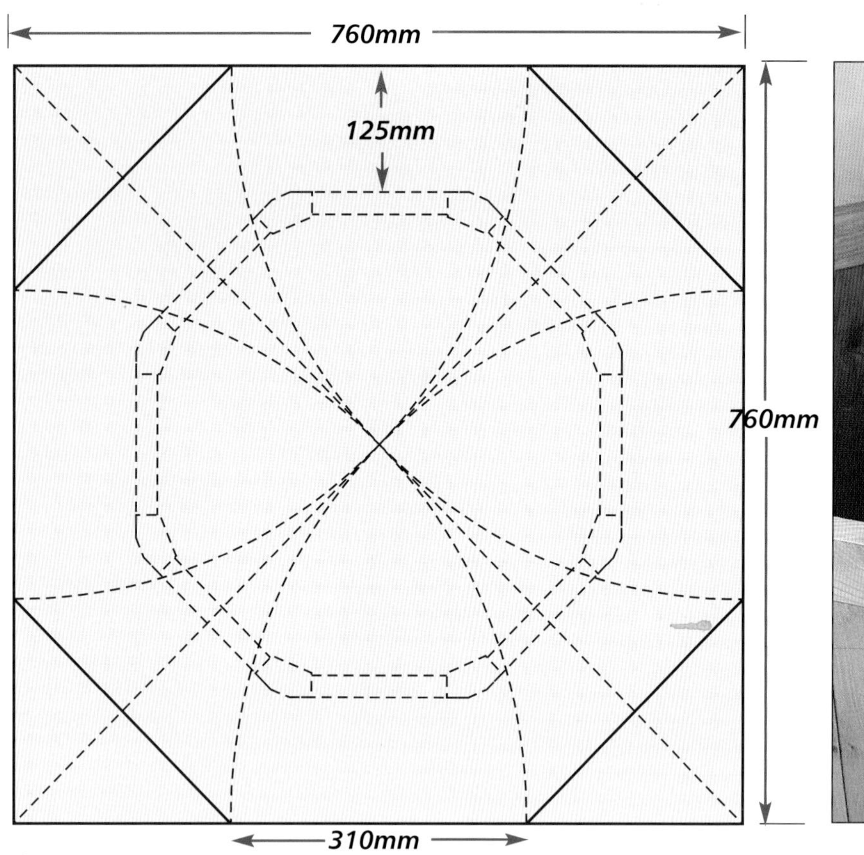

Fig 1 **Top geometry**

Routing hinge recess

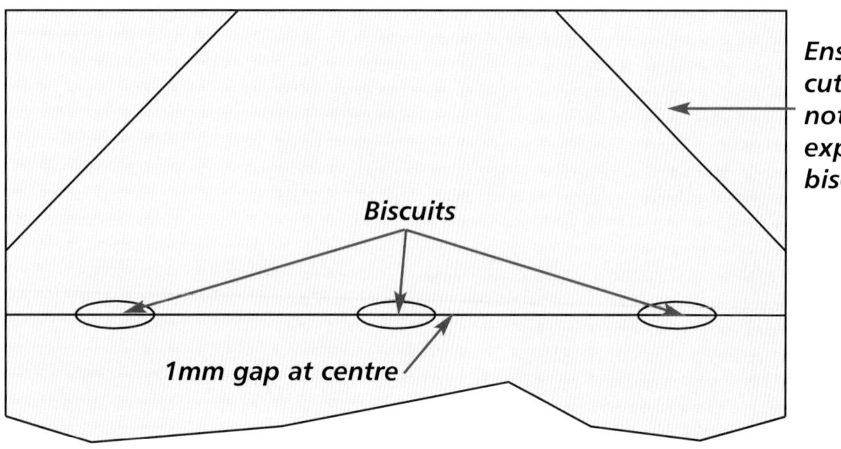

Fig 2 **Edge joint**

figure and least stability. Dutch elm is not as dark, has straighter grain, with fewer figures, and is more stable. Wych elm is even straighter-grained still, with a paler colour – often with a green streak – and the most stable of the three. Beware when buying, so that it matches previous work! Though Dutch elm disease affects all three types, there are still reasonable supplies of timber available, mainly from the North. It is being replanted in the South.

Going Dutch

The variety I was using was Dutch, and despite being more stable still had to be thoroughly acclimatised to its end-use conditions. I selected what I required, and marked out the various components about 10% oversize. The pieces for the top were cut from the best-figured boards. All the pieces were stacked, sticked and put in my conditioning cabinet for a month. If you do not have access to a conditioning cabinet the pieces should be placed, similarly stacked and sticked, for as long as possible in the room in which the table will eventually live. The boards were 38mm (1 1/2in) thickness, which easily dressed down to 30mm (1 1/8in) for the top boards abd 32mm (1 1/4in) for the leg posts, and was deep-sawn into 12mm (1/2in) boards for the panels.

For the top I selected boards from the centre of the log, which were effectively quarter-sawn, and therefore the most stable. However, given the wild grain of elm, each board still had a cupping direction. I don't normally alternate this – I find that it only produces a ripple effect – but at least if everything's trying to cup in the same direction it's easier to brace flat! I decided to make a 760mm (30in) square top and cut off the corners to form an octagon. First a pattern was cut in hardboard, to establish where the joint lines would be, and ensure that the strengthening biscuits would not be exposed by the cut.

To form an equally sided octagon from a square, first mark the diagonals. Taking half the length of the diagonal as a radius, mark an arc from each corner, and then join the points where the arcs cut the sides of the square to form the octagon (Fig 1). This established that the sides of the octagon were approximately 311mm (12 1/4in). I was using 75 x 255mm (3 x 10in) boards for the top so the corner cut would not cross a joint. The boards were matched for the most pleasing figure and the joining edges planed. The fit of the joining edges was slightly concave, touching at each end with a 1mm (1/32in) gap at the centre. This helped the clamps pull up tight and allowed for extra shrinkage at the ends when drying out (Fig 2).

The joining edges were biscuited to add strength and make the clamping-up easier. The biscuits were set well short of the cut which would be made across the corner to form the octagon. Cascamite was applied to

Top open, head on, showing braces

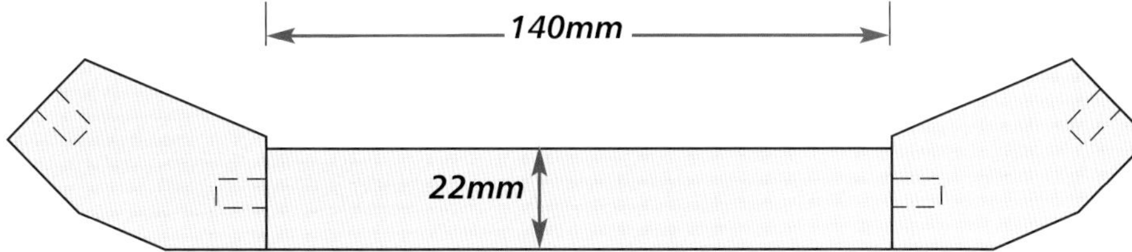

Fig 4 **Frame joint**

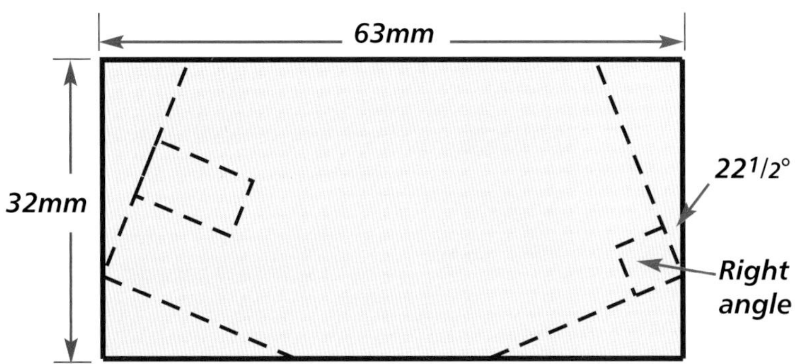

Fig 3 **Post cross section**

Vertical profile cutter used on fielded panels

"An old elm in the bottom field had been killed by Dutch elm disease"

the edges and the biscuits, and then the top was clamped up, checked to ensure it was flat and left to set.

Going postal

The posts were cut from 32 x 63 x 417mm (1 1/4 x 2 1/2 x 16 1/2in) pieces. First the sides were carefully angled on the planer by setting the fence to 22 1/2°. I use pre-set fixed templates to set the angle, finding it quicker and more accurate. They appear to have been dropped from the APT catalogue, but Veritas do a Poly Gauge for the same purpose. Once the angles had been cut, the mortices were cut at right angles to that edge on the router table. The mortice for the bottom rail was set up 12mm (1/2in) so that the rail was 12mm (1/2in) clear of the floor and the end of the post formed a foot. The front faces were planed at right angles to the edges to form three facets on the front of the post (Fig 3).

The top and bottom rails were cut to size and a tenon formed on each end. Slots were cut 6mm (1/4in) deep on the router table on the inside edges of the rails and posts to take the panels. They were also cut on the bottom inside face of the posts and bottom rails to take the 6mm ply base, the slot on the post taking account of the offset to make the foot. All the joints were tested dry and adjusted as necessary (Fig 4).

On the panel

The panels had been deep-sawn on the bandsaw from pieces of the 38mm (1 1/2in) elm and thicknessed to 12mm (1/2in); then sticked and stacked with a heavy weight on top and replaced in the conditioning cabinet to let the stresses and moisture levels even out. They were then cut to size, allowing 6mm (1/4in) all round to fit into the slots in the posts and rails. A vertical profile cutter, with the router on the table, was used to cut the fieldings around the edges of the panels. Several shallow passes were made and the resultant cut needed very little work with a sharp shoulder plane, then a light final sanding to finish nicely.

That's base

The hardboard template used for the top was cut down by the 125mm (5in) by which the top overhung the pedestal, plus the thickness of the rails, less the depth of the slot cut to fit the base. I cut it a little oversize then made adjustments by trying it in the dry-assembled pedestal until the fit was correct. The template was then used to mark out the base which was cut and test-fitted dry.

The assembly

This wasn't straightforward and needed to be thought out carefully (Fig 5). I considered making up four complete frames and panels first, then joining them up with the rails and panels between. Experimenting with blocks to hold the posts at the correct angle in the clamps, I found a tendency not to pull up evenly, or to damage the edge. I decided to

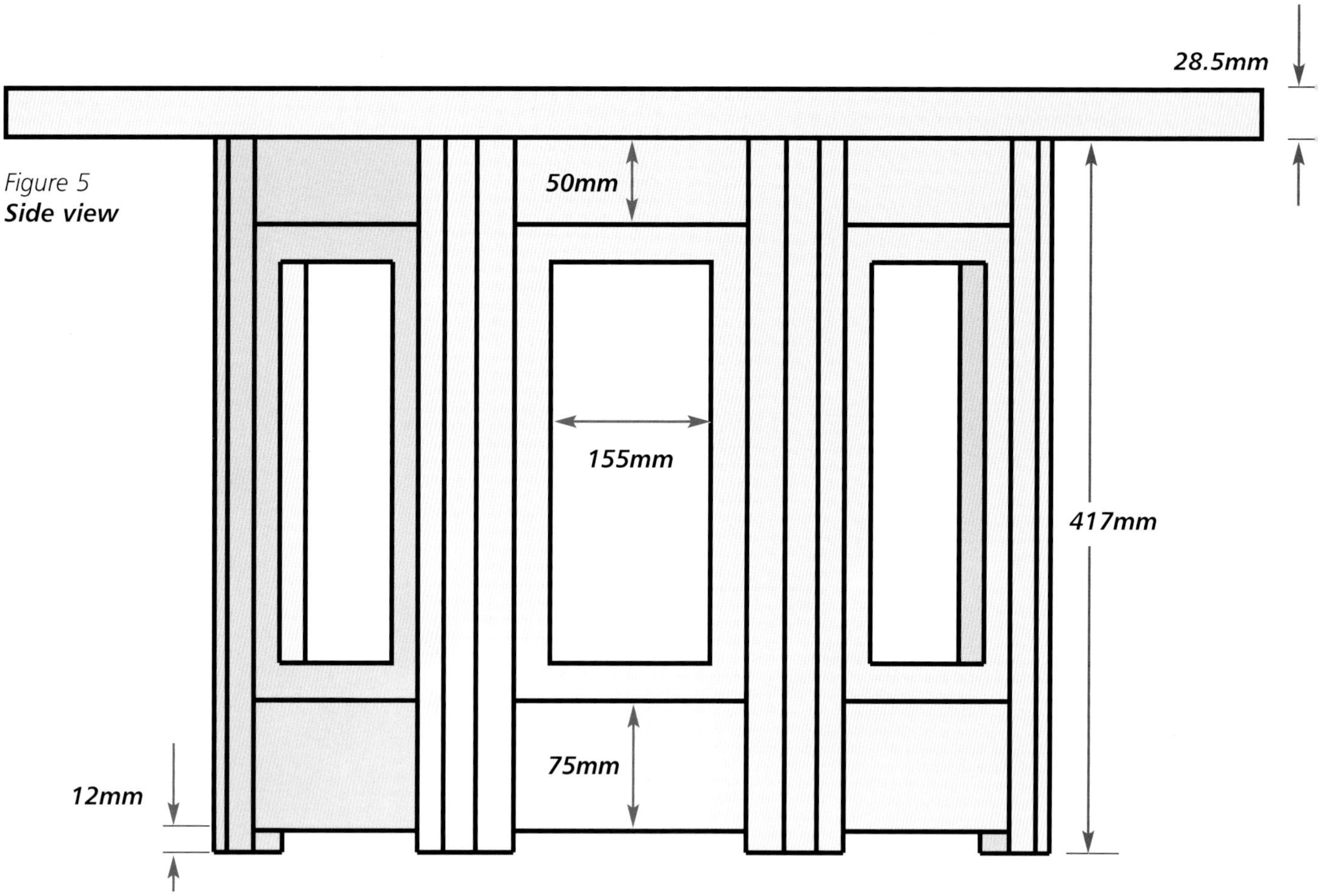

28.5mm

Figure 5
Side view

50mm

155mm

417mm

75mm

12mm

Clamping arrangement

use strap clamps and go for the whole assembly in one go, like coopering a barrel. All the joints were check-fitted dry again, then the workshop was cleared and everything laid out to hand. Then the old military adage 'Time spent in reconnaissance is seldom wasted' flashed into my mind, so I assembled the whole pedestal with the base in position, dry, as a final check. I then fitted the strap clamps and pulled it all up tight. It went together well, and I found that judicious use of a couple of sash clamps across the top pulled it into the exact shape. Having the base in position to clamp against kept the bottom of the pedestal true.

The whole thing was disassembled and laid out ready. I decided to use Cascamite because of its relatively long working time and lack of initial 'grab' – I wanted everything to be fluid until I had finally checked the measurements and adjusted all the clamping. I took a deep breath and started to spread glue – it all went very well, and I got it together and clamped into position quickly without any real problems. I was relieved and smug at the same time – perfect planning prevented p***-poor performance!

Belt and braces

Once the pedestal had set I put the top in position, carefully lining up the sides of the pedestal with those of the top, and marked round it with a pencil. When I took off the top I drew a line inside that octagon to allow for the thickness of the frames, and marked

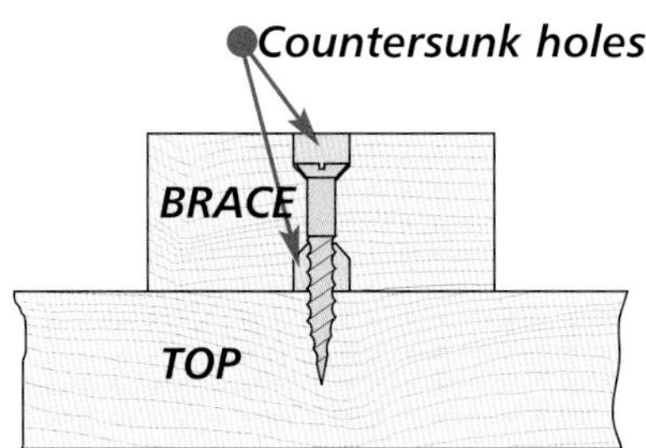

Figure 6 ***Double-countersunk hole***

the positions for the braces. These were cut to size and shape, and the top face edges rounded over to 6mm ($^{1}/_{4}$in) radius with a bearing-guided bit. They screwed into position through double-countersunk holes (Fig 6), which allow lateral movement but hold the top flat. The holes on top of the screws were filled with dowel plugs cut from scrap elm to tidy the job up.

Hinge & Bracket

The top edge of each side of the pedestal was only 190mm ($7^{3}/_{8}$in) so I decided to use a strip of piano hinge, with extra countersunk holes half-way between the existing screw holes to double up the screws. Even though the lid was heavy, the overhang prevented it opening much past the vertical and straining the hinge fitting. I cut the rebate for the hinge in the top edge with the small router and squared it off with a chisel. The top was then replaced and the hinge position marked. The hinge was fitted to the top first and then the other leaf located into the rebate in the top of the side, and screwed into position.

To the finish

As indicated in the design brief, this table was going to get fairly robust use. I chose a Danish oil finish, not so much because it's tough but because it's renewable. I carefully checked for glue marks and finally hand-sanded everything down to 320 grit. Then I followed my normal practice of a liberally applied first coat of oil, renewed every hour or so for a day until the wood would really take no more. At that point I removed all surplus oil, to prevent any build-up on the surface, and left it to dry and harden in a warm, dry place for 24 hours. This surface was cut back by hand with 320 grit, followed by a light coat every 24 hours for a week, then cut back between coats with a Scotchbright grey pad. Ten days were then allowed for final hardening before use.

The surface has since been renewed several times by cutting the surface right back with a Scotchbrite grey pad and applying a further light coat of Danish oil. This method works well as long as the surface is well cut back to ensure no build-up of oil. I usually do this just before we are going away for a few days, to give the new coat plenty of time to harden before use. Minor improvement between renewals can be made with a very light coat of linseed or teak oil. I prefer to cut back with the grey pad every time before I put any more oil on the surface, to prevent that 'syrupy' look. Often the grey pad treatment is enough, with no further oil required.

Left ***Top open side on***

Not just for Christmas...

I made several pieces out of this tree. The one described here has been in use in both our previous cottage and our current one for several years, and is still giving good service. I'm pleased to have a piece of furniture from something that was so much a part of our view for so long. It seems fitting to me that the tree lives on as a piece of furniture, still appreciated in a different way. ●

SUPPLIERS

APT - Veritas Poly Gauge - 0800 371822

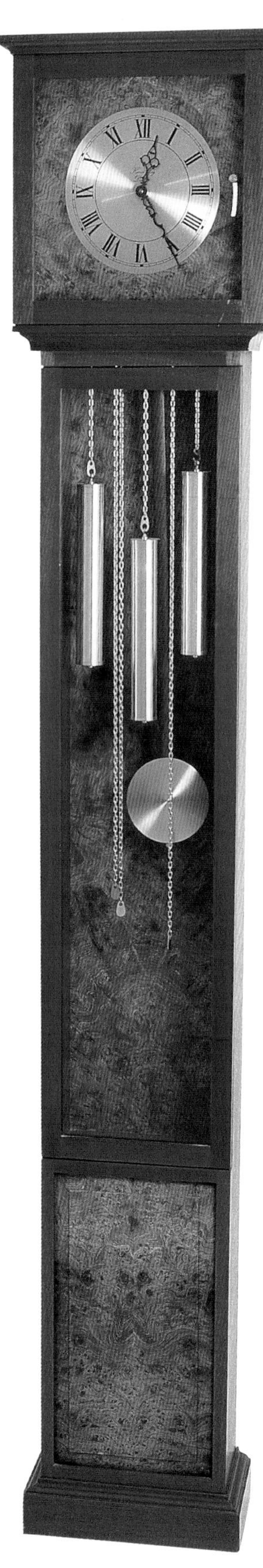

BIG time

Shaker design inspires a very British grandfather clock

A client contacted me to discuss her requirement for a longcase or grandfather clock. She did not want a reproduction of one of the massive, ornate, dominating monsters that abound, but something more elegant and simple in style, scaled to fit a cottage room.

Some time ago I made such a clock in sycamore, based on a Shaker clock design in Thos. Moser's excellent book *How To Build Shaker Furniture*.

It is a fairly standard Shaker design, used elsewhere with small modifications. Typically, it has simple lines and no ornamentation. Having said that, it was too big. The example shown in Moser's book was 2135mm (84in or 7ft) tall, made of pine and painted dark red! I have never really understood how the Shakers reconciled their philosophy of simplicity and non-ornamentation with their habit of painting their furniture in garish colours.

For my Shaker-style clock (shown far left) I chose a subtle blend of sycamore and ripple sycamore, with fumed oak detail which I felt complemented the design.

design concept

Although my client was keen on the lines and proportions of my clock, she found the sycamore too plain for her taste. She had seen a chest I had made in fumed mahogany and burr elm and was dead set on that combination for her clock. She also wanted to be able to see the pendulum and brass weights. We decided on fumed, oiled, Brazilian mahogany for the case with a burr face board. The back behind the weights and the front panel were also to be in solid burr.

A traditional three-weight movement with a Westminster chime and strike, brass dial, and black serpentine hands, were chosen from the Yorkshire Clock Builders catalogue.

When making a clock of this nature it is necessary to choose the movement and adjust the dimensions of the case to fit the pendulum length and swing, front-to-back clearances of the movement, and any chime assembly, and the drop required for the weights. All this information was given in the catalogue, or made available from Yorkshire Clock Builders, who were extremely helpful with advice.

The clock was to be 1981mm (78in) high to suit the ceiling height, so I cut the front-to-back and side-to-side measurements pretty fine to keep the slim, elegant look. This resulted in a small footprint that could give some instability to a piece of this height. Gripper rods at the edge of fitted carpets would also accentuate the problem by tending to tilt the clock forward.

A clockmaker I spoke to said that he always chocked the front of tall clocks to give a slight backwards lean for added safety. Yorkshire Clock Builders confirmed that this would have no effect on the working of the movement.

This 'lean-back' feature was often built into Victorian tall bookcases. The plinths were cut lower at the back so that the weight of the full bookcase was against the wall behind it.

I decided not to build the lean into the clock case, but to chock the front with hidden, thin pieces of ply held in position with Blu-Tack. This would have the advantage of being adjustable. Floors and walls, especially in cottages, are not always true and level!

timber selection and preparation

I raided my store of burr elm harvested from local hedgerows over the years by my log supplier, Martin. Burr elm is mainly an isolated hedgerow tree, often not commercially viable to timber merchants, and it frequently ends up as logs. It is worth harvesting, but, having decided some time ago that I am a furniture maker and not a timber merchant, my days of roaming remote places, deeds of derring-do with the chainsaw, and protracted negotiations with local farmers, are over.

Nowadays Martin brings it to me in exchange for money! The timber is planked at a local sawmill (£15 per nail hit), stick-dried, and finished in my wood store which has a dehumidifier.

The main problems encountered when working burr are wild grain, live and dead knots of all sizes, ingrowing bark, cracks and blemishes. It can be very hard and quite soft all in the same board. Being a hedgerow tree often means nails, barbed wire, even a horseshoe are found deep in the tree! It is worth checking the site it came from. I once saw a lovely piece in a wood yard near Catterick army base, only to be told it came from near the grenade range!

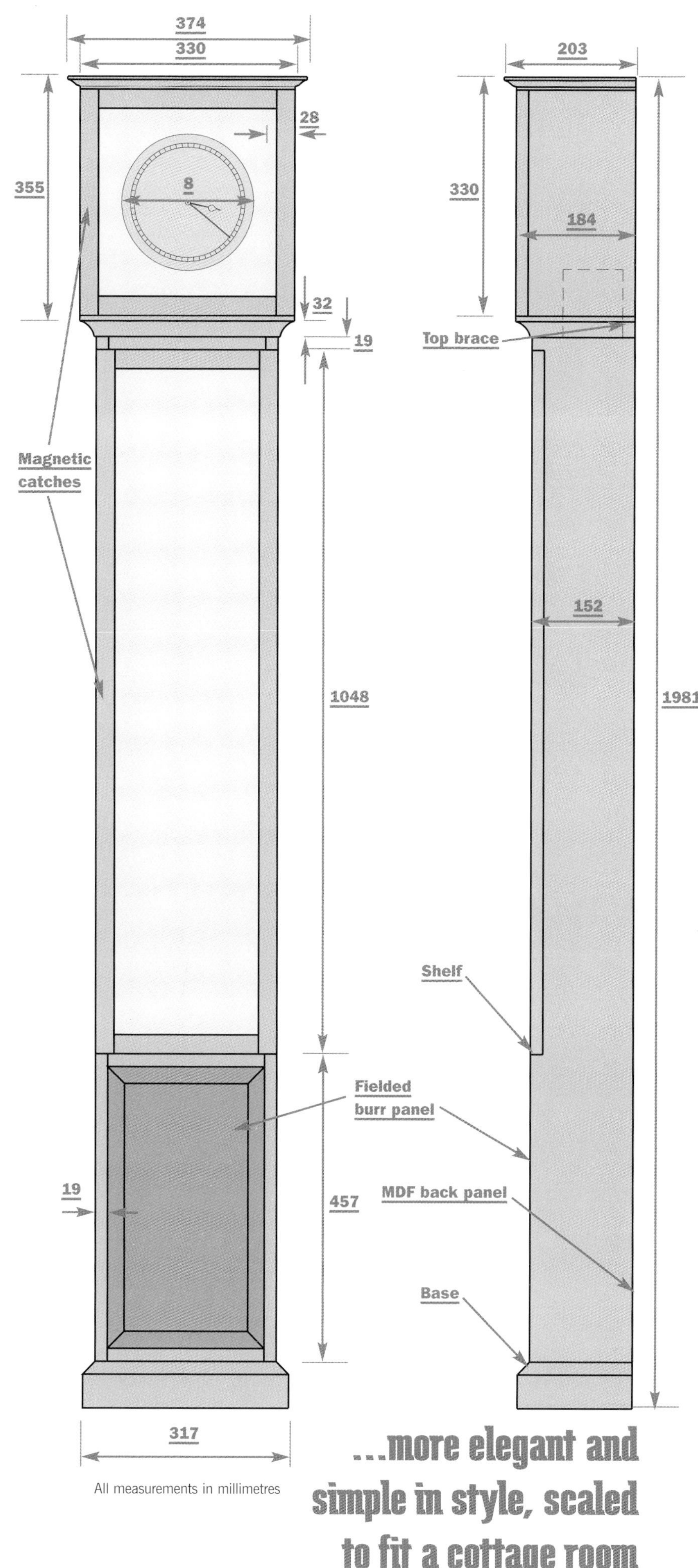

All measurements in millimetres

...more elegant and simple in style, scaled to fit a cottage room

Above Close-up of face, door open
Right Close-up of face, door closed
Below right Back showing seat and chime boards, back removed

Humidity has a serious effect on burr, as it takes in and gives up water relatively easily, causing movement. Careful seasoning and selection of the wood, sharp tools, adequate tolerances and a thoroughly sealing finish are all required to tame the beast.

I managed to find two sequential pieces 38mm (1½in) thick, which could be deep-sawn on the bandsaw to make bookmatched panels: one long enough to make the back panel, the other to make the face board and the fielded front panel. Choosing sequential boards and bookmatching them ensured the figure and colour would be consistent.

The mahogany was easier to select, with its straight, uniform grain and figure. Its stability would be essential to contain the movement in the beautiful, but wild-grained burr.

The burr was deep-sawn, and the pieces to make the panels were cut oversize. They, and the selected pieces of mahogany (also cut oversize), were stacked with sticks between the boards, weighted on top, placed in my conditioning cabinet with its dehumidifier set to domestic conditions, and left for a couple of weeks to stabilise.

carcass construction – sides

The sides were cut to size, with the tops stepped back above the line of the top moulding, to run between the bottom braces of the bonnet. The sides protrude into the bonnet to finish just under the seat-board rails.

Two housings were cut to take the base and the shelf. The positioning of the shelf is determined to some extent by the drop required by the weights.

The base and shelf were both cut to size in solid mahogany, with the grain running in the same direction as the sides. The sides were morticed to take the top braces, which were cut to size and tenoned to fit.

The top back brace, the sides as far as the shelf, and the top of the shelf were slotted to take the burr back panel that would be dry-fitted to allow for movement.

The sides below the shelf, the base, and the underside of the shelf were slotted to take the lower MDF back that would be glued into position for rigidity. They were also slotted to take the fielded burr front panel that would be a dry fit, again to allow for movement.

The sides were shouldered back below the front top brace and above the shelf to allow the door to sit under and inset, top and bottom. Then the face was fitted over the front edges of the sides. This was done to avoid using a door pull, and enabled the hinges to be hidden, thus keeping the lines as clean as possible.

Humidity has a serious effect on burr, as it takes in and gives up water relatively easily, causing movement

burr panels

The burr panels were made up to size from the conditioned pieces. They thickness to 12mm (½in), thick enough to reinforce the centre join with plenty of biscuits. Reinforcing the join is essential, as gluing burr to burr is a bit hit and miss: the grain is so wild that you can end up with short grain to short grain and little effective grip.

The join was also planed slightly hollow in the centre to allow for extra shrinkage at the ends, which dry out more than the centre.

assembly

All the pieces of the lower case were finished, dry-fitted and glued where appropriate, then clamped, checked for square and left to dry.

A support bar for the plinth front was fitted between the sides, screwed through and biscuited to the base above it. The plinth pieces were given an ogee moulding on the top edge with a router, cut to length, and mitred on the radial-arm saw. I used a negative-rake crosscut blade for a good finish and to prevent 'climbing' over the work. Adjustments were made by hand with a plane on a shooting board.

Biscuits were used in the mitres. Apart from the obvious benefit of extra strength, this method proved useful in preventing the joints from slipping when clamped.

The plinth front was fitted by screwing and gluing it onto the support bar from the back. The first 50mm (2in) of the plinth sides were also glued to the sides with PVA (which allows a little movement) and clamped into position. The remainder of the plinth was were left dry. They were fixed at the back from the inside through an oversize hole with a screw and washer (**see Fig 1**). This allows for any movement in the sides across the grain.

The mitres were tapped over where necessary and sand-finished when dry.

mouldings

The top and bottom mouldings were made and fitted with mitred corners. I used two different sizes of a simple cove profile which I felt was appropriate. The actual profiles used are a matter of personal taste and the cutters you have for your router, spindle moulder, or moulding plane. The mouldings were screwed from the inside, using double-countersunk holes to allow for movement (**see Fig 2**).

bonnet construction

The bonnet top was cut to size. The housings were also cut for the sides and an ogee moulding formed on the front and side edges. A stopped slot was cut for the fixed back, and a stopped housing for the face board.

The sides were cut to size and the housings were cut for the fixed back and the face board. The bottoms were morticed for the braces, and the tops shouldered back 6mm (1/4in) to fit the stopped housings in the top. The seat-board rails were screwed on, again in double-countersunk holes.

The braces were cut to size and tenoned to fit

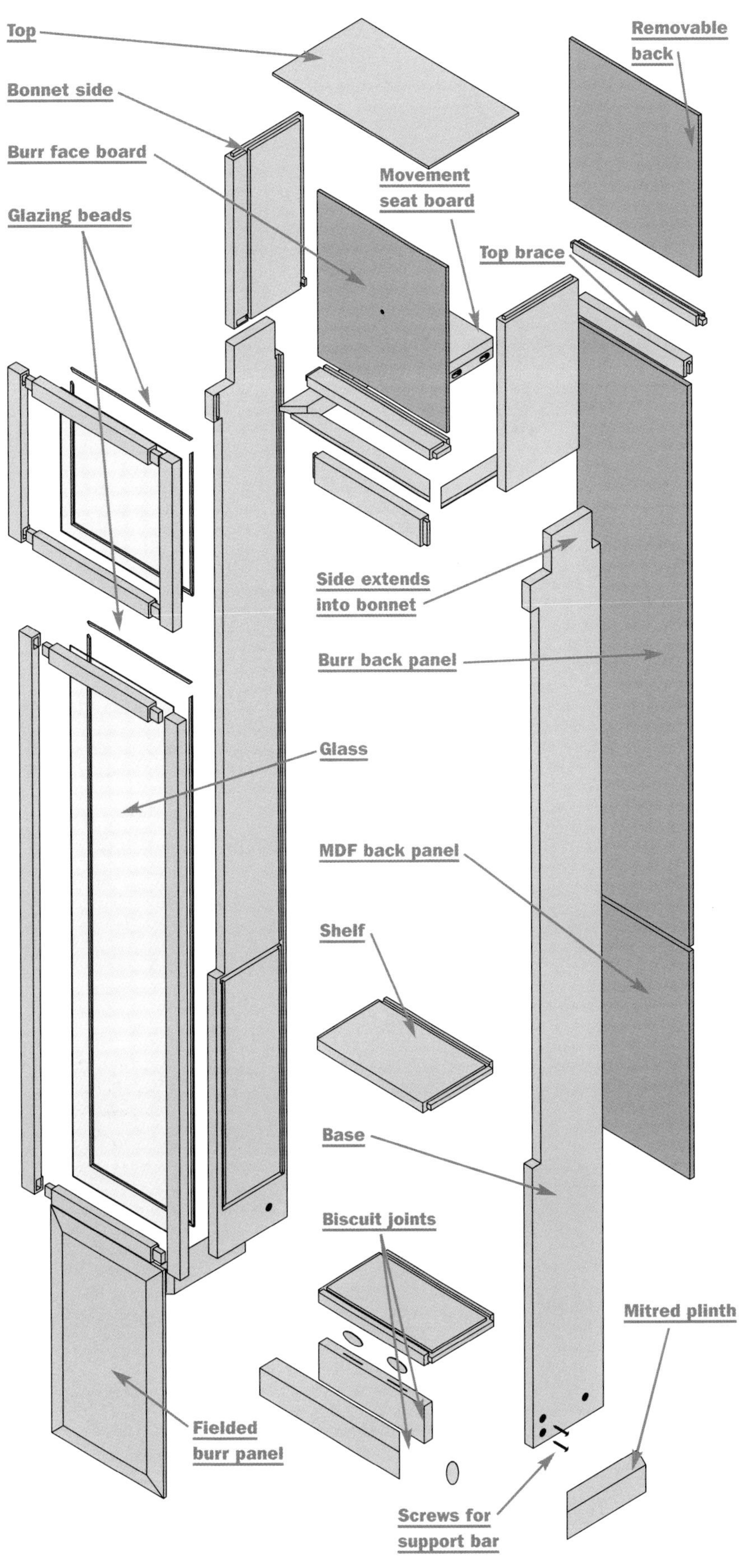

Exploded plan

Above Close-up of burr front panel

the pre-cut mortices. Housings were cut for the face board, and all parts were finished and fitted dry, then glued and clamped, checked for square, and left to dry. A piece of mahogany-faced MDF was cut to size, and a rebate cut with the router in the lower part of the back, to fit it. A turn catch was made to hold it in position. The bonnet was fitted to the lower carcass and adjustments made.

doors

I did not want anything on the doors to break the line, so I used magnetic button catches behind the frames and recessed 292mm (11½in) brass butt hinges as far in as possible. The doors were face-fitted to the sides, so the edge is easily accessible for opening.

The frame pieces were cut to size, the top and bottom rails morticed, and the side rails tenoned to fit. Rebates were cut on the insides of the frames for the glass and glazing bead. The glass was fitted into the frames on a very thin bed of clear silicone mastic. The glazing bead was then pinned into position: the pins were countersunk and filled, and the doors fitted.

fuming

Fuming has a significant effect on mahogany. It brings out the deep red colour, without any discernible effect on burr. The clock was wiped over with white spirit to show any glue marks (these were removed) and was left to dry, then hand-sanded to 320 grit. It was placed in a polythene tent with some saucers of 890 ammonia and left for 24 hours.

This process must be undertaken with care and appropriate chemical safety measures. Ammonia has a particularly adverse effect on the eyes and contact causes permanent damage.

finish

I decided to finish the clock before fitting the movement, but I did do a dry run first to check that everything fitted!

To bring out the colour of the fumed mahogany and the colour and ornate figure in the burr, I used a Danish oil finish. I applied three coats with a sponge, rubbed the surface down with a Scotchbrite grey pad between coats to de-nib, and finished with two coats of clear wax, buffed to a soft sheen. The burr was quite porous and soaked up plenty of the oil, thus sealing it well.

Author adjusting pendulum

movement

The bonnet was removed from the lower case and the door and back from the bonnet. The movement seat board was cut from 12mm (½in) ply to the detailed dimensions provided with the movement, and screwed to the rails inside the bonnet. The movement was offered to the back of the face board and the position for the hands spindle was marked. A hole was drilled for the spindle and, using this to locate the face, it was glued to the face board with epoxy.

The detailed fitting and adjustment of the movement was not complicated or difficult, and full instructions were provided with the movement from Yorkshire Clock Builders.

It would be worth checking that the supplier you use provides the instructions for fitting, and is willing to give advice, if required. I found it relatively easy to adjust the clock to an accuracy of +/-10 seconds a week.

There are several choices of movement for this type of clock. A battery-driven quartz movement with false weights and a moving pendulum is available. You could even put a quartz movement in the bonnet and use the lower case as a cocktail cabinet. I saw this in a pine furniture catalogue – dead tasteful!

conclusion

I enjoyed making this clock. There seems to be some mystique about these longcase clocks. People viewing my work, in the full knowledge of what I do for a living, are surprised that I made the clock, but are not surprised that I made far more complicated pieces. The clock is only a couple of boxes, after all.

SUPPLIERS

Yorkshire Clock Builders, tel 0114 255 0786

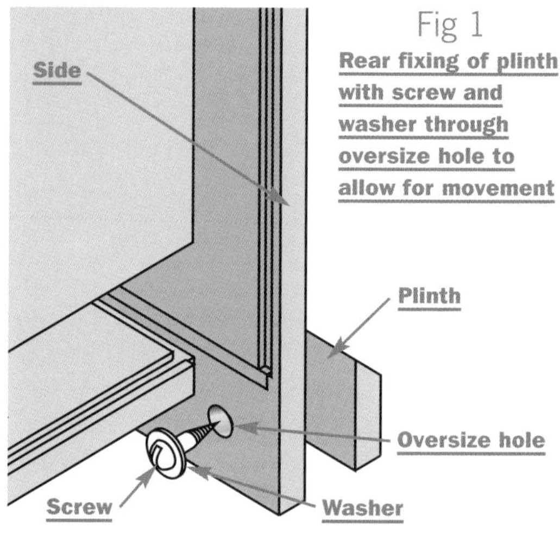

Fig 1
Rear fixing of plinth with screw and washer through oversize hole to allow for movement

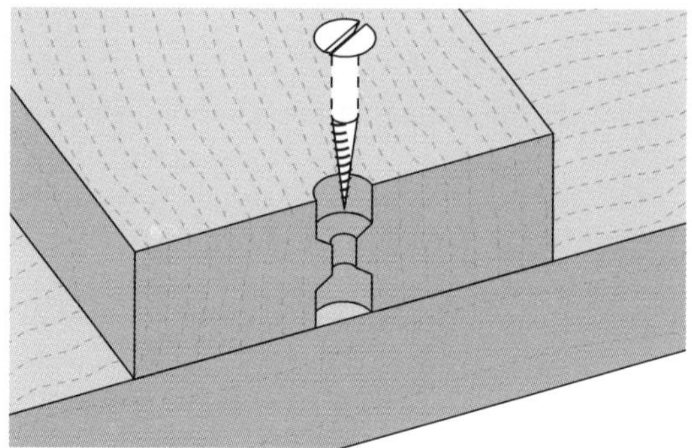

Fig 2
Double-countersunk hole for screw, allowing lateral movement

A cottage kitchen

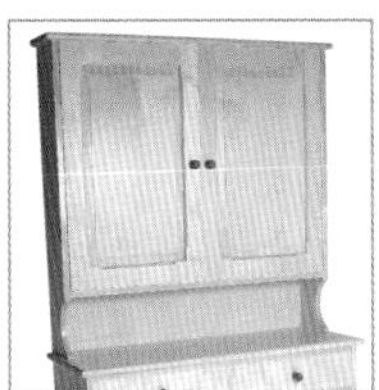
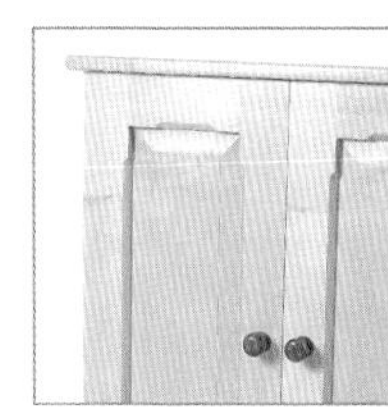

A chip off the old block

Making a multi-purpose kitchen trolley

The trolley provides flexible and versatile additional workspace

When we bought our cottage three years ago my wife thought it perfect – just a few small adjustments were required, one of which turned out to be a complete makeover of the kitchen. Now I understood why it had been so easy to convince her that setting up the workshop was a top priority after we moved in.

The kitchen had fitted units, quite functional but not pretty. The layout and lighting were very poor and the work surfaces badly planned, with insufficient clearance under the top cupboards. A kitchen is, of course, just another workshop, so I applied the same basic principles to the overall design.

The first major improvement was to remove the centrally positioned three-way spotlight cluster – which meant that no matter where you tried to work you would be in your own shadow – and replace it with several low-voltage lights, positioned over the areas where light was required. Strip lights were also fitted under the top cupboard bases to light the working surface.

Design

My next step was to provide more usable working surfaces. The main requirement was for a mobile area on which knives could be used to increase flexibility. Hence the basic design of a butcher's block on wheels was born.

It seemed logical to store the knives on board and use the space underneath the top to store a tea tray; an extra cutting board for raw meat; a tiled board to use as a stand for hot items; and, on the lower shelf, the bread bin.

I felt a 4½ litre supercharged V8 would round it off nicely, but was overruled! The trolley would fit under a standard-height worktop but could be moved to any part of the kitchen as required.

Timber selection

The units in the kitchen were standard DIY-shed gear in a lovely shade of simulated dark oak – much too sombre for a low-ceiling kitchen not over- endowed with windows. We decided to redo it in pale sycamore to lighten things up. This timber is a lovely creamy-white colour with a uniform, straight grain, a fine, close, even texture and a natural lustre.

I ordered all we required, kiln-dried, for the whole kitchen project from Duffield's. Having used them for years, I know they're careful to end-rear the

Cutting board, tiled hot stand, bread bin

The various trays

The double-sided raw meat cutting board is made from two pieces of burr, bookmatched and jointed in the centre, using biscuits and Cascamite with a hardener. A recess is routed in the centre of each face at each end, using a 12mm (½in) core-box cutter set to cut 6mm (¼in) deep, thus providing finger grips.

To make the hot stand, a piece of 19mm (¾in) ply is cut to size and tiled on one side with some spare tiles left over from the kitchen walls. A piece of burr is then biscuited to each end, with the same finger-grip arrangement as the cutting board.

A simple box is made from sycamore as a bread bin. The corners are butted and reinforced with biscuits. A sycamore faced-5mm (3⁄16in) MDF base is glued into a slot cut in the base. The lid is made from burr and a slot cut in the underside to locate it over the sides. This lid also doubles as a breadboard for cutting on.

The trolley slides neatly away

"A kitchen is, of course, just another workshop, so I applied the same basic principles to the overall design"

boards to make sure the inevitable marks, from the sticks separating the boards, do not penetrate below the surface.

I selected the wood and checked with a small plane just to be sure. To add a little visual detail interest to the sycamore used throughout the kitchen, I decided to use burr elm *(Ulmus* sp.*)* pulls on the doors and drawers. I had some big lumps of burr, rescued from a log pile, which had been drying at the back of my timber store for about 12 years. Their time had come, and despite the derision and hilarity of the editorial staff at *F&C*, I decided they would provide a nice, heavy, unsplittable top to the trolley, with the off-cuts used for the door and drawer pulls.

Timber preparation

Even though the big irregular chunks of burr had been drying for so long, the moisture content in the middle would still be higher than close to the surface. There were also plenty of faults and blemishes, so to get a decent-size top, clear of faults, I had to make it up from several pieces. They were cut about 10% oversize and stacked with sticks between them in the workshop to let the fibre stresses and moisture content stabilise, before finally making them up.

The sycamore *(Acer pseudoplatanus)* pieces wee also cut a bit oversize, stacked and sticked in the workshop to condition before starting. Even though this was kiln-dried, and had been in my timber store with its dehumidifier for a long period, time was still needed to allow the fibre stresses to stabilise after cutting. Note, the workshop is kept at end-use conditions so the conditioning process continues during the making.

Legs and rails

The legs were all cut to size, and the shoulders on the inside edges of the top of the front legs cut on the bandsaw. The bulk of the waste for the recesses in the tops of the rear legs was removed with a router and squared off with a chisel. The side edges were stop- chamfered on the router table and finished with a scraper, and the bottom edges rounded over to 6mm (¼in).

I had decided on double biscuit joints to attach the rails to the legs, flush with the outside edge; so the rails were cut to size and the biscuit positions marked. The biscuit slots were cut at the same time, using only one depth adjustment.

The sides were assembled first, using four no. 20 biscuits on the top rail and two on the bottom, clamped up, measured across the diagonals to ensure all is square, and left to set. The bearer rails for the tray and boards were then screwed to the sides under the top and the sides joined together by fitting the front and back rails, again with biscuits. Once it was clamped, all the diagonals were checked to ensure the whole trolley was square and true, then it was left to cure.

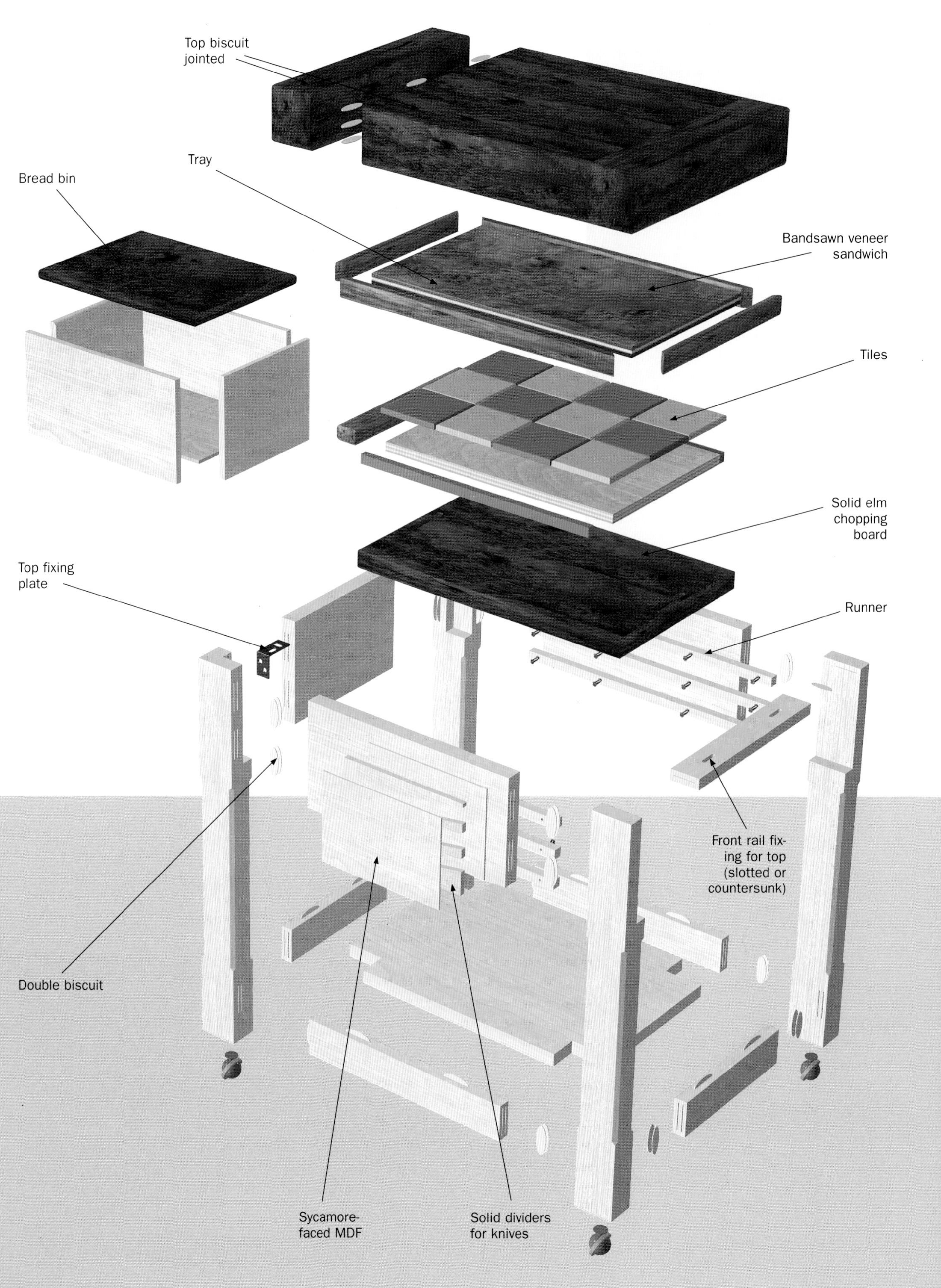
Top biscuit
jointed
Tray
Bread bin
Bandsawn veneer
sandwich
Tiles
Solid elm
chopping
board
Top fixing
plate
Runner
Front rail fix-
ing for top
(slotted or
countersunk)
Double biscuit
Sycamore-
faced MDF
Solid dividers
for knives

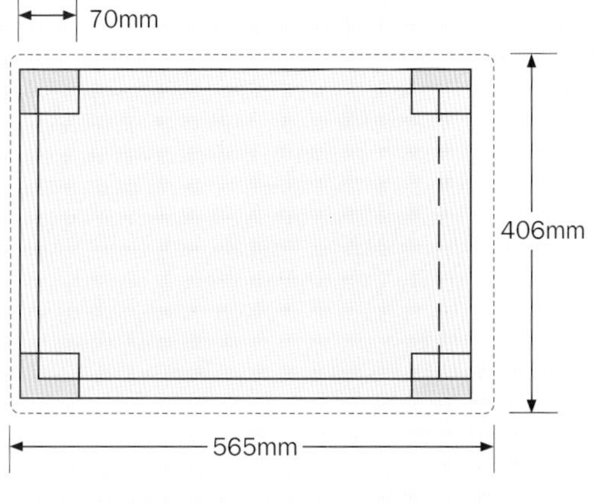

"The floor in the kitchen is riven slate and, therefore, slightly uneven. I managed to find some casters with 'soft' wheels; this considerably improved the ease of movement and reduced noise"

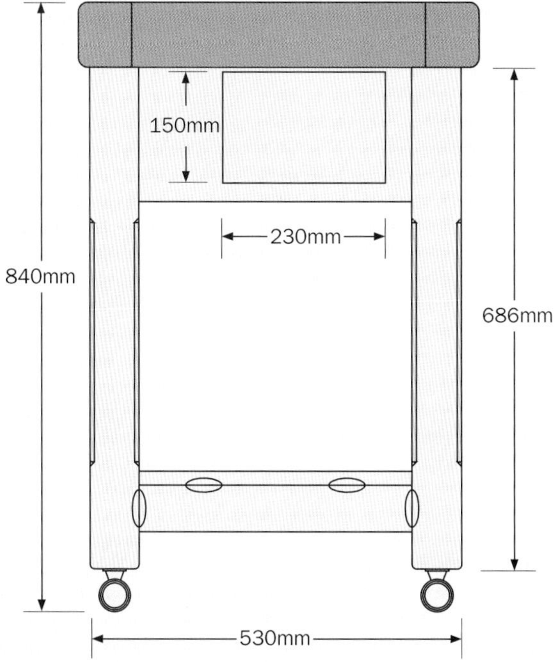

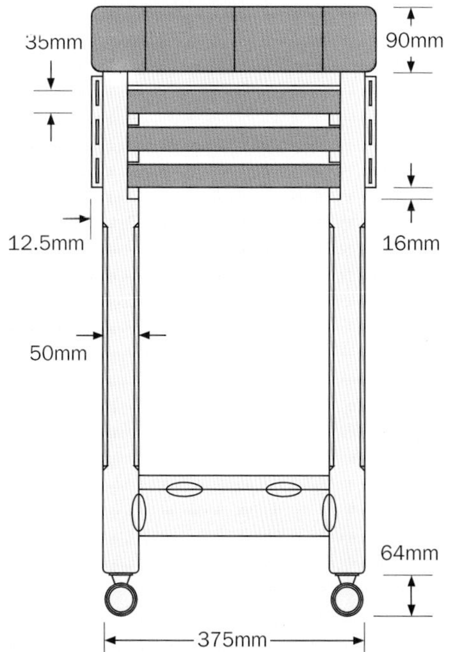

Shelf and knife holders

The bottom shelf was cut to size and the corners – to fit round the legs – cut out on the bandsaw, then dropped onto the bottom rails and fixed with biscuits.

The knife holders were made up from two pieces of sycamore-faced MDF separated by thin strips of solid sycamore to form the slots for the knives. The positions for the strips of wood were marked out around the actual knives, and the strips glued in place using a fast-setting PVA. The size and spacing of the strips of wood were adjusted so the knife holders on each side are the same size, regardless of the size of the knives they are holding. The knife holders were then glued to the sides of the trolley with Cascamite.

"The trolley has proved to be of enormous general use, giving great flexibility in the kitchen"

Top

The top was now made up from the six pieces which had been cut from the raw lumps. Burr has such a wild grain it's difficult to assess whether one is gluing end or side grain, and it'll probably change along the join any way! I decided to multi-biscuit all the joins and use Cascamite glue with K10 hardener for strength and waterproofing – bearing in mind the top would be washed and oiled regularly. The top was then fixed to the frame using screws through double- countersunk holes up through the front rail, and with expansion plates to the back rail. The plates were fixed to the back rail directly with screws through countersunk holes, and to the top through the slots. There are two slots at right angles to each other, and – remembering wood will move across the grain – I made sure to put the screw into the right one. This allowed for the inevitable movement of the top, while holding it flat, and left the clearance required for the underslung tray and boards.

Wheels and tray

The floor in the kitchen is riven slate and, therefore, slightly uneven. I managed to find some casters with 'soft' wheels; this considerably improved the ease of movement and reduced noise.

I made the tea-tray base by bookmatching two pieces of 12mm (½in)

Knife holder under construction

The top is double-biscuited all the way round

From the side, showing knife storage

Suppliers

Soft wheel castors:
Archibald Kenrick & Sons
tel: 0121 553 2741
Acrylic finish:
Satin Aqua Cote
mail order from Barfords
tel: 01277 622050

burr and edge-jointing them, not using biscuits.

When they were set I made sure both faces were planed flat, and split it in half by deep-sawing through the middle on the bandsaw. The planed side of the resultant, approximately 6mm (¼in) 'veneers' was glued down to each side of a piece of 5mm (3⁄16in) three-ply, again using Cascamite. It was then placed on the bench, covered with a piece of thick ply and concrete blocks placed on top, as a makeshift press. When it had cured I put it through the thicknesser a couple of times on each side to reduce the thickness.

The tray was completed by putting a simple frame, mitred at the corners, around the base, which was set in the centre of the frame height to give a double-sided tray, with a finger grip at each end to pull the tray out.

Finish and hygiene

All the sycamore was finished with Barford's satin-finish acrylic water-based floor varnish. I decided on three coats; it was touch-dry in 20 minutes, but should always be left for the full two-hour drying time before cutting back between coats. This finish is very tough and helps to prevent the sycamore yellowing.

The tray and ends of the tiled hot stand were finished with four coats of yacht varnish to protect and allow constant wiping with a damp cloth. The cutting boards were finished with olive oil as they would be in contact with food. Oil is a renewable finish and the most suitable for a surface which will be constantly scored. Re-oiling should take place as required.

The wooden cutting boards should, of course, be kept clean, so a kitchen anti-bacterial cleaner is ideal, but I use an anti-bacterial spray as well.

At least one side of one chopping board should be kept exclusively for raw meat and not used for any other food.

Conclusion

This is a wonderful sandwich-making workstation. One can creep off to a quiet corner and, almost unnoticed, get on with the important business of making a bacon butty. The trolley has proved to be of enormous general use, giving great flexibility in the kitchen.

Over the following pages I will describe the main cabinetmaking elements involved in the complete kitchen project. ■

Dress to thrill

The kitchen makeover continues with a dresser in pale sycamore

Interior detail

The makeover of our kitchen also required the provision of more storage space, this time in the form of a dresser. To continue with the project, whilst still trying to live there, I decided to make the dresser next and use the space provided to house the contents of the other cupboards as the alterations progressed.

I've always preferred a mix of fitted and free-standing units in a kitchen. The effect is less clinical and you can take the free-standing items with you when you move. Or at least that's the theory. When we sold our last house, the buyers bought a lot of the furniture with it, including the kitchen dresser. It was quickly missed, and its replacement took on some considerable urgency!

Timber selection

We decided on sycamore (*Acer pseudoplatanus*) with burr elm (*Ulmus* sp.) detail for the whole of the kitchen. Sycamore is a lovely creamy-white colour, with a uniform, straight grain, a fine, close, even texture, and a natural lustre. It would lighten up an old, underwindowed room with a heavy oak-beamed ceiling.

I ordered all the wood required – kiln-dried – for the whole kitchen project, being most careful to check the boards, which had been end-reared to minimise the inevitable drying marks left by the sticks separating them. Just to be sure, I selected the wood and checked with a small plane that they did not penetrate below the surface. When checking through the sycamore in the workshop I was lucky enough to spot some with ripple grain. Ripple sycamore is the same as ordinary sycamore in all respects except that it has ripple grain, running at right angles to the main grain direction, catching the light and giving a figure almost like satin or silk. It's frequently used for musical instruments, especially violin backs, and is sometimes called 'fiddleback' sycamore.

The ripple was not as pronounced as on timber sold specifically as ripple sycamore but I was pleased to find there was enough to make the door panels and drawer fronts for the whole project, just enough to give that extra bit of interest and detail. Similarly, there was plenty of burr elm left over from the kitchen trolley (pages 62–6) for the door and drawer pulls.

Timber preparation

The sycamore pieces are cut slightly oversize, and stacked and sticked in the workshop to condition before starting. Even though the wood was kiln-dried, and had been in my timber store with its dehumidifier for some time, the fibre stresses needed to stabilise after cutting. The workshop is kept at end-use conditions so the conditioning process continues during the making. The backs were cut to size from sycamore-faced 5mm (3/16in) MDF.

The burr elm was cut into blanks of a suitable size for the pulls and left in the workshop to condition. It was in small pieces and pretty dry from years in my timber store, so unlikely to move much. I have in the past dried wet burr in small pieces in an hour or so by boiling off the water in a microwave. This backfired on one occasion when trying to dry some 100 by 100 mm (4 by 4in) pieces for bun feet. I didn't know there was an old nail buried in the centre of one of the pieces – it became red-hot and turned the block of wood into a very efficient smoke grenade!

Carcass construction

All the components were thicknessed to 22mm (7/8in) and cut to width and length. The top was made up first, from three of the best widths, the figure matched carefully to run through and disguise the join, and the joint strengthened with biscuits. The edges were planed on the surfacer, finished by hand, and left slightly hollow in the middle, so when clamped the ends would be under pressure. This allows for extra shrinkage

Free-standing furniture allows you to take some of your kitchen with you when you move!

Design

The most important aspects of this design are storage and accessibility. It's no use having a cupboard with shelves two feet deep to store small items when it all has to be unpacked to find anything! The arrangement I have arrived at over the years is this one. It employs a shallow top cupboard, with racks or shelves on the insides of the doors, where small, light items – such as spices and sauces – can be stored and are on full display when the door is opened. Inside are shallow shelves suitable for tins or jars, which are stored one or two deep and also on full display. The deeper bottom unit is suitable for bulk storage and/or larger items, and the drawers will take anything flat like table mats and napkins.

To arrive at the shelf depths and clearances for each individual dresser, I line up all the likely contents to be stored and arrange them by height and depth, then decide, with the client, which need to be on the most easily reached shelves and tailor the shelf sizes and spacings to fit. This is, after all, what custom-making is all about: helping the client to identify, then fulfilling an exact requirement of function and aesthetics.

It has been a successful design and I have made several for personal use and for other clients. I am still surprised that users of kitchens are so impressed by the arrangement; it seems only logical to me, but fitted kitchen cupboards tend to be too deep, hence the popularity of small racks for spices, eggs and other foodstuffs. These small racks, in turn, produce clutter and make cleaning more difficult.

Stopped chamfer detail on doors

Fielding panels on router with vertical profile cutter

Fitting doors, showing wedged steel rule spacer

Turning the pulls

Detail of door shelves

at the ends, as the end grain loses water more quickly. The drawer frames were made up from 75 by 22mm (3 by 7/8in) sycamore with biscuited joints, and the bottom one shouldered front and back to go into the stopped housings in the sides. The front biscuits are glued but those at the back are not, and an expansion gap was left to allow for movement in the sides.

The work space was organised so the components could be sticked and stacked flat during making – with free air flow to all faces – for even drying.

Housings

Practically the whole of this piece is held together with housing joints, and as some people are sceptical about these joints I'll explain how they work in some detail.

The housing joint should be a compression fit and require knocking home with a hammer and block. About 1mm (3/64in) of the leading edge can be very slightly bevelled to assist in starting the entry. The glue should be spread quite thinly with a brush along the top edges of the housing, and thinly on the leading edges of the entering piece. It initially provides lubrication, then swells the wood to give a mechanical fit like a biscuit, and finally gives some, if limited, glue bond. It's a mechanical joint; a sloppy fit relying on glue as a filler is ineffective.

The joint is least strong in the direction from which it is assembled, but has strength in all other directions. The housings in the tops, together with the glued and screwed back and the biscuited bracket feet, provide strength against outward spreading forces to the carcass. Stopped housings for the shelves and bottom drawer frame, 22mm wide by 6mm deep (7/8 by 1/4in), were cut with a router in the sides of the top and bottom units, and in the sides of the bottom unit to take the base. Similar stopped housings were cut in the undersides of the tops to take the sides, and in the topside of the base unit top to locate (without glue) the ends of the sides of the top unit.

The top drawer frame was to be fitted to the sides with biscuits, glued at the front and back but dry in the middle. Countersunk slots were cut in it so the screws could go through it into the top, helping to hold the top flat but allowing for movement.

A slot was cut in the sides and tops, 5mm wide by 6mm deep (3/16 by 1/4in) to take the backs, the front face of the backs being 10mm (3/8in) in from the back edge of the sides.

The sides, shelves, bottom drawer frame and base of the bottom unit were all shouldered and partially dry-fitted into their respective housings. Then the front edges of the shelves, and the front and sides edges of the tops, were rounded over to 10mm (3/8in) radius.

The curves on the bases of the top unit sides were cut on the bandsaw and finished with a spokeshave and scraper. The cut-outs were also made on the bandsaw to form the feet in the sides of the base unit.

Assembly

I assembled the top unit first. The shelves were glued and tapped into position and the back was fitted dry to help hold everything square. Clamps were applied, the diagonals checked to ensure it was square, and left to set; then the top was fitted.

The base unit was assembled in the same way. The top was screwed and glued down to the top drawer frame front and back rails – and screwed only through the side and centre rails.

When the glue in both units had thoroughly cured, and before gluing the backs in, all the surplus glue was removed from the joints and the internal surfaces finished.

Backs and doors

Glue was applied to the back edges of the shelves, drawer frames and base, the

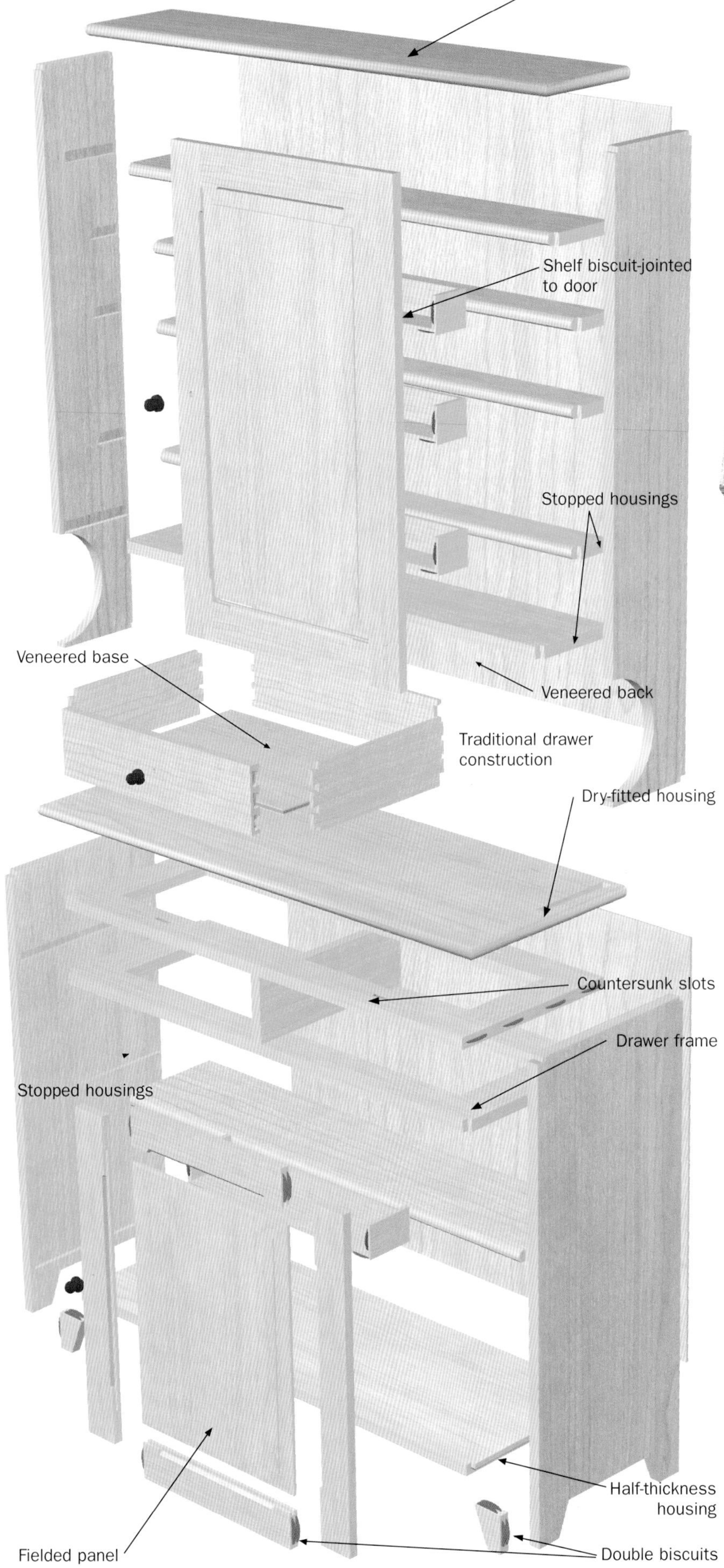

Housed top

Shelf biscuit-jointed to door

Stopped housings

Veneered base

Veneered back

Traditional drawer construction

Dry-fitted housing

Countersunk slots

Drawer frame

Stopped housings

Half-thickness housing

Fielded panel

Double biscuits

"This was the centre piece of the kitchen and made a big difference right away"

A few burr door/drawer pulls!

Suppliers
Satin Aqua Cote: mail order from Barford's, tel: 01277 622050

slots in the sides and tops – except the slot in the topside of the base unit top, which is, like the ends of the sides, a dry fit. Then the pre-sanded back was placed carefully in position and screwed through to the shelves, drawer frames and base with 3 by 12mm (1/8 by 1/2in) countersunk screws to give extra strength.

The stiles and rails of the doors were cut to size and a double biscuit joint used at each corner. The doors were dry-assembled and the measurements for the fielded panels taken, allowing them to recess 6mm (1/4in) into the frame.

I made the door panels by deep-sawing selected ripple sycamore and match-jointing, with biscuits for extra strength, in the middle. The panels were cut to size and fielded using a vertical profile cutter from Wealden; the results are good, with minimal hand-planing and sanding needed. The panel faces were finished, a slot was cut on the inside edges of the rails and stiles to take the fielded panels, and then the inside edges of the frames were finished.

The stopped chamfers on the front side edges of the frames were cut with a chamfer bit on the router and finished with scraper and sanding block. The doors were assembled, glued and clamped, checked for square and wind, and left to set.

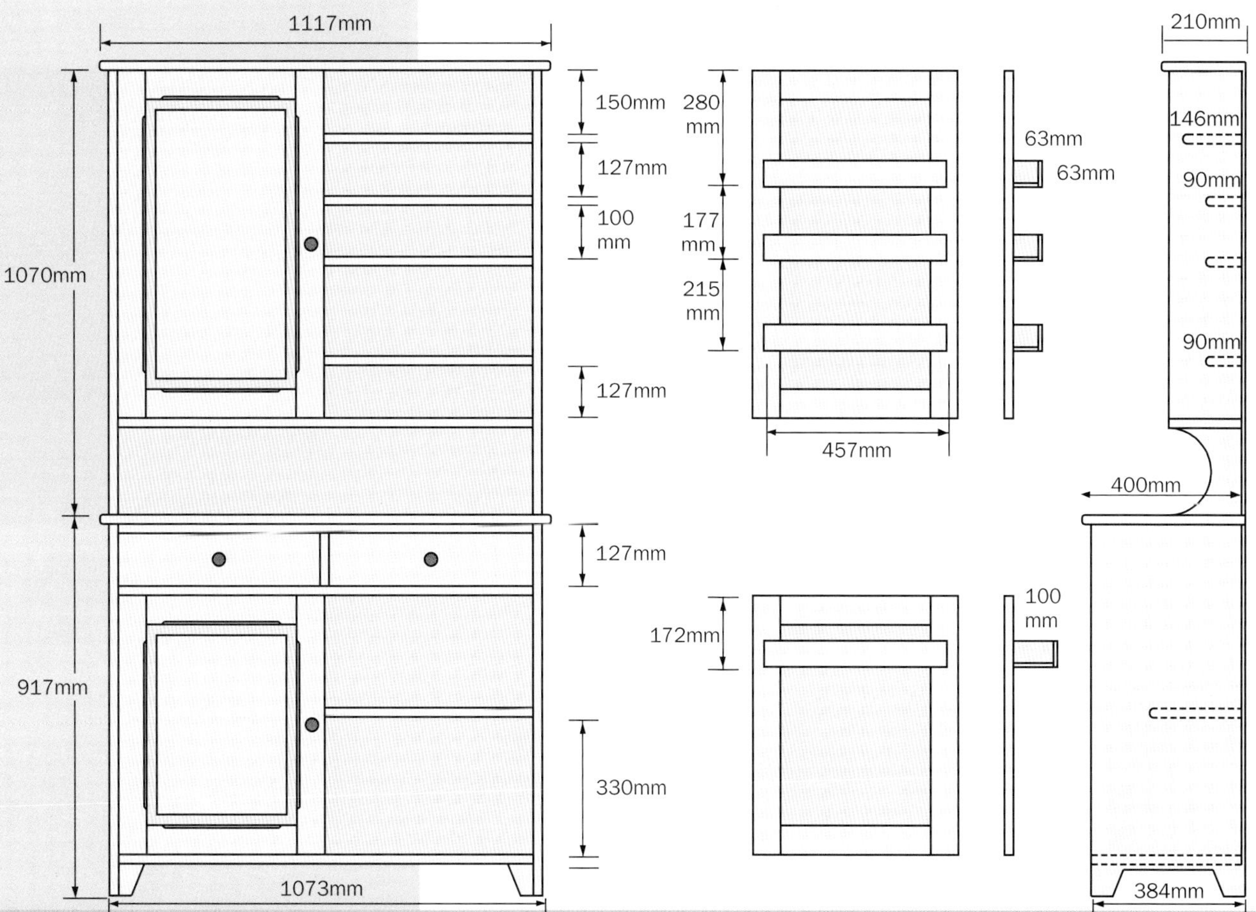

The shelves for the insides of the doors were made up by biscuiting the front onto the sides, all of which were slotted to allow a ply base to be glued in. The complete units were fitted to the doors by a biscuit between each side and the door frame.

Fitting the doors

Once set, the faces of the frames were sanded and the completed doors fitted to the opening, leaving about 1mm (3/64in) clearance all round, to be adjusted to 2mm (5/64in) on final fitting. Full-length piano hinges were used on these doors as they give extra strength, leave a neat line, and even out the load – bearing in mind the doors are carrying shelves! The hinges did not need to be recessed, and a self-centring hinge pilot drill along with my power screwdriver made short work of fitting them. The position of the hinges was marked on the inside face of the cupboard and a cutting gauge used to scribe the screw line. The doors were held at the correct height by a metal rule wedged as a spacer underneath them.

The screw line was centred in the hinge screw hole and the self-centring pilot drill used to drill one pilot hole at the top and one at the bottom of each hinge. The screws were driven home and the door checked for fit; adjustments made, the remaining holes drilled and screws driven. Brass double ball catches were fitted and the springs adjusted to get a satisfying 'clunk-click'.

Drawers

All the pieces for the drawers were cut to size, fitted and marked: the fronts from 22mm (7/8in) sycamore, the carcasses from 10mm (3/8in) sycamore and the bases from 5mm (3/16in) sycamore faced MDF. The sides were slotted for the bases, taped together, and the tails cut on the bandsaw.

I marked the pins on the drawer fronts and backs, one at a time, from the corresponding tails, and the majority of the waste was then removed with a router. I finished each joint individually with a sharp chisel. The drawers were then assembled with the MDF base glued in all round and pinned at the back, checked for square and wind, and left to set. They were finally fitted, finished and put to one side.

Door and drawer pulls

These were turned from the prepared blanks of burr. I don't undertake a lot of turning so I try to standardise and repeat each action. I find sizing tools invaluable and have at least two, set to the relevant diameters. A piece of hardboard with the profile on one side, and the positions for marking the major cuts on the other, is also very helpful. I did all the pulls for the whole project in one go, with some 'insurance' extras. Those not used are useful for future one-off jobs. The pulls were then oiled and buffed on the lathe to a nice deep finish.

Finish

To keep the pale creaminess of the sycamore I again chose Aqua Cote satin finish from Barford's; this is water-based acrylic floor varnish. I applied three coats with a sponge, rubbing down between coats to de-nib. This is my preferred water-based varnish; it dries quickly and hardens to a tough satin finish. At the time of writing it has been in use in the kitchen on all the surfaces – including the work-tops – for nearly two years and shows no sign of wear.

Conclusion

This was the centre piece of the kitchen and made a big difference right away. It also provided the facility to empty the existing cupboards – which required modification in the grand plan. At last, tranquillity was established in the Ley kitchen!

My kitchen refit continues on the following pages. ■

The original kitchen – dark is not light enough!

Remake, remodel

As the kitchen refit proceeds, a wall cupboard is given a much-needed makeover

Once the dresser was complete and available for storage, I was able to continue the kitchen makeover by emptying the existing wall units and giving them a new look. I had tried to improve their use on a temporary basis as soon as we moved in – by putting strip lights under them – but they were badly positioned, with insufficient clearance underneath to allow the work-top space to be used.

Timber

The solid sycamore *(Acer pseudoplatanus)* and sycamore-faced MDF were from the same stock as used for the kitchen trolley and dresser, all of which had been conditioning in the workshop during the whole of this project. I made good use of offcuts and thin strips.

Carcass

After removing the doors, I took the carcasses to pieces by removing the plastic dowel screws. The whole carcass was made from chipboard faced on the outside of the sides with a plastic-covered photographic paper, simulating dark oak (*Quercus* sp.). The outside of the top and bottom, and all of the inside, was a light-coloured, practical, wipe clean, plastic surface – not a million miles from the sycamore in colour. The shelves had the same surface and were adjustable in a wide range of positions. The outside of the top and bottom would not be visible in use, so they were left with the plastic surface, but the dark oak sides needed to be changed.

Not being too sure which glue would bond to the outside surface, I experimented with a belt sander and found its 'beauty' was merely a thin skin and I was quickly through to the substrate chipboard. To this I glued some 5mm (3/16in) sycamore-faced MDF, using Titebond. All the sides were then stacked on top of each other between some pieces of scrap work-top, and left overnight weighted with a couple of concrete blocks on top, to set.

The front edges were then planed clean and true, and lipped with a 6mm (1/4in) strip of sycamore. This was glued with Titebond and the sides placed between sash clamps, front edge to front edge so even pressure would be applied.

Once the edging strips had set, the sides were attached to the top and bottom using a biscuit in the centre and countersunk chipboard screws on the outside edges.

The back panels were fixed in their slots in the sides and top using polyurethane glue. Bison from Adquick comes in a handy squeeze tube and doesn't go off. It bonds to the wood, plastic surfaces and gaps, correcting the loose fit of the panels in their slots. The bottom edge was screwed and glued with Bison to the bottom shelf. Everything was checked for square and left to set. The carcass was now solid and strong enough to take the loss of structural strength always sacrificed to adjustable shelves.

To echo the design of the dresser and change the very utilitarian look of the cupboard, I decided to fit a half-round, overhanging edging strip of sycamore to the top and bottom edges – wide enough to overhang the top and bottom

Design

The overall aim was to lighten the whole kitchen by replacing the visible dark oak-effect surfaces with lighter, creamy-white sycamore. The units themselves were sound enough, and it was far cheaper and more convenient to reorganise and alter them – rather than replacing everything – to achieve this lighter, cottage-like effect.

We found we could reorganise the shelving in two of the cupboards, using extra shelves from the others. This made more efficient use of the space and halved the amount of covered storage we needed, allowing us to lose the inefficient and inaccessible corner cupboard, and giving some open shelves for display storage and ornaments. The whole unit could then be raised, which, combined with the extra clearance under the centre shelving, enabled the work top to be actually usable. The same lighting units could then be transferred to the new unit to provide light above and in front of the work area.

Above: Stop-chamfering doors

Below: Completed unit showing adjustable shelves

The old oak-effect unit

of the doors at the front, thus making them partially inset. This strip was cut from solid sycamore and rounded over on the router. It was fitted with biscuits to the top and bottom of the front and sides of the carcass, but taking great care in positioning the biscuits on the sides as they had to clear the countersunk screws and the central biscuit used to fix the sides to the top and bottom.

Doors

The original doors were from solid oak but the standard 'cathedral' style. I decided to replace them with solid sycamore doors with fielded panels and stop-chamfered frames to match those in the dresser.

The stiles and rails of the doors were cut to size and a double biscuit joint used at each corner. The doors were dry-assembled and the measurements for the fielded panels taken, allowing them to recess 6mm (1/4in) into the frame. As the doors were quite narrow, panels were deep-sawn from some ripple sycamore and bookmatched to give a matching pair of panels in each cupboard.

The panels were cut to size and fielded using a vertical profile cutter from Wealden. The results are very good, needing minimal hand planing and sanding. The panel faces were then finished, a slot was cut on the inside edges of the rails and stiles to take the fielded panels, and the inside edges of the frames finished.

The doors were assembled, glued and clamped, checked for square and wind, and left to set. The stopped chamfers on the front inside edges of the frames were cut with a bearing-guided chamfer bit on the router, and finished with scraper and sanding block.

Fitting doors

The original concealed, adjustable hinges were removed from the old doors. These hinges are ugly and only allow face-fitting of the doors, but they have several advantages for this type of cupboard: they are self-closing, have special fittings for the chipboard sides, require no catches, and can be adjusted for correct alignment. I decided to use them to fit the new doors.

The hinge is located in a 35mm (1 3/8in) hole drilled in the correct position in the door. I bought an inexpensive 35mm hinge cutter from Screwfix, which worked extremely well in my pillar drill. Suitable cutters for drills and routers are also available from Wealden. This size of cutter needs a pillar drill or a variable-speed router for safe,

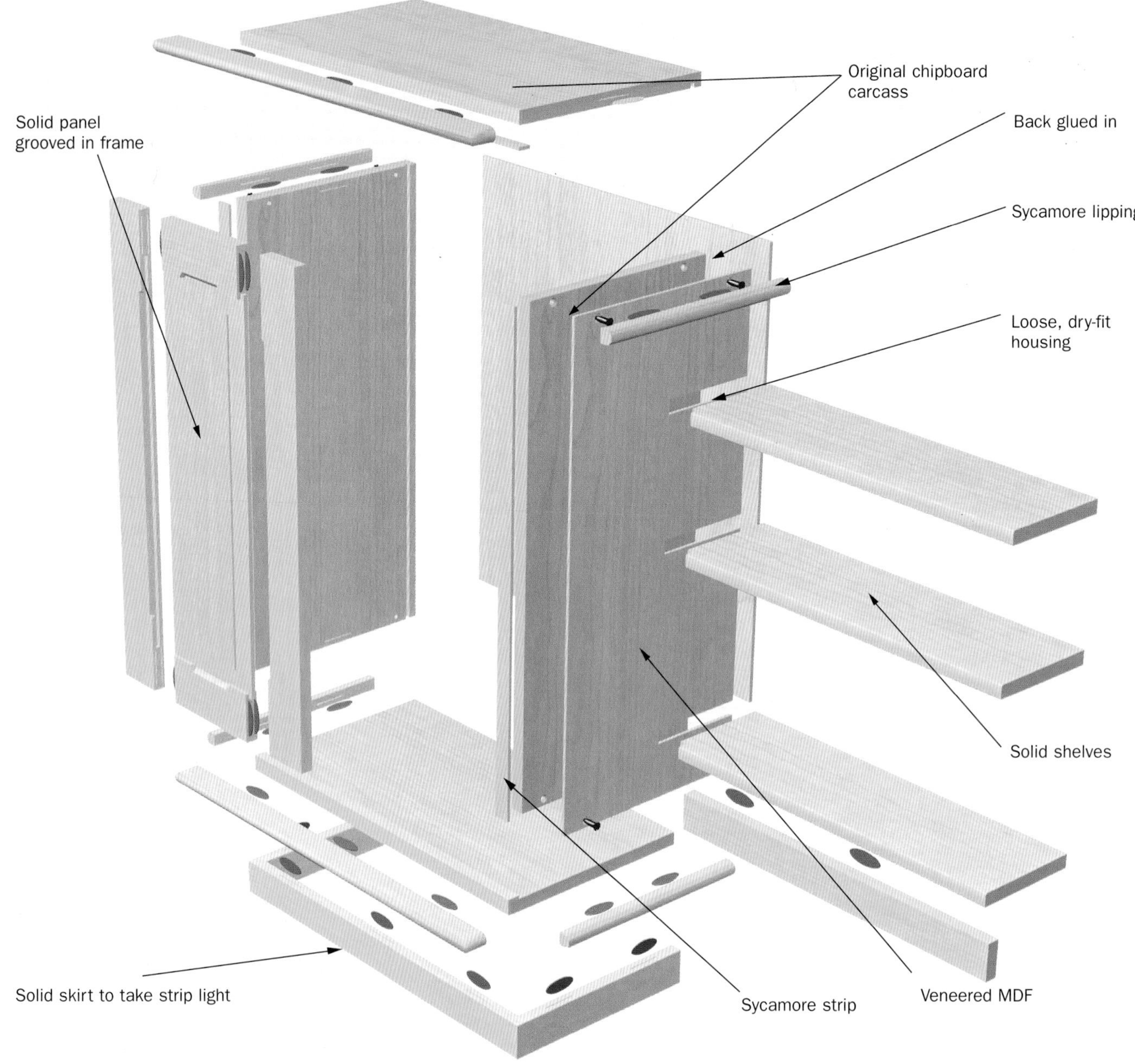

accurate use. Holes were drilled in the sides for the special chipboard screws, and the other end of the hinge fitted.

A 6 by 19mm (1/4 by 3/4in) strip of sycamore was glued and pinned inside the cabinet at the top and bottom for the doors to close against. Previously they had closed onto the front edge of the top and bottom, but they are now inset under the newly fitted half-round edging.

Adjustments were relatively simple and the doors fitted and functioned well. Burr elm (*Ulmus* sp.) pulls were selected and fitted from the stock I'd made for the entire project during the making of the dresser.

Shelves

For ease of construction, movement, and fitting I decided to loose-fit the shelves, without glue, into housings in the sides of the cabinets. Once both cabinets were fitted to the wall, the shelves would be secure.

The shelves were made from 22mm (7/8in) sycamore and the fronts rounded over to the same profile as the edging strips on the top and bottom of the cupboards. The ends were shouldered back 10mm (3/8in) and housings cut in the sides of the cupboards, in the correct positions. These housings are a relatively loose fit, as these joints are not intended to contribute to the overall strength of the construction, just to serve as supports for the shelves.

Lights

Linkable strip lighting – specifically for this sort of use and available from Screwfix – was fitted under the cupboards and shelf, providing good even light where it's required, with low energy consumption. Skirts 63mm (2 1/2in) deep were fitted with biscuits to the sides and fronts of the bases of the cupboards, and the underneath front of the bottom shelf, to hide the lights and fittings.

Finish

To keep the pale creaminess of the sycamore I chose a satin-finish water-based acrylic floor varnish. I applied three coats with a paint pad, rubbing down between coats to de-nib. The advantage of the acrylic finishes on pale woods is that they have a minimal initial 'yellowing' effect and prevent long-term darkening by filtering out UV light.

Barford's Aqua Cote is my preferred water-based varnish. It dries quickly, enabling up to four or five coats in a day if necessary, and cures in a few days to a very tough, durable surface. I also use the new matt finish extensively; it has a much lower sheen than the satin

Fielded doors with stop-chamfering

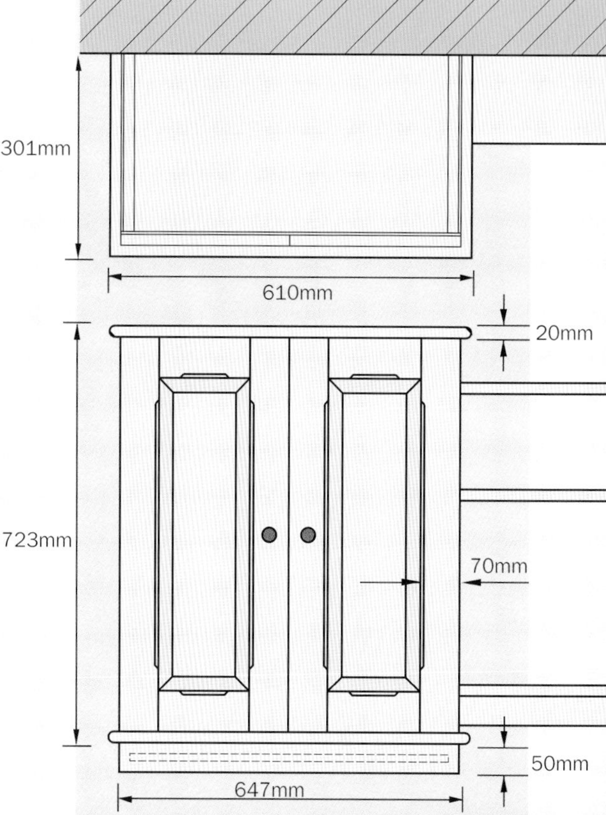

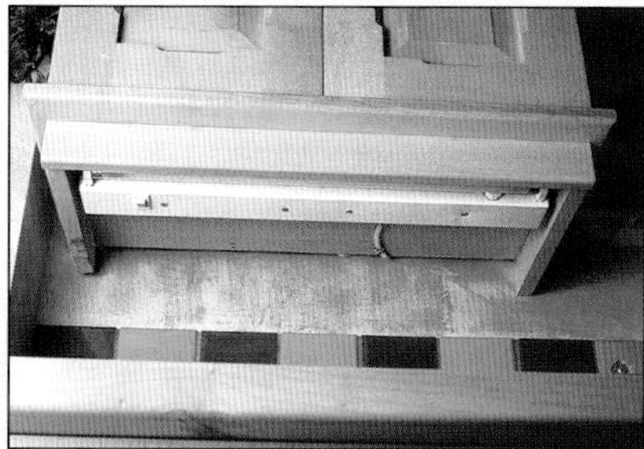
Underneath, showing strip light

"The overall aim was to lighten the whole kitchen by replacing the visible dark oak-effect surfaces with lighter, creamy-white sycamore"

Suppliers

Adquick for Bison polyurethane glues tel: 01223 412373
Wealden for router hinge cutters tel: 0800 328 4183
Screwfix for hinge cutters and link lighting tel: 0500 41 41 41
Barford's for Aqua Cote acrylic varnish tel: 01277 622050

The result: some wing correction needed here, squadron leader!

and is just as tough and durable.

Conclusion

The alterations to these cupboards provided a satisfactory result for minimum time and expense. The same principles were applied to the remaining fitted units in the kitchen, with the fitting of a butler's sink and 38mm (1½in) thick solid sycamore worktops completing the makeover.

I made best use of the positive features of the existing units and personalised them to achieve the look we wanted, and it was pleasantly surprising to achieve so much, relatively quickly and inexpensively with a minimum of inconvenience. But, having covered the main items of free-standing furniture and the elements of the alterations to the existing fitted units, I'll leave it to those interested to apply the general principles and their own variations. ■

Very simple, very country

The final part of this kitchen refit series sees the making of a table and chairs

Last but not least

I've just made a kitchen dresser for a client who, like me, prefers a mixture of fitted and free-standing kitchen furniture. Hers was a modern house in York stone in a small, pretty village in Yorkshire, and she had achieved a nice blend of modern, functional, fitted units, with some traditional free-standing pieces from me. The major free-standing piece was the large dresser in local elm (*Ulmus* sp.). The client wanted a table and chairs in a different native hardwood but one sympathetic to that piece.

Timber prep

After some deliberation my client chose native ash (*Fraxinus* sp.) for this project. This wood is cream to pale tan in colour, with a dark, sound heartwood. It's tough, with a straight, coarse, open grain, and the figure is quite similar to the wych elm (*Ulmus glabra*) I had used in the dresser. To add interest to the table top I had some olive ash, which is the light to dark brown heartwood colour all over, with a marbled effect similar to Mediterranean olivewood (*Olea* sp.).

All this timber had been seasoned for some time in my timber store, so its moisture content wasn't a problem, and I felt the construction would allow swelling or shrinking movement without noticeable effect. The main concern was that all the stresses in the timber should be stabilised before construction. To this end, all the pieces for the table top and chair seats were dimensioned slightly over size, sticked and stacked in the workshop. The stacks were initially either weighted on top or put in clamps, so the stresses stabilised, after cutting the fibres to size it. The weights were removed and the clamps slackened over a couple of weeks to ensure the pieces were all stable. A small amount of wind on the top or seat would alter the length of the legs!

Table top

This is made from four pieces: the centre pieces from olive ash and the two outside pieces of ordinary white ash (*Fraxinus americana*). The figure is carefully matched, running through the join to mask it – the overall effect is like a wide through-and-through board of ash with a lot of heart.

The edges of the boards were planed on the jointer and finished by hand to

Design

The brief was for something a bit different: simple, solid, and very 'country'. The table had to be as big as possible, without getting in the way, and to seat four adults.

It so happened that I was friendly with a local butcher based in the village and to whom I'd taken the odd pig to be prepared for the freezer – in my 'Good Life' days of attempted self-sufficiency. His butcher's block – which had a top about 760mm (2ft 6in) square and was a massive 305mm (12in) thick with four legs hammered straight into holes in the underneath – sprang to mind, and became the inspiration for the table. The top of a butcher's block is often end-grain up to give better recovery from chopping and cutting. The depth of the top is to stop it splitting through, and to provide serious weight, to resist the forces applied to it.

We decided to make a stylised version with a fairly thick top, but with a normal 'long-grain up' surface, and collars to fix the legs. To keep the table user-friendly in the limited space available in the kitchen, the corners and edges were rounded off. The legs were refined a little by making them octagonal rather than square in cross section.

The chairs were a logical progression, incorporating influences from a milking stool and an antique spinning chair I'd been asked to repair by some friends. The same rounding over was applied to the seat and back shape and edges. The legs fitted directly into the seat, with a fox wedge, and the back was held in position by pegs under the seat.

It's worth bearing in mind that the dimensions of the table only just allow it through a standard 760mm (30in) doorway with the door off; so it was worth checking the entry route and restrictions before starting work!

Above: Side view of the table

Right: Front view of chair

"The brief was for something a bit different: simple, solid, and very 'country'. The table had to be a big as possible, without getting in the way, and to seat four adults"

remove the ripples. The centre of the join was left slightly hollow – when they were pulled up in the clamps this would cause extra pressure on the ends, allowing for the extra shrinkage as the ends dry out more than the centre. The joins were reinforced with double biscuits, and all was glued up with Cascamite, clamped checked for wind, and left to set. The diagonals were marked on the underside to enable the leg-fixing collars to be positioned.

The corners were rounded off to a 150mm (6in) radius on the bandsaw and finished with a belt and drum sander. The top and bottom edges were rounded over using a 12mm (1/2in) bearing-guided radius cutter in a hand-held router.

Leg collars

Scrap pieces of 45 by 165 by 165mm (1 3/4 by 6 1/2 by 6 1/2in) ash were used to make the collars to attach the legs to the top. The diagonals were marked to find the centre, and the screw fixing holes were drilled on these diagonals.

A 50mm (2in) hole saw was used to produce the angled hole for the legs. The angle was found by drawing the table side and end cross sections, full size, on hardboard and making ply angle setters. These are pieces of ply cut to the correct fixed angle, taken from the full-size drawing and used to set the angle of the work to the drill.

Then a jig was made to raise one corner of the collars to the correct height so the holes drilled by the perpendicular pillar drill are at the correct angle, giving the required splay on the table legs.

Legs

The legs were cut 25mm (1in) too long and planed 55mm (2 1/4in) square. The planer fence was set to 45° and the corners planed off to make the octagonal cross section. The tops of the legs were turned to fit the holes; if a lathe is not available they can be pared with a spokeshave. A saw cut is then made in the top of each leg, at right angles to the line of the grain on the collar, and a wedge made of some scrap oak to fit.

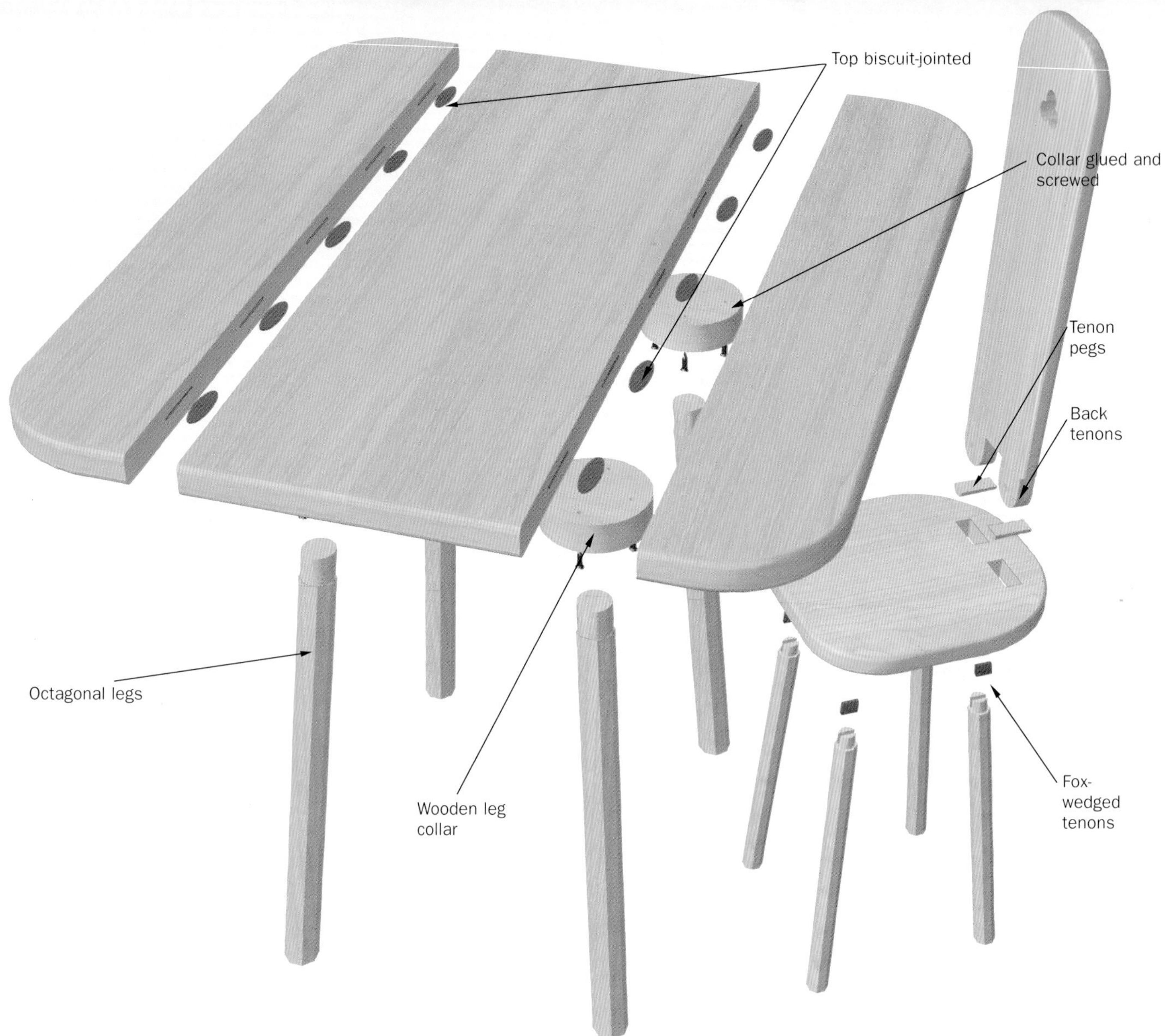

The legs were finished down to 240 grit with a random orbital sander. Cascamite was then applied to the inside of the holes, and the leg tops pushed through until the low side was flush with the top surface of the collar; the wedge was tapped home, and the glue left to set.

With the glue set, the tops of the legs were planed flush with the top surface of the collars. The collared legs were then positioned on the underside of the table top, using the diagonal lines marked on the collars and the table top to locate them accurately, and dry-fitted with screws only. The table was stood on a known level surface – I have a 1830 by 1220mm (6 by 4ft) piece of 25mm (1in) MDF, levelled as a reference surface, on the floor of the workshop.

Draw a line on each face of the leg by placing a 150mm (6in) metal rule on the level surface, and drawing a line along its top onto the leg which is parallel to the floor. A line parallel to this is drawn in the correct position, and the legs removed and trimmed to correct length on the bandsaw.

The legs were then glued and screwed into position, with the grain in the collars running in the same direction as the grain in the table top. If there are any access problems for the assembled table, leave out the glue and increase the number of screws so the legs are detachable.

Once the legs were fitted, the table top was finished down to 240 grit.

Chair seats

The rectangles of 32mm (1 1/4in) ash were cut for the chair seats. The positions of the holes for the legs were then marked and holes 25mm (1in) in diameter and 25mm (1in) deep drilled for the legs. Then, using the same method as for the table legs, gauges were cut from ply to set the angle of the work to the drill, and jigs made to repeat the holes for all eight front and back legs. A Forstner bit was used: its centre pin is short and will not penetrate the seat top surface.

A router, with a chock under one side of the baseplate to set the correct angle, was used to cut the two 25 by 63mm (1 by 2 1/2in) through mortices for the back. The seat was then shaped with a 100mm (4in) radius cut on the front corners, and a 150mm (6in) radius on the rear. The top and bottom edges were rounded over with a 12mm (1/2in) bearing-guided router cutter, and the seats finished to 240 grit.

Legs

The legs were cut 25mm (1in) over length and the octagonal cross section formed on the planer. To fit the holes in the seat, the top 32mm (1 1/4in) was turned on the lathe. I used a fox wedge in the top of the leg to ensure a tight fit. A saw cut was then made in the top 20mm (3/4in) of the leg and a wedge made to spread the join when the leg was hammered home. This wedge must be very accurate – just a tad wider than the saw cut – and nearly parallel so it will go right in, spreading the leg end to a tight fit, but not binding on the bottom of the hole, so preventing it going in to its full depth. I think modern glues make just as strong a job, without the uncertainty and complication of the fox

Underside of table, showing leg collars

One of my own set, made some time ago, showing the back tenon pegs

Cleaning up the glue on the chair legs

wedge, particularly the gap-filling ones – not that I've ever had a loose joint in my life!

Certainly, my more recent versions have been glued up with Bison from Adquick; it has the added advantage of setting in about 10 minutes at normal temperatures, and reassuringly foaming out of the join to let you know it is full. When set, the foam is slightly compressible, allowing slight movement without breaking the bond. Any surplus is easily cut away with a chisel.

Alternatively, the hole can be drilled right through the seat and a normal wedge used in the top of the leg. When wedging any tenon, make sure the wedge line is at right angles to the grain run around the hole or mortise, to avoid splitting!

Once the legs were finished, fitted and set, the seat was stood on the bench and the legs trimmed parallel to length, in a similar manner to the table legs. The bottoms of the legs were marked by placing a short straightedge, 12mm (1/2in) high, against each face of the leg, and drawing a pencil line,

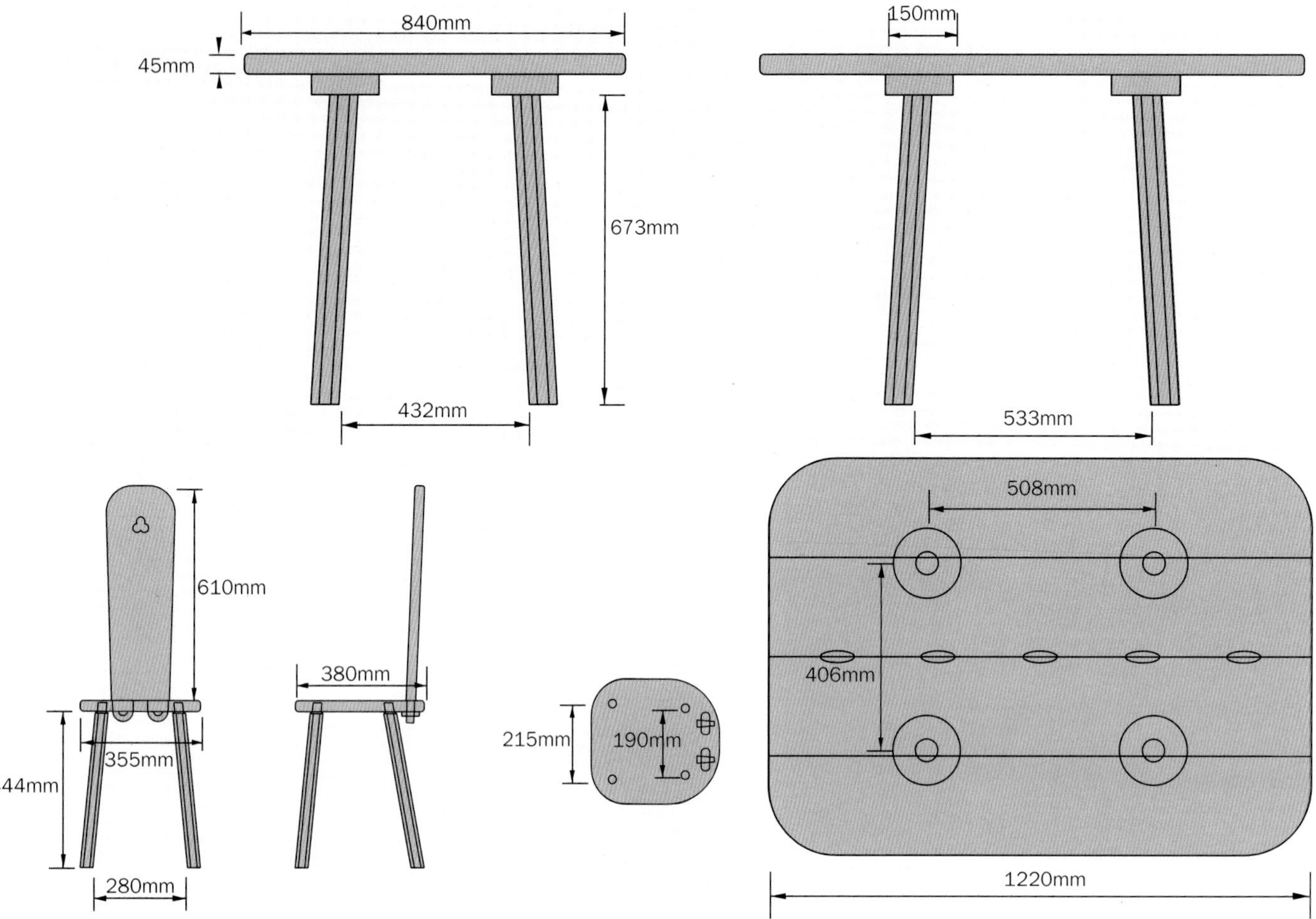

parallel with the bench top, on the top edge. A line was drawn parallel in the correct position and the cut made on the bandsaw.

Backs

The backs were cut from 25mm (1in) ash. Before any shaping took place, the end tenons were cut and fitted through. With the tenons in position in the seat, the 3mm (1/8in) shoulder was marked – similar to the way the legs are trimmed – by placing a straightedge on the seat and drawing a line on the top edge. The actual cut line was marked parallel to this line, in the correct place. The cut was made with a tenon saw and planed flush to the remainder of the tenon with a shoulder plane. The bottom edge of the seat was marked on the tenons, and the 25mm (1in) peg holes drilled with their centres just inside the mortice, above the bottom line of the seat.

Pegs were made by turning 30mm (1 1/8in) dowels on the lathe and splitting them in half, down the length, on the bandsaw. The resultant half-round pegs were trimmed and pared to fit, and finally trimmed to length once they had been hammered home. The tenon ends were rounded to give a 20mm (3/4in) edge around the peg holes.

Shamrock fingerhole

The three overlapping holes in the back were drilled with a 25mm (1in) Forstner bit to form the shamrock shape. A pillar drill was used and the holes drilled from both sides to avoid breakout. This feature is not only decorative but gives a useful finger-grip for lifting the chairs. Finally, the back was shaped on the bandsaw, finished with the belt sander, and the edges rounded over, using the 12mm (1/2in) bearing-guided cutter in the router. It was finished and fixed in position, with the pegs hammered home and trimmed to size.

Finish

The assembled table and chairs were finally hand-finished down to 320 grit and wiped over with white spirit prior to varnishing.

Five thin coats of satin polyurethane varnish were applied with a sponge pad and allowed to build up to a smooth finish. Each coat was left to dry for 24 hours in my warm, dry workshop. The first two coats were cut back with 320 grit on a hard sanding block to allow the grain to fill. Further coats were cut back with a Scotchbrite grey pad to give a soft sheen. Although the final coat dries in 24 hours or so, it's better left for 7 to 10 days to cure fully before use. The result is a very durable, wipe-clean, easy-to-maintain finish.

Conclusion

I've made several sets of these tables and chairs over the years, in a range of woods and finishes. It's a simple, useful project which is easily modified to give an individual touch. My favourite is a set I made in sycamore (*Acer pseudoplatanus*) with an unsealed table top which is scrubbed clean and bleached occasionally to remove difficult stains and to keep it hygienic. This was the norm for kitchen tables in the past, and looks and feels quite distinctive. ■

Dining-room suite in English oak

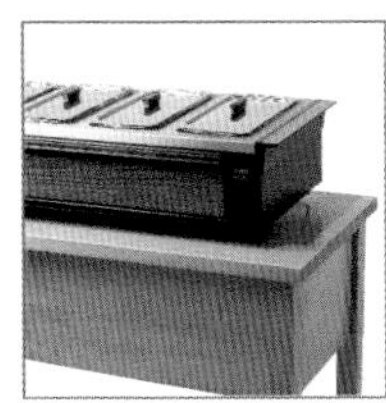

Table

This sturdy dining table in English oak pays respect to the legendary Robert Thompson... but what happened to the mouse?

Photo 1 **The appealing simplicity of the twin-leg design**

The Officers' Mess at the RAF Regiment Depot in Catterick, North Yorkshire, contained several very nice pieces of furniture by Robert 'Mousey' Thompson. This legendary carver, designer and maker worked from Kilburn, a small village nearby. Many of his pieces are ecclesiastical, exclusively in English oak, and distinguished by a carving of a mouse, somewhere on the piece.

There are several stories about the origin of the mouse, but the one I like best is quoted in James Thompson's book, *The Mouseman of Kilburn*. Robert (Thompson) was carving a cornice for a huge church screen with a co-worker, who made a comment about being 'as poor as church mice'. Robert light-heartedly carved a mouse on the cornice and then realised that he had hit on a lovely trademark. He saw it as signifying industry in quiet places.

It was certainly an astute move as his work is now distributed all over the world. The business is now run by his grandsons, and the furniture, still with a mouse carved on it, is still known as 'Mouseman'.

When I left the RAF Regiment many of my friends asked what I was going to carve on my own work as a trademark. The many suggestions were varied and interesting – but most were too difficult to carve!

DESIGN

I had, of course, visited the Mouseman workshop and showroom, and been impressed by the simplicity and honesty of the solid, very English designs. When we needed a dining table and chairs for our own cottage, I was influenced by what I had seen. Something in the English oak, country furniture genre, suitable to double as a display piece for potential clients, was required. A simple refectory-style table and traditional chairs fitted the bill, and in this article I will cover the table; the chairs follow on pages 88–92.

The size of the top was governed by the number of people it was required to seat. The norm is about 580mm (23in) of edge per sitter, at a height of 735–760mm (29–30in). This one was to seat 6–8 normally and 10 at a squeeze.

Refectory tables are usually narrow – 760–915mm (30–36in) – but here the width was increased for flexibility, to give

service

Photo 2 **End-grain oak always looks good, with the combination of annual rings and rays**

Photo 3 **The stopped chamfer on the legs is an essential ingredient to that very traditional 'English' look**

the possibility of squeezing two on each end if required, and allowing room in the centre for serving dishes. This extra width also gave a decent overhang to tuck the chairs under. The narrow tables often have narrow benches, as opposed to chairs.

An ideal table has, of course, no legs; the top should just hang conveniently at the right height, with no visible means of support to get in the way of knees and chairs. Until the arrival of anti-gravity oak, however, I had to keep the legs as far out of the way as possible (**see Photo 1**). Paired legs, close together, with a foot below and a bearer for the top above, achieved this. The arrangement also looked more suited to a dining table than the alternative slab end, shaped or plain, often found on a less formal kitchen piece.

The legs were stop-chamfered on the edges, and this shape was reflected in the chair legs, to link the whole set together.

TIMBER SELECTION

I went to Duffield's of Ripon, my usual timber supplier, to select the English oak. I found some nice kiln-dried 44mm (1 3/4in) quarter-sawn, waney-edged stock for the top. There were also some 100 x 100mm (4 x 4in) random lengths which had been air-dried for some years after cutting square, from which I was able to select suitable pieces to make the legs and underframe with minimum waste. I prefer air-dried stock at this thickness; kiln-drying can lead to defects such as face cracking, case-hardening or honeycombing.

TIMBER PREPARATION

I cut five straight-edged boards for the top, a little oversize, and dressed both faces to get a good look at the figure. The 4 x 4s (100 x 100mm) were also dressed and the best pieces cut, 25mm (1in) over length, for the legs. From the remaining 4 x 4s I deep-cut 4 x 2 (100 x 50mm) for the feet, bearers and rails. Everything was then sticked, stacked and placed in my conditioning cabinet for some weeks to settle, prior to final dimensioning. The conditioning cabinet is a large airtight box with a dehumidifier set to domestic conditions.

After this conditioning period, all the pieces were cut to size and brought into

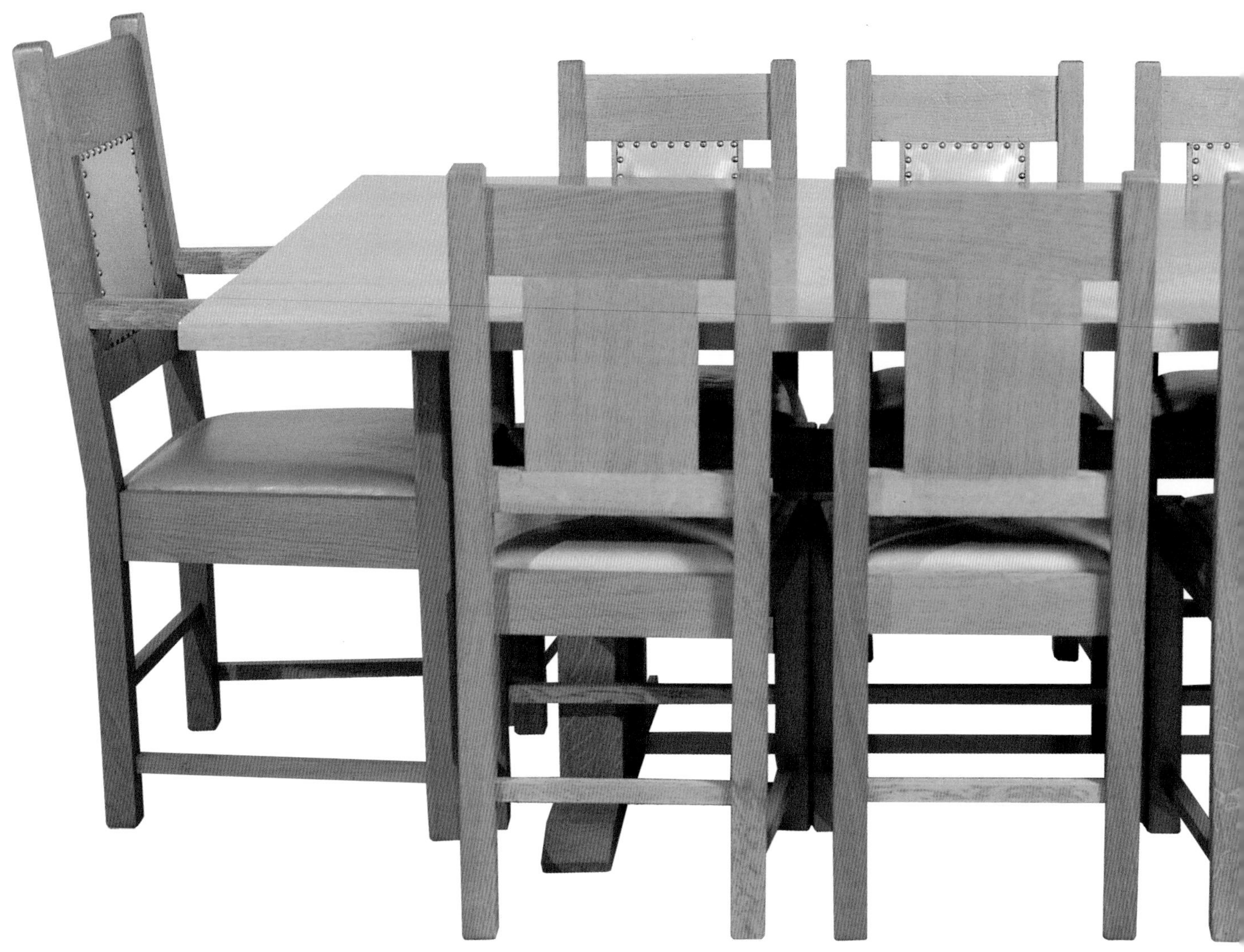

the workshop. Final conditioning takes place during making in the workshop, which I keep warm with a stove, and dry with another dehumidifier. The importance of correct conditions for timber storage and furniture making cannot be over-emphasised. The closer the temperature and humidity in the workshop are to the end-use conditions, the better.

TOP

The top was made up from five boards, which were laid out and the arrangement adjusted until the most pleasing result was achieved (**see Photo 2**). The wood was well figured and the quarter-sawing, apart from giving stable boards with a minimum of potential movement, had exposed the 'flash' of the medullary rays. I tried to ensure that the figure ran through the joins to disguise them.

The individual boards were quite heavy and difficult to edge over my planer, even with its 1.5m (5ft) table. For safety and efficiency I lined up roller stands to effectively increase the length of the table, and take the weight as they went over.

Once they had been edged, the machine ripples, which would weaken the glue joint, were removed and final adjustments made with my no. 7 jointing plane.

The fit of the joining edges was slightly concave, touching at each end with approximately 1.5mm ($^{1}/_{16}$in) gap at the centre. This helps the clamps pull up tight, and allows for extra shrinkage at the ends, which dry out quicker, (**see drawing**). The joining edges were then slotted for a loose ply tongue to add strength. The boards were marked where they would be finally cut to size, and the slots stopped short of those marks, so that the final trimming would not expose the tongue.

Cascamite glue was applied to the slots, edges and tongues, the top was clamped up, checked to ensure it was flat, and left to set. Surplus glue was removed with a scraper, and a belt sander was used to flatten the top, finishing it down to 150 grit.

LEGS

The legs were cut to length, and dimensioned to 90mm (3$^{1}/_{2}$in) square cross section. All four faces were finished with the belt sander down to 150 grit. The stopped chamfers were cut with a router, all starting 90mm (3$^{1}/_{2}$in) from the ends.

"An ideal table has, of course, no legs; the top should just hang conveniently at the right height, with no visible means of support to get in the way of knees and chairs."

Photo 6 **The matching dining and carver chairs are described on pages 88–92**

Photo 4 **The author busy screwing the top on; note the long expansion slots for the screw heads to allow for seasonal movement**

They were finished with a sharp scraper, and hand-sanded using a sanding block (**see Photo 3**).

FEET AND BEARERS

The slope chamfers on each of the ends of the feet and bearers were cut on the bandsaw and finished with a no. 5½ jack plane. The cut-outs on the undersides of the feet, to leave the three floor-contact pads, were formed with the router and sanded to a finish. The slots in the top bearers, through which the top fixing screws would fit, were also cut with the router. Make an outside 19mm (¾in) slot, 25mm (1in) deep to take the screwhead and washer, and a central 6.3mm (¼in) through slot to screw through into the table top (**see drawing**).

DOWELS

The top bearers and feet were positioned on the legs and dry-clamped. Holes for the 25mm (1in) dowels were drilled through the feet and top bearers, into the legs. This enabled the holes to be drilled by hand and ensured that they lined up accurately. The dowels could be fox-wedged into the blind holes and top-wedged into the open holes, if required, although I did not feel it necessary.

The legs, feet and bearers were all finished to 150 grit with the belt sander, then finally finished with the random orbital sander, glued up with Cascamite, clamped, checked for square, and left to set.

RAILS

The mortices for the top and bottom rails were cut on the inside edges of the feet and bearers. The rails were cut to length, and tenons formed on their ends. The edges of the rails were rounded over to 6.3mm (¼in) radius with a router and, again, finished on the belt and random orbital sanders.

ASSEMBLY

The underframe was put together by gluing the rails to the leg assemblies, again with Cascamite. They were clamped, checked square, and left to set. Then the top was positioned on the underframe and fixed with screws through the expansion slots in the top bearers (**see Photo 4**).

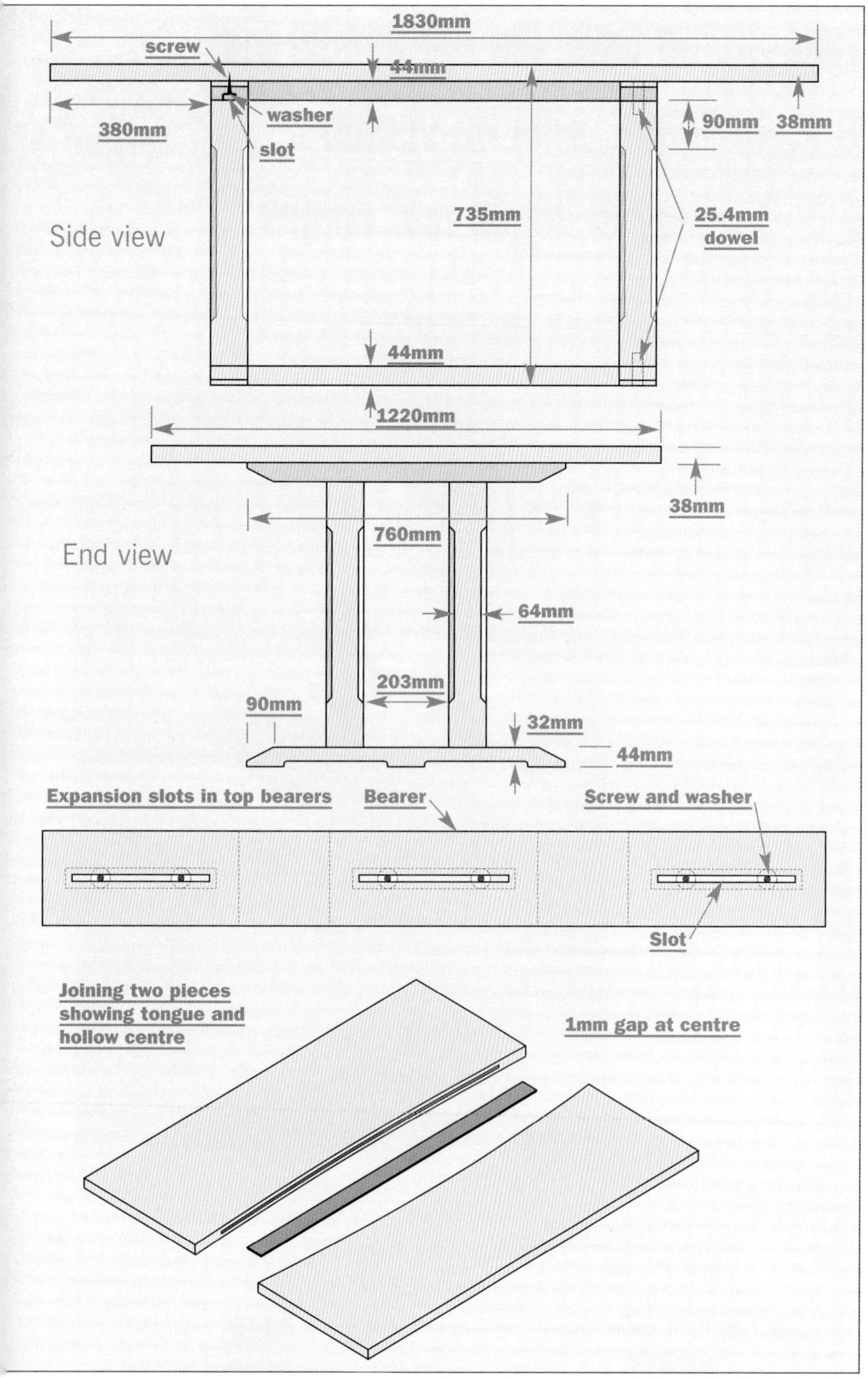

Side view

1830mm
screw
44mm
washer
slot
380mm
90mm
38mm
735mm
25.4mm dowel
44mm

End view

1220mm
38mm
760mm
64mm
203mm
90mm
32mm
44mm

Expansion slots in top bearers
Bearer
Screw and washer
Slot

Joining two pieces showing tongue and hollow centre
1mm gap at centre

FINISH

All the components had been finished prior to assembly, except the top face of the table top. This was now finally finished with the random orbital sander, and then the whole piece hand-sanded down to 320 grit.

An oiled finish really suits this sort of piece in oak, and that was what I wanted for the table and chairs, but I had my doubts about its durability on the table top. This would have to endure hot dishes and alcohol, and I could see a constant need for re-oiling.

I contacted the technical department of Liberon and was assured that polyurethane varnish would key to a single subcoat of their finishing oil, provided it was allowed to dry for at least 24 hours.

I gave everything one coat of Liberon finishing oil, which I find thinner and more penetrative than some other Danish oils, carefully wiping off all surplus with kitchen tissue. This coat gave the main colour change to the wood. Thereafter all but the top was given the usual five or six thin coats of oil, at 24-hour intervals, wiping off all surplus, and cutting back with a Scotchbrite grey pad between coats.

Then the top was given six thin coats

"There was nothing complex about this piece."

Photo 5 **A superb finished table complete with leather-upholstered chairs**

of satin-finish polyurethane varnish, applied with a sponge pad, again at 24-hour intervals, and allowed to build up to a smooth finish. The first two coats were cut back with 320 grit on a hard sanding block to allow the grain to fill. Further coats were cut back with the grey pad, again on a block, to give a very similar sheen to the oiled finish. The top was not used for a full week after the table was moved into the cottage, to allow the polyurethane to cure fully .

The overall effect was of an oiled finish but with a durable, easy-to-maintain top. I was extremely satisfied with the result (**see Photos 5 & 6**).

CONCLUSION

There was nothing complex or tricky about this piece. The main things to watch are the sheer weight and sharp edges of some of the pieces. As a one-man show, I had to make provision with stands and gloves to avoid damage to my little pink body. The table has been the scene of dinners large and small and is still in full use in our new cottage. Long may it live!

Side chair

Carver

A set of chairs to match the dining table

FIRSTSITTING

Having completed the dining table on pages 82–6, I set about making the chairs to accompany it. The most time-consuming factor when constructing chairs is making jigs and setting up the machines and stop positions. It is essential to make all the components you are likely to need, as it's preferable to have too many than to set everything up again just to make a couple more. This is a useful point to make to clients who are not sure whether to have six or eight chairs. Believe it or not, the cost of making two chairs later on could be up to three times more than constructing them at the same time as the rest of the batch!

We decided on six side chairs and two carvers. Only four of the side chairs would be in regular use, with the two spares kept in my study.

DESIGN

The chairs had to reflect the design of the table, and I opted for a simple and sturdy English country style, reminiscent of the legendary Robert 'Mouseman' Thompson. The measurements of this type of chair were fairly standard, being averaged out to suit the main range of variation in human size. Of course this will not necessarily concur with individual size and taste, but years of experience have taught me that it's the most practical solution available.

I was asked some time ago to make 30 chairs for a memorial chapel in a local church. They were designed by the Diocesan Committee who came up with a seat height of 355mm (14in). I had been told categorically not to change the design. A mock-up of the chair in softwood was sent along to the committee and, after making some fairly heavy landings on the

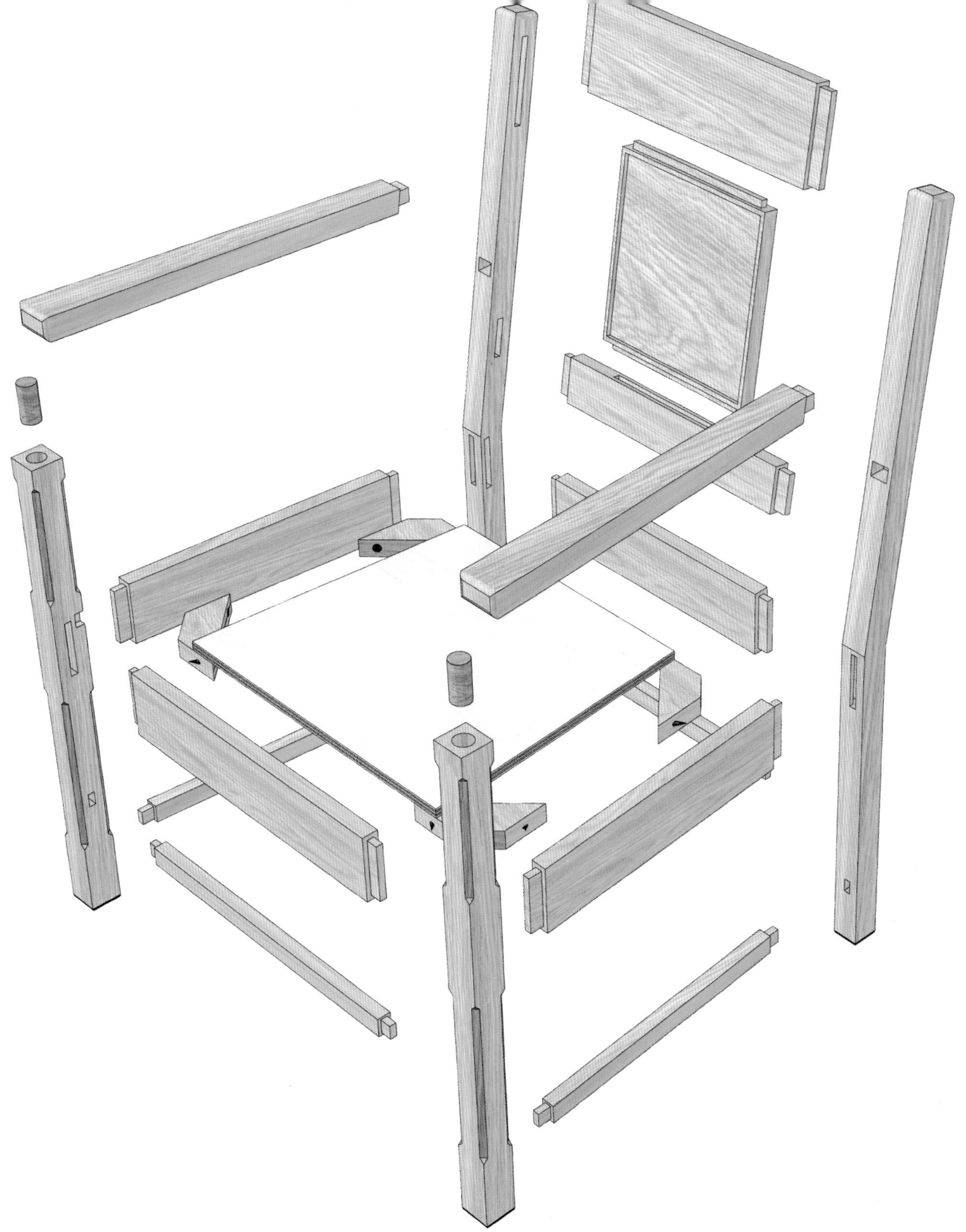

chair, they asked for the seat height to be raised. Naturally I had tried to explain to them about the standard height, for the reasons cited above. Still, they say that 'A camel is a horse designed by a committee'.

TIMBER SELECTION

The timber selection in this case was fairly simple as I had ensured that there was enough timber left over from the table to make the chairs from the offcuts. With any project, when cutting out it's important to use the larger pieces with the best faces for the most visible areas and work down in quality for the other components. Plain or even blemished timber can be used, so long as it is in an unseen area of the construction. Very small pieces of timber can be used for the rails and braces.

TIMBER PREPARATION

All the oak for both the table and chairs had been sticked, stacked, and placed in my conditioning cabinet for a few weeks prior to final dimensioning. This cabinet is a large air- and vapour-tight box with a dehumidifier set to domestic conditions.

After the conditioning period, all the pieces for the table were cut to size and then brought into the workshop.

The remaining timber for the chairs got extra time in the cabinet, ensuring it was out of the way while the table was being made.

Final conditioning would take place during making in the workshop, which I kept warm with a stove, and dry with another dehumidifier. Correct conditions for timber storage and furniture making are essential. The basic principle is to try and get the temperature and humidity in the workshop as close to end-use conditions as possible.

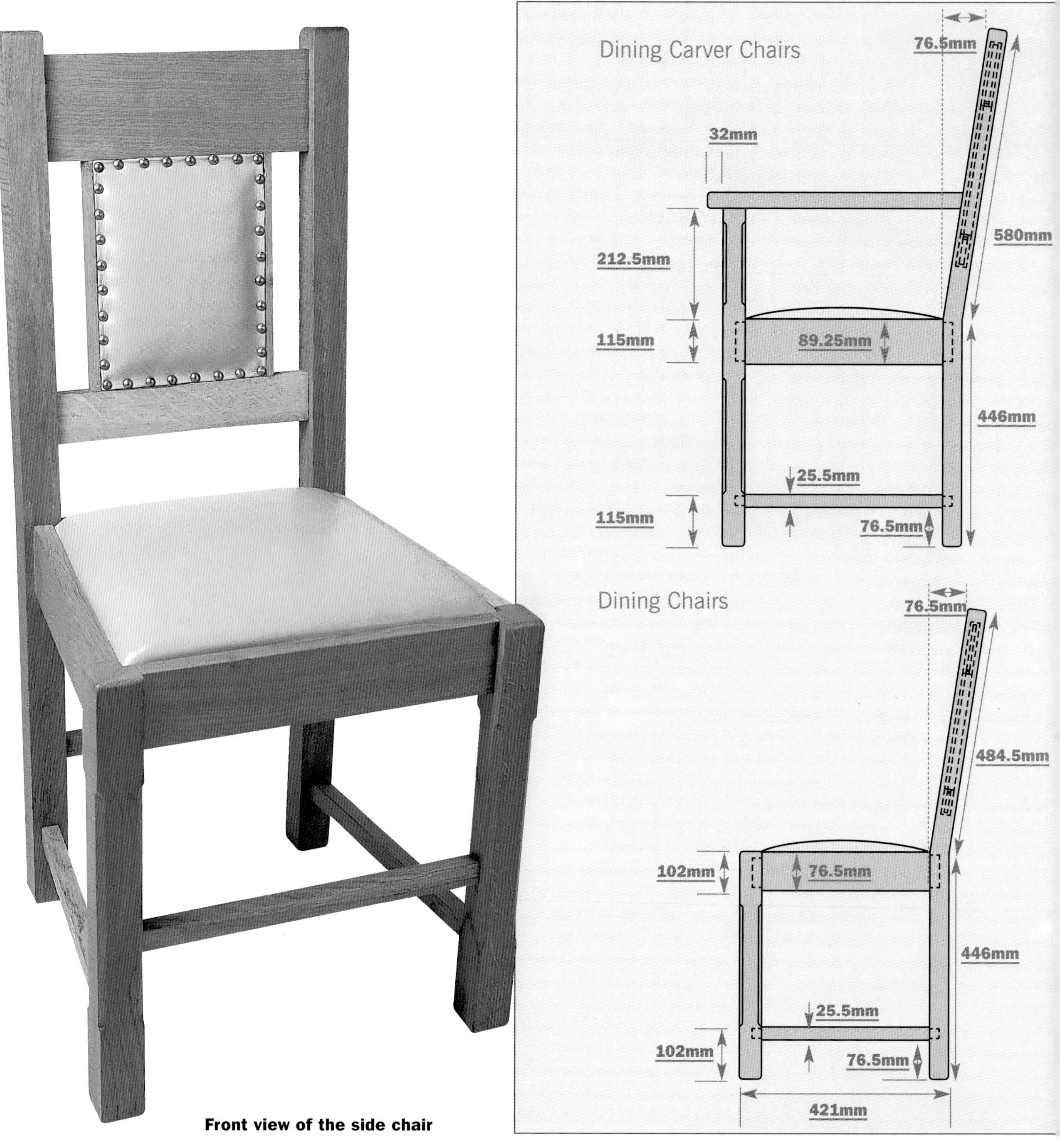

Front view of the side chair

The pieces of the timber that were to make up the chairs were all fairly small, with no large cross-grain areas. They should have little movement, and almost all are exposed on all sides and faces to allow even drying. The joints in a chair are particularly critical to its strength, and I didn't want any detrimental shrinkage once the mortices and tenons had been machined and fitted.

BATCH PRODUCTION

The essence of batch production is accuracy, care and organisation. Accurate cutting lists, careful sequencing of actions, and the use of rods and jigs for measurements to be repeated, are all of crucial importance. I made a pattern in hardboard for the back legs and another of the seat plan in order to work out the patterns for the angled tenons in the seat and leg rails.

I checked that I had the correct number of each component, with the left- and right-hand pieces clearly marked. All the cuts at one machine setting were done at the same time and I double-checked the measurements of the first piece, to ensure that I didn't make multiple mistakes.

SIDE CHAIRS

FRONT LEGS

I dimensioned the front legs and routed all the mortices with a straight cutter. Using a 45° cutter I then made the stop chamfers, finishing them with a scraper. I used a 6mm (1/4in) radius cutter to round over the tops and bottoms, leaving the top inside edges (i.e. the mortice faces) intact.

I then finished to 150 grit with both a belt and an orbital sander.

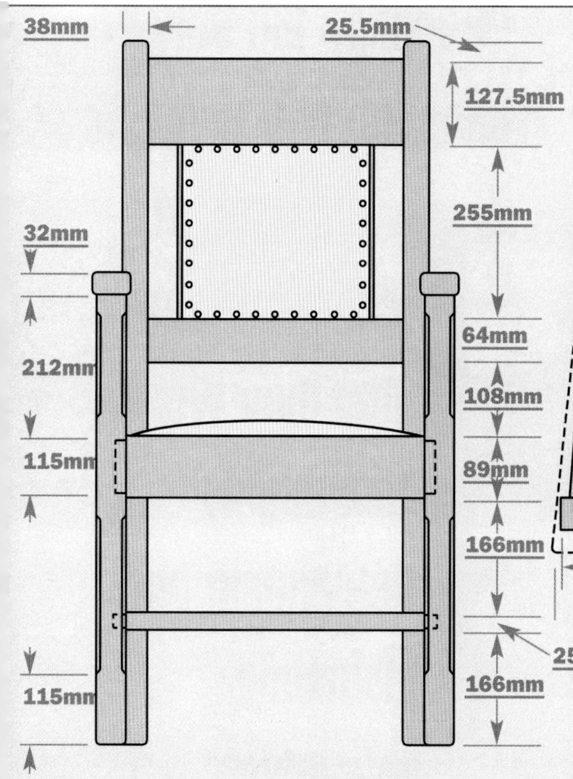

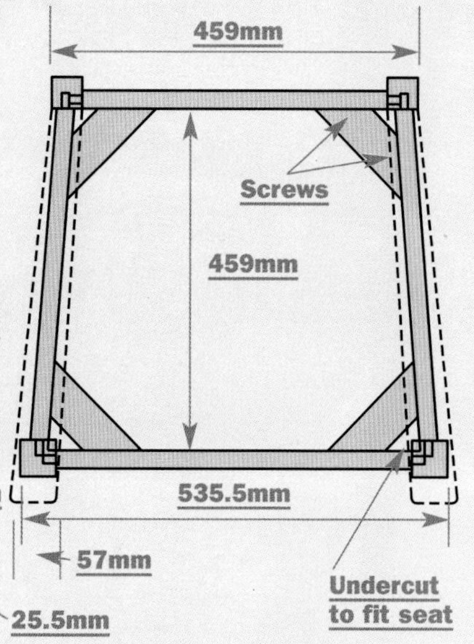

"Great care should be taken when cutting these tenons..."

Note rounding over of the top of the leg, and cut-out for seat

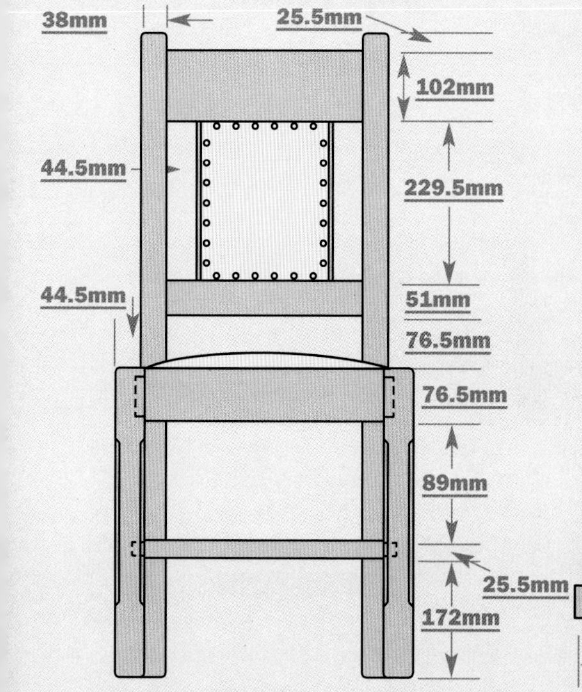

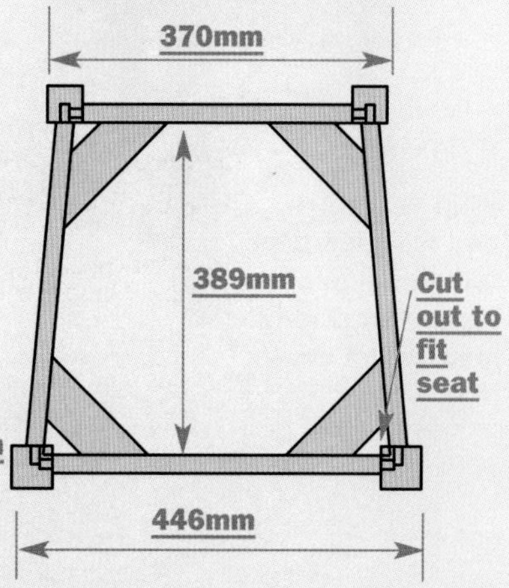

Seat supports and braces are clearly visible

BACK LEGS

The back legs were cut out on the bandsaw and finished with a plane and scraper. As with the front legs, the mortices were routed out, the tops and bottoms were rounded over and sanded with belt and random orbital sanders.

FRONT AND BACK RAILS

The seat, back and leg rails for the front and back of the chair were cut to size and tenoned in the usual way. In this case I used the radial-arm saw to make multiple cuts, although a bandsaw, router or even a tenon saw would have done the job just as well.

SIDE RAILS

The side rails were a bit more complicated as the tenons needed to be cut at the required angle for the front-to-back taper of the seat. The angle was taken from the full-size drawing and patterns made in hardboard to mark the tenon. The main destructive force on a chair is from front to back, which can cause it to collapse, so the side tenons take virtually all the strain. Great care should be taken when cutting these tenons to make them as accurate as possible. I cut them slightly oversize on the bandsaw, then planed them individually to a tight fit using a small shoulder plane.

BACK PANELS

The back panels were cut to size, with a tenon cut to fit the long shallow mortice in the rails above and below them. The outside edge of the panel was flush with the rails above and below. The centre of the panel was 3mm (1/8in) shallower, so the edge of the leather butted up to the wood at the edges when it was upholstered. The top and bottom rails were glued and clamped to the panel to complete the back panel units. Once set they were machine-finished with 150 grit.

ASSEMBLY

The front and back 'units' were assembled first. All the joints were put together dry to make sure they fitted. Titebond glue was applied to the top edges of the mortices and brushed onto the tenon faces, the joints pushed together, clamped, checked for square and left to set.

Once the front and back units were assembled and set, they were connected in a similar way to the side rails to form the complete chair. It is important to assemble the chairs on a flat, level surface so that they are truly square. I have an 1830 x 1220mm (6 x 4ft) piece of 25mm (1in) MDF, levelled as a reference surface, on the floor of the workshop. Failure to do this before the glue sets will produce some very wonky chairs!

In a perfect world all joints are a perfect fit, but as we all know, a perfect world it ain't. If a tenon is loose, a piece of veneer glued to the appropriate face normally solves the problem. Modern glues of the gap-filling 'I can't believe it's not nails' variety, or the foaming polyurethane Bison or Gorilla brands, are also an excellent standby.

SEAT BRACES

Once the chairs were assembled, seat braces were screwed and glued across the corners of the seat area to act as a support for the drop-in seat and increase the chair's overall rigidity.

SEAT

I made the seats out of 12.7mm (1/2in) ply to drop between the seat rails and sit on the corner braces. I checked with the upholsterer who told me to leave a 6mm (1/4in) clearance all round to allow for the edge padding and cowhide we intended to use for the upholstery. A cut-out was chiselled in the tops of the front legs to allow the seat to drop in.

CARVERS

The carvers were a scaled-up version of the side chairs with longer front legs dowelled into the arms, which were tenoned into the front face of the back legs. The front legs were cut to size along with the stopped chamfers above and below the seat rails. The tops were drilled for a 25mm (1in) dowel.

As the legs continue past the seat, they had to be undercut at the seat front corners to allow it to slide in. Start with the front edge and then drop the back into position.

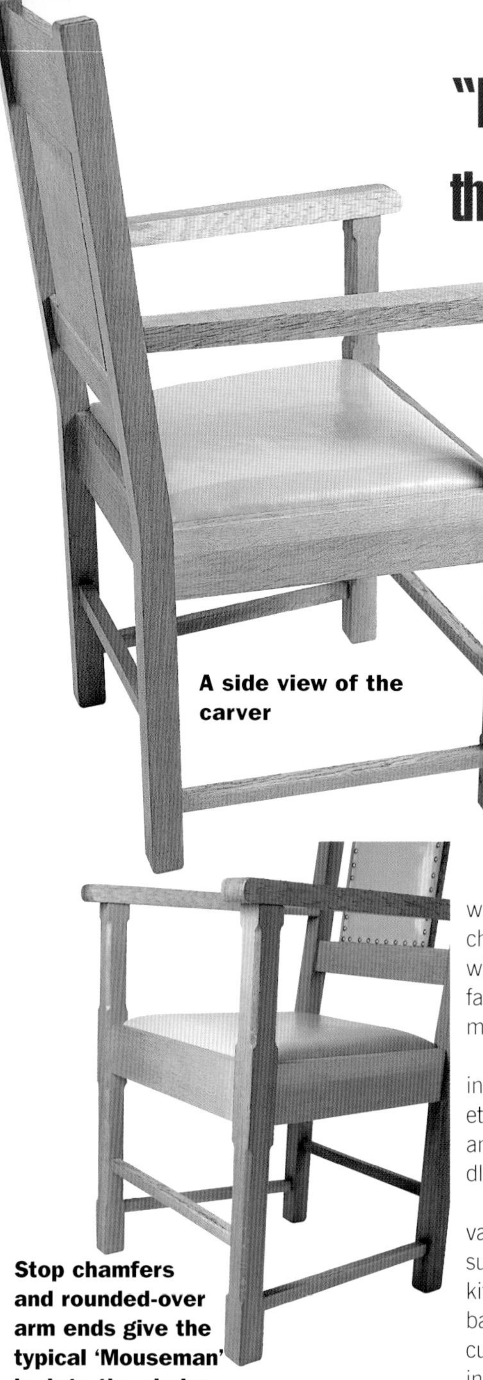

A side view of the carver

Stop chamfers and rounded-over arm ends give the typical 'Mouseman' look to the chairs

"Perhaps the only thing the two projects did have in common was that they were thoroughly demanding and ultimately enjoyable."

The only difference to the back legs, apart from the size, was the extra mortice in the front face to take the tenon on the end of the arm. The assembly method and sequence was the same as for the side chairs, and the arms were added after the seat braces had been fitted.

ARMS

The pattern for the arms was taken from the full-size drawing. They were cut to size and shape, with the front ends rounded over using a 12mm (1/2in) radius cutter. A tenon was cut on the end which fitted to the back, and a 25mm (1in) blind hole drilled in the underside at the front for the dowel to the top of the front leg. The arms were glued and clamped, and left to set.

FINISH

All the components had been machine-finished prior to assembly. All the oozing glue was removed and the complete set of chairs were hand-sanded with 320 grit. A wipe over with white spirit cleaned the surface and showed up any glue marks I had missed.

I applied several coats of Liberon finishing oil, which I find thinner and more penetrative than some other Danish oils. Oil is an ideal finish for chairs which are too fiddly to varnish.

The coats were applied at 24-hour intervals in the warmth of the dry workshop. All surplus oil was carefully wiped off with kitchen tissue, and the surface was cut back with a Scotchbrite grey pad once fully cured. After a couple of weeks' curing time in a warm, dry room, the chairs were finally buffed to a silky sheen with a soft cloth.

UPHOLSTERY

The upholstery was relatively simple but, as it was to be in cowhide, I decided not to attempt it myself. We were able to select a nice caramel colour to complement the honey colour of the oak, and were very satisfied with the end result.

CONCLUSION

Making the chairs was a totally different type of project from the table. Whereas the table involved a few large pieces, a few joints and large areas to finish, the chairs entailed batch production, lots of small pieces, repeat cuts and many accurate joints. Perhaps the only thing the two projects did have in common was that they were thoroughly demanding and ultimately enjoyable. I was particularly pleased with the end result and both the table and chairs are still well used.

Photo 1 - Side table with food warmer on top

The host with the most

This side table in English oak is an elegant alternative to a hostess trolley

We liked the idea of having an electric food warmer to keep food warm close to the table, especially for those big family meals. But we couldn't stand the metal trolley with the woodgrain-effect finish that came with it! We then discovered that the food warmer was available without the trolley – though still with the same wood-effect finish – so we bought one and decided that I would make a suitable piece of furniture in which to hide it.

The food warmer is quite bulky and difficult to store, and is not the sort of item to be left out on view. Although invaluable when required, it would be used at relatively infrequent intervals. The design features a table with a deep frame that forms a box; the lid is hinged for access. We also decided that it did not need to be on wheels.

The food warmer is stored inside when not in use, enabling the table to be used as a normal side table most of the time. On the occasions when the food warmer is required, it's placed on the top, with the side table becoming its stand.

SELECTION AND PREPARATION OF TIMBER

The existing dining-room furniture is all made of English oak in a nice, simple country style (the table and chairs have already been described on pages 82–92). The side table is complementary in style and is also made of English oak. We decided on the final measurements, essentially building around the size of the internal box required, under the lid, to contain the food warmer. I retired to draw up the final piece on the computer, in Autosketch.

Once the design and measurements had been finalised, and approved by senior management, I set off to my usual timber merchants where I managed to get some nice English oak to match the existing furniture.

Photo 2 Side table closed with food warmer inside

Photo 3 End view, table closed, shows top braces let into side

Photo 6 Inside of lid, with braces and plugged double-countersunk screw holes

Photo 7 Close-up of leg, showing stopped chamfers

Photo 8 Finishing stopped chamfers with scraper

Back in the workshop, the wood was laid out, marked up, and cut oversize to allow for final trimming. The best-figured pieces were chosen for the frame front and the top. It was then faced and thicknessed, checked for faults, figure, colour, and marked. Next it was sticked, stacked, and placed in the dining room to settle and adjust. Two weeks later it was brought into the workshop and dimensioned to its final sizes.

I keep my workshop as close as possible to normal domestic conditions of temperature and humidity, so any final conditioning takes place during the making. The importance of correct conditions for timber storage and furniture making cannot be overemphasised. The closer temperature and humidity in the workshop and woodstore are to end-use conditions, the less likelihood of future movement, warping, twisting, and subsequent damage and disappointment.

CONSTRUCTION DESIGN

The legs were cut to length and dimensioned to 40mm (1 5/8in) cross section. The mortices were cut for the front, back, and sides of the frame, using a router with a 12mm (1/2in) cutter. The floor ends of the legs were rounded over to 6mm (1/4in) radius, using a roundover cutter in the router, to prevent splintering and aid sliding on carpets (**see Fig 1**).

The stopped chamfers were cut on a router using a 45° cutter, all finished with a sharp scraper (**see Photos 7 and 8**) and sanded finely, using a sanding block, so as not to lose the straight edge.

The front, back and sides of the frame were dimensioned and the tenons cut to fit the mortices in the legs. The back was made 3mm (1/8in) narrower and set 3mm (1/8in) lower than the front to form the rebate between the back legs for the lid hinge. The sides were made 25mm (1in) narrower and set 25mm lower than the front and back to allow clearance for the top braces (**see Photo 3**).

These joints were dry-fitted to check for accuracy. It was particularly important that they were a really good fit, as they needed to be as strong as possible; there would be no bottom rails to complete the square and brace the legs. However, given the length of the mortice and tenon join between the legs and the frame, I felt that there was sufficient strength in the construction.

Using a router with a 6mm cutter, the 6mm (1/4in) housing for the oak-faced MDF base was now cut in the sides, back, front and legs. The base was cut to size, allowing 6mm (1/4in) all round for the housing, and the cut-outs made for the legs. The base was fitted dry and checked, and adjustments made. The frame pieces and the legs were now finished down to 150 grit.

Photo 9 Author fitting hinge

"The food warmer is stored inside when not in use, enabling the table to be used as a normal side table most of the time."

Photo 4 Table open, showing food warmer inside

PVA glue was applied to the mortices in the legs for the front and back pieces, then the front and back tenons were pushed home, clamped, checked for square, and left to set.

When the front and back were set, glue was applied to the mortices for the sides and the base housing. The sides and base were fitted to the assembled front and back, clamped, checked for square, and the whole carcass left to set. Incidentally, the base was glued in all round as it was of MDF, and not subject to movement. This provides a lot of extra strength to the whole construction.

TOP CHOICE

The top was made up from two boards which were faced and thicknessed, and matched for the most pleasing figure and colour, trying to ensure that the figure ran through the join to disguise it. The most pleasing effect prevented alternating the cupping tendency of the boards, so I decided to ignore that factor. I am not convinced about the value of this practice anyway. I prefer to address the likely movement in one direction rather than risk the corrugated-iron effect!

The joining edges were machine-planed on the jointer, then hand-planed to remove the machine ripples which would weaken the glue joint.

The fit of the joining edges was made slightly concave, touching at each end with approximately 1mm (1/32in) gap at the centre. This helps the clamps pull up tight, and allows for extra shrinkage at the ends, if there is any further drying out.

The joining edges were then slotted for biscuits for extra strength. The boards were marked where they would be finally cut to size, and the biscuit slots stopped well short of those marks, so the final trimming would not expose the biscuit. PVA glue was applied to the slots, edges and biscuits, the top clamped up, checked to ensure it was flat, and left to set.

I then fitted braces under the top to keep it flat (**see Photo 6**). However, the grain in the braces is running across the width of the top boards, so that although the top will expand and contract across its width, the length of the braces will remain unchanged. This would cause the top to crack and/or buckle.

To prevent this, the braces are screwed to the top through double-countersunk holes. These give clearance to allow the screw to move from side to side, with the top movement, while still holding it flat (**see Fig 2**). Of course the braces are not glued to the top. I plugged the surface holes in the braces with matching oak dowels to improve the look.

The braces were fitted over the sides, which had been set 25mm (1in) lower to

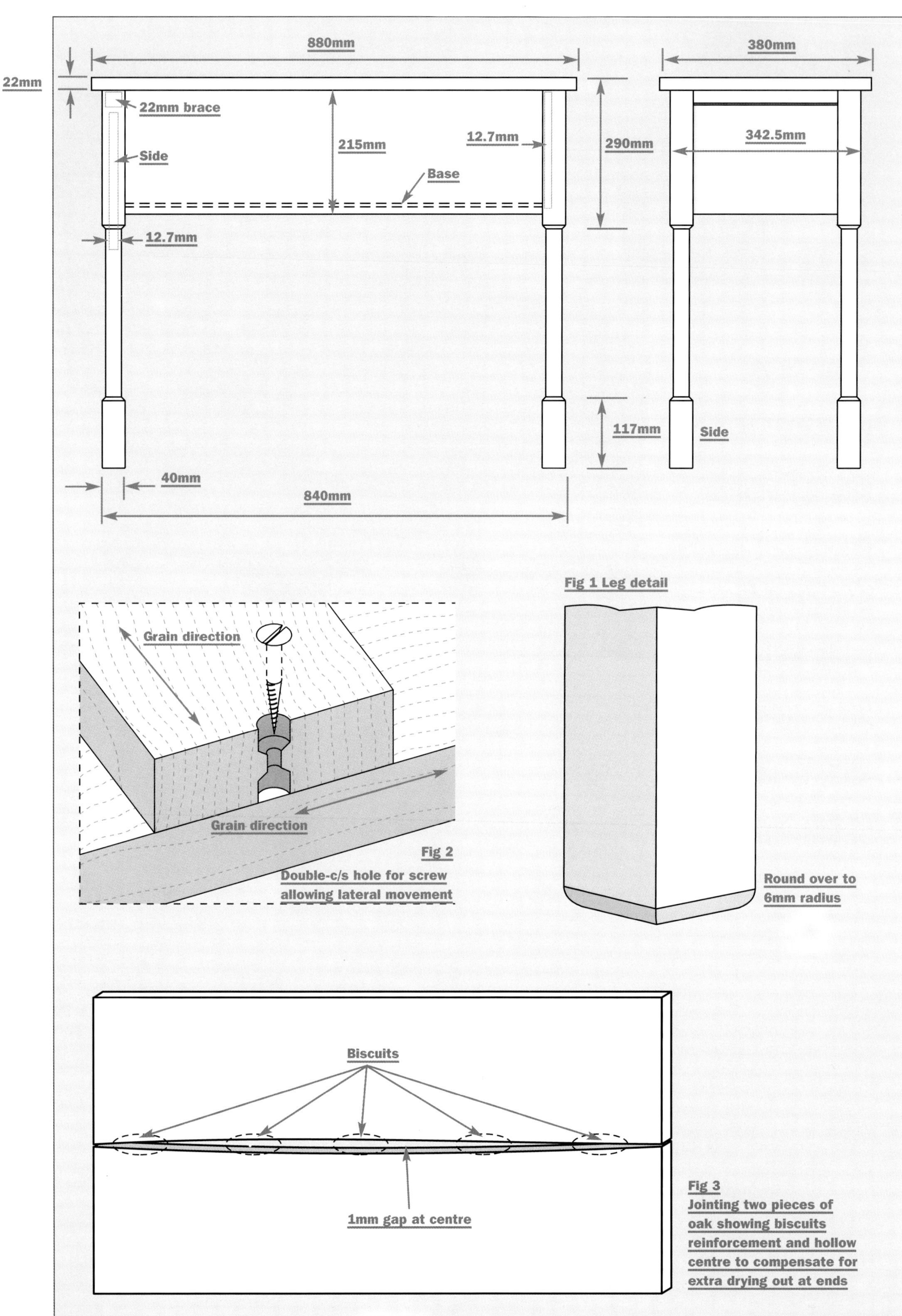

Fig 2
Double-c/s hole for screw allowing lateral movement

Fig 3
Jointing two pieces of oak showing biscuits reinforcement and hollow centre to compensate for extra drying out at ends

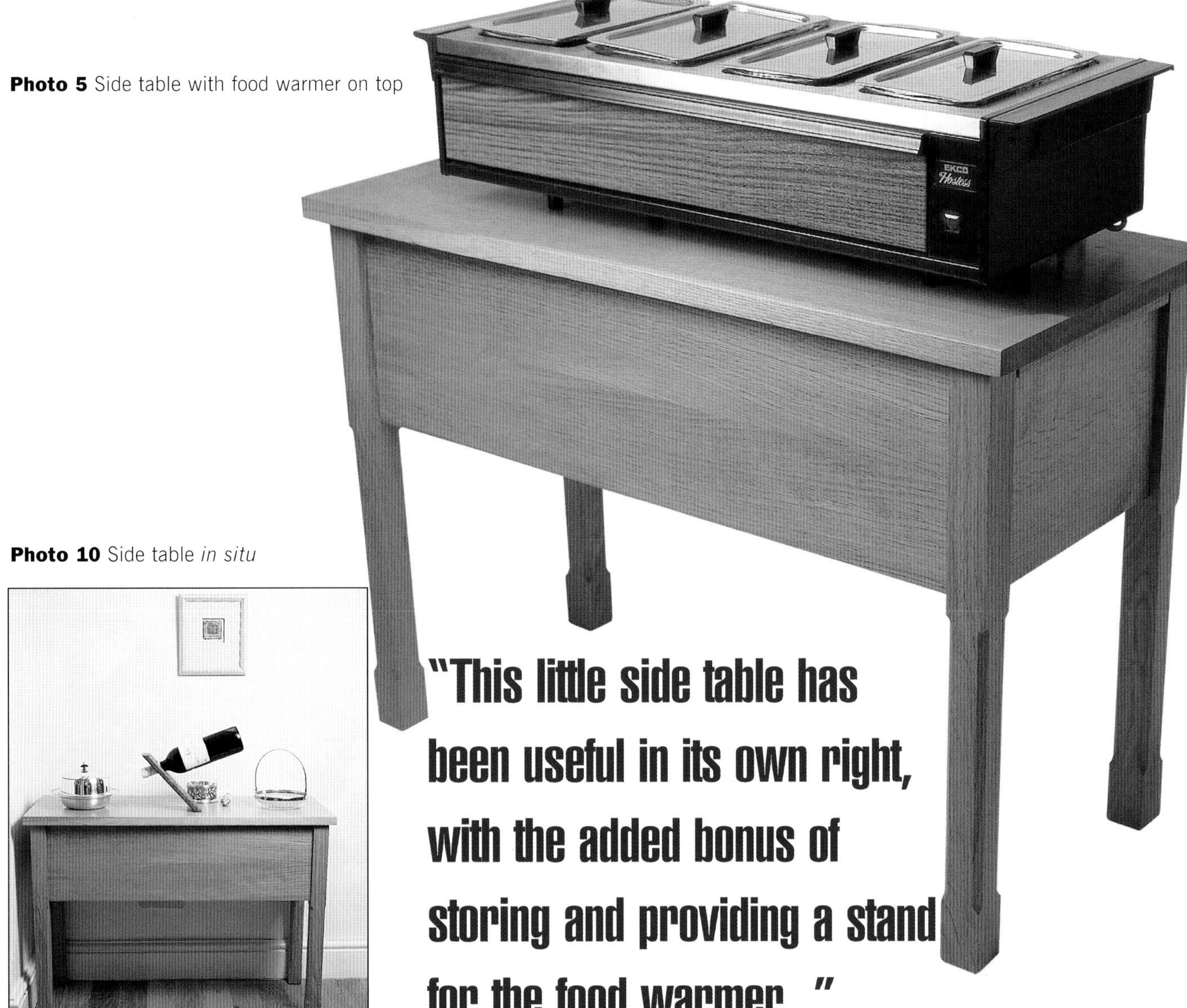

Photo 5 Side table with food warmer on top

Photo 10 Side table *in situ*

accommodate them. This was to avoid having to allow for this extra 1in clearance on the depth of the frame, which was already deep enough!

The top is hinged to the back with a piano hinge and overlaps the sides, back and front of the legs by 18mm (3/4in). This overlap at the back holds the lid open just past the vertical. Once set, the top was fitted to the carcass with the piano hinge, set flush in the rebate already left in the back top edge, and proud on the underside of the top (**Photo 4**). At this point I checked that the top closed down evenly all around onto the top of the frame, and made any necessary adjustments.

FINISHING

An oiled finish was preferred for this table to match the existing furniture, but I had my doubts about its durability on the top, as I had on the original dining table. The oak was coarse-textured, and the principle of an oiled finish is not to build up a layer on top of the wood, but to soak it into the top surface, wiping off any surplus.

I felt there would be an unavoidable build-up of oil on the surface and that it would mark easily. The likely use for the table would entail contact with hot and cold objects, liquids, and alcohol. I could forsee a constant need for re-oiling.

I decided to use the same solution I had used on the dining table, to give everything one coat of Liberon finishing oil and carefully wipe off all surplus with kitchen tissue.

This coat gave the main colour change to the wood. Liberon told me that their polyurethane varnish will key to their finishing oil, provided it is a single subcoat and allowed to dry for at least 24 hours.

Thereafter, all but the top was given the usual five or six thin coats of oil, at 24-hour intervals, wiping off all surplus, and cutting back with a Scotchbrite grey pad between coats.

The top was given four thin coats of satin polyurethane varnish applied with a sponge pad, which was allowed to build up to a smooth finish. The first two coats were cut back with 320 grit on a hard sanding block to allow the grain to fill. Further coats were cut back with the grey pad to give a similar sheen to the oiled finish.

The end result was extremely satisfactory: the overall effect was of an oiled finish, but with a durable, easy-to-maintain top.

CONCLUSION

This little side table has been useful in its own right, and the added bonus of storing and providing a stand for the food warmer more than justifies its place in the dining room. You will note that the bottle of Rioja on it is from the estate of 'Baron de Ley' (**see Photo 10**).

Shaker-style bedroom set

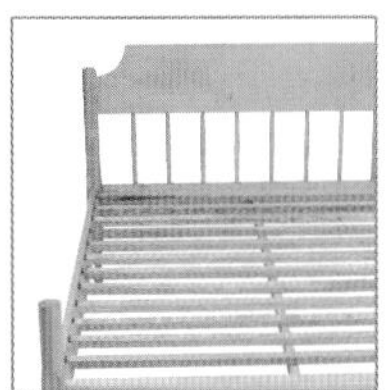

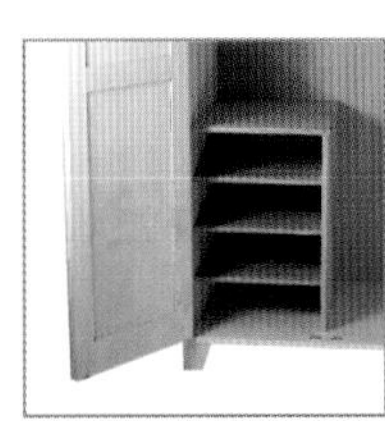

SHAKER

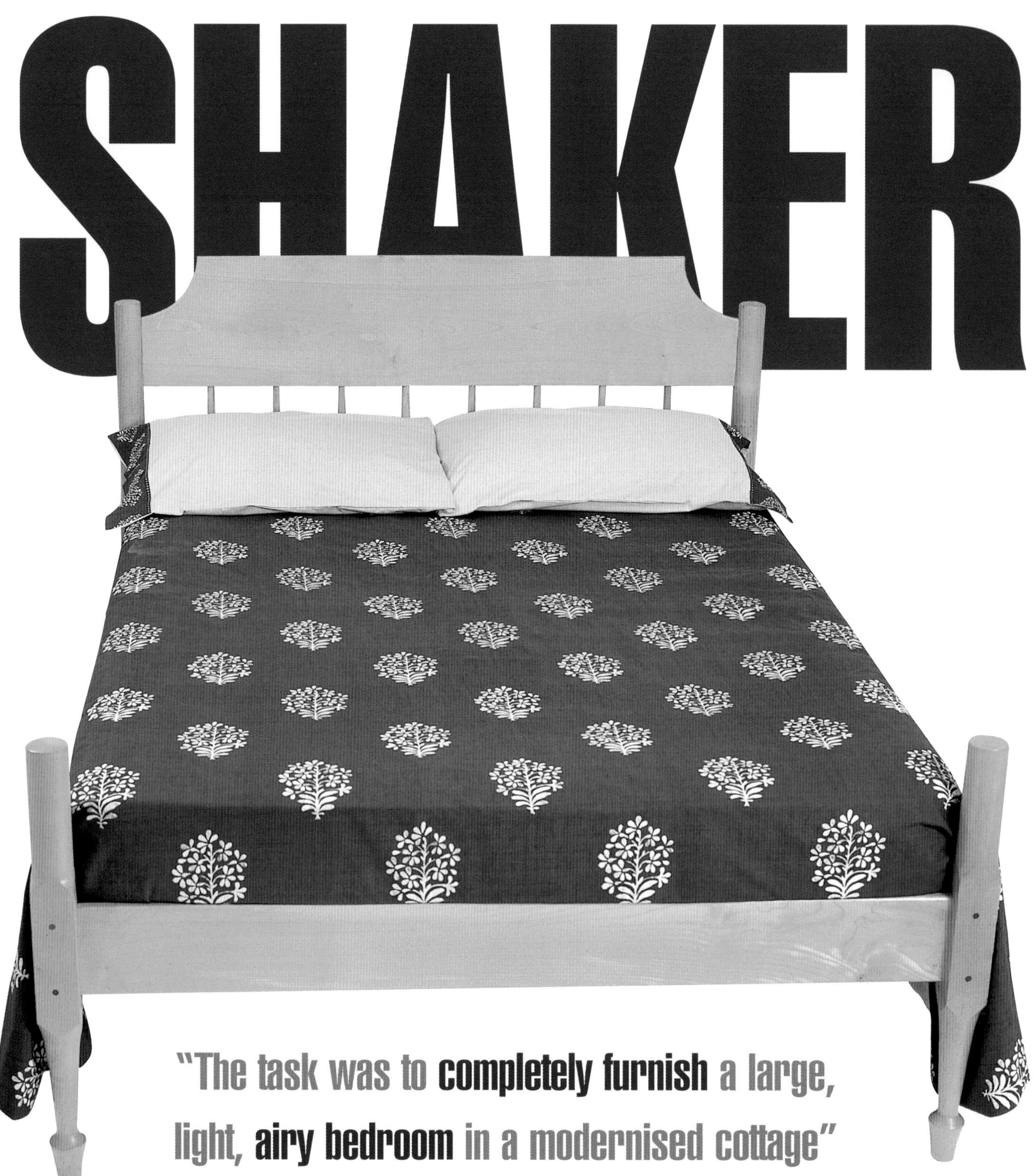

"The task was to completely furnish a large, light, airy bedroom in a modernised cottage"

This bed is a standard double for a 1880 x 1370mm (74 x 54in) mattress. It could also be made as a single or king-size. As mattresses are not necessarily of a standard size, it is wise to measure yours first, and build the bed around it.

DESIGN

The task was to completely furnish a large, light, airy bedroom in a modernised cottage. My client preferred a simple, uncluttered look and was quickly impressed with some Shaker designs in Thos. Moser's excellent book, *How to Build Shaker Furniture*.

We found a bed design which could be modified to the necessary requirements and decided on the Shaker theme for the whole room. This bed consists of an internally sprung mattress on a slatted base. I established that the bed linen would be a fitted bottom sheet, with a duvet over. This way no clearance was required in the slatted recess for bulky blankets to be tucked in around the mattress. The corners of the mattress were slightly rounded and would compress to accept the projecting corners of the squared centres of the legs. This tight fit would hold the mattress and sheet firmly in place.

The head and foot are permanently jointed with glued mortice and tenons, while the side rails and slats are dry-fitted and removable. This allows the bed to be handled in more manageable pieces.

The side rails have a deep tenon into the legs at each end, which is fixed from

BED

How to construct a bed in Shaker style

"Sycamore is a moderately priced British hardwood and there is generally a plentiful supply"

the inside with three countersunk screws. The slats are dropped into position between fixed spacers and, again, screwed into position on a bearer rail which is glued and screwed to the side rail. This is where power screwdrivers really come in handy. You can use lighter and springier slats by incorporating a centre-support rail directly under them.

TIMBER SELECTION

The timber selection was easy – my client had been impressed by an earlier commission for a writing desk which she had seen on display in the Bowes Museum in Co. Durham. It was made in sycamore with fumed oak detail and she particularly liked the contrasting colour and the texture of the fumed oak.

Sycamore is a moderately priced British hardwood and there is generally a plentiful supply, although it is very important that it has been correctly felled and seasoned. Felling should only take place in winter, when the sap is down. Prior to kilning, the wood should be stood upright (end-reared) after being converted into boards. This is to prevent deep staining from the sap and penetrating sticker marks.

When buying timber, try to get a guarantee that the job has been done properly because the staining is an ugly, dirty grey, which I have not found any satisfactory method of removing. Ironically, bleaching seems to turn it to an equally ugly green.

Sometimes there is only a light surface stain which comes off on the first pass over the planer — thus it pays to test the wood with a small plane before buying.

Oak is fumed to a rich, dark, plain chocolate colour by leaving it in an atmosphere of ammonia. In this case there were only the 16 dowel pegs to be fumed, so they were made first, placed in a plastic box with a small quantity of ammonia 890 and left for 24 hours.

Sycamore reacts to the fuming process by going a greyish colour and I wanted to keep it as creamy-white as possible. Therefore I ensured that once the fuming was done, all traces of ammonia were dispersed before any sycamore was cut.

Be careful with the ammonia — it has a particularly adverse effect on the eyes and any contact can cause permanent damage. Wear eye protection and, if possible, do the whole thing outside.

TIMBER PREPARATION

I bought the sycamore from my usual supplier, 25mm (1in) kiln-dried for the main parts, and air-dried 75 x 75mm (3 x 3in) posts for the legs. I bought the latter because no kiln-dried was available at this thickness. I chose 25mm (1in) air-dried ash for the slats and bearers, due to its strength and springy quality.

All the pieces were cut out slightly oversize, and stacked and sticked in my wood store with its dehumidifier. I left them there for a couple of weeks to settle. All the pieces were then dimensioned to their final thickness and stacked and sticked in the workshop.

My workshop is kept warm and dry with heaters and a dehumidifier so that conditioning takes place all the time the piece is being worked on. It is no use spending a lot of money on quality dry wood, and having it deteriorate in a cold, damp workshop.

CONSTRUCTION

LEGS

The legs were cut to length and the mortices cut with my old MOF 98 heavy-duty router, while the legs were still square. The centres were then marked on each end and shaped on my lathe. The tops of the legs were turned round as close to the full 65mm (2⅝in) diameter as possible.

I cut a profile in hardboard and, using pre-set sizing tools to get the reference diameters, shaped the bottoms of the legs. I don't do much turning, so I use all the help I can get to achieve an acceptable result!

Once the legs had been shaped and sanded on the lathe, the tops were slightly domed over, leaving a very small plug of wood where the centre was holding the top end of the leg onto the lathe. The leg was removed from the lathe and the plug was cut off, chiselled flush, and the top end finally hand-sanded to a finish.

The bed complete with bedclothes & bedside tables

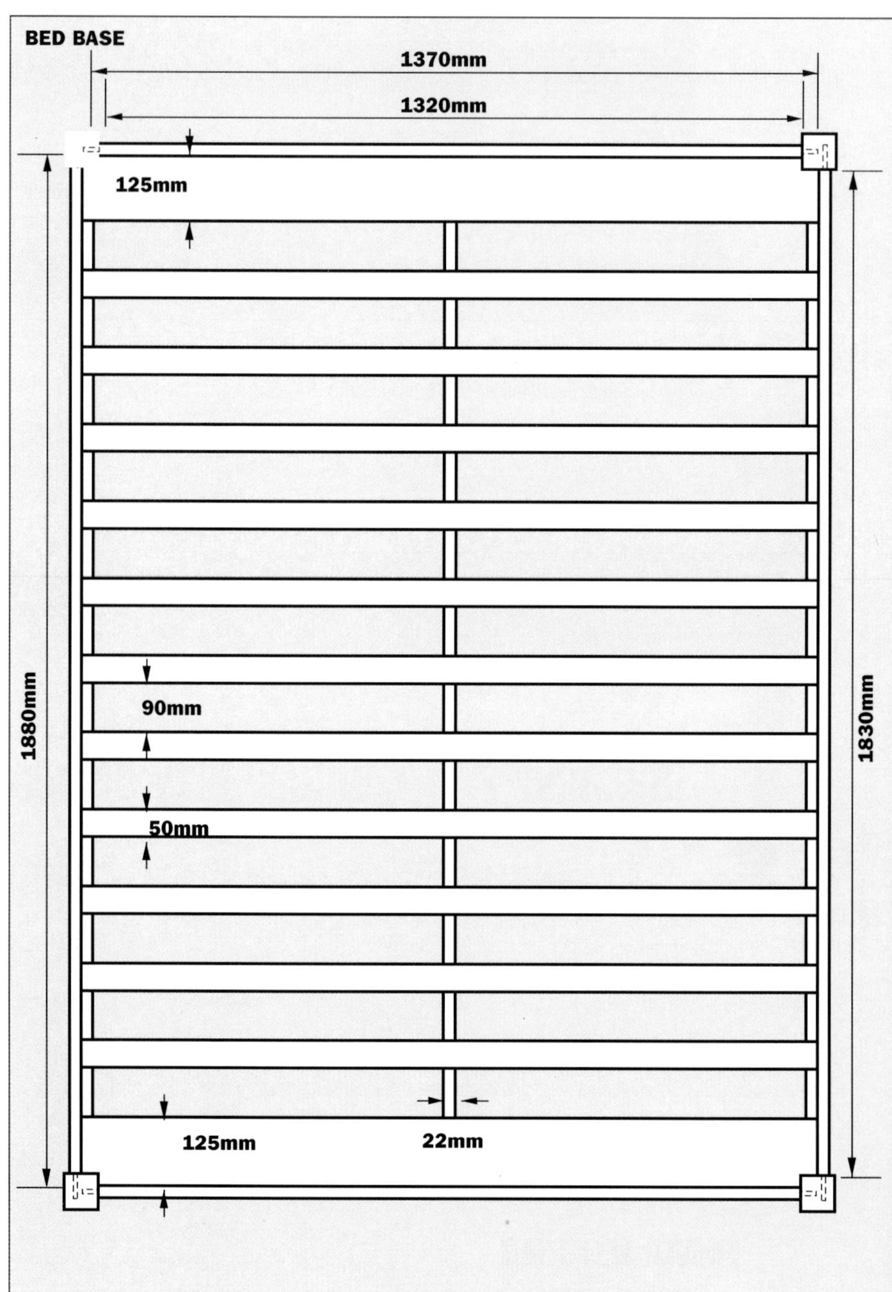

Close-up of the head

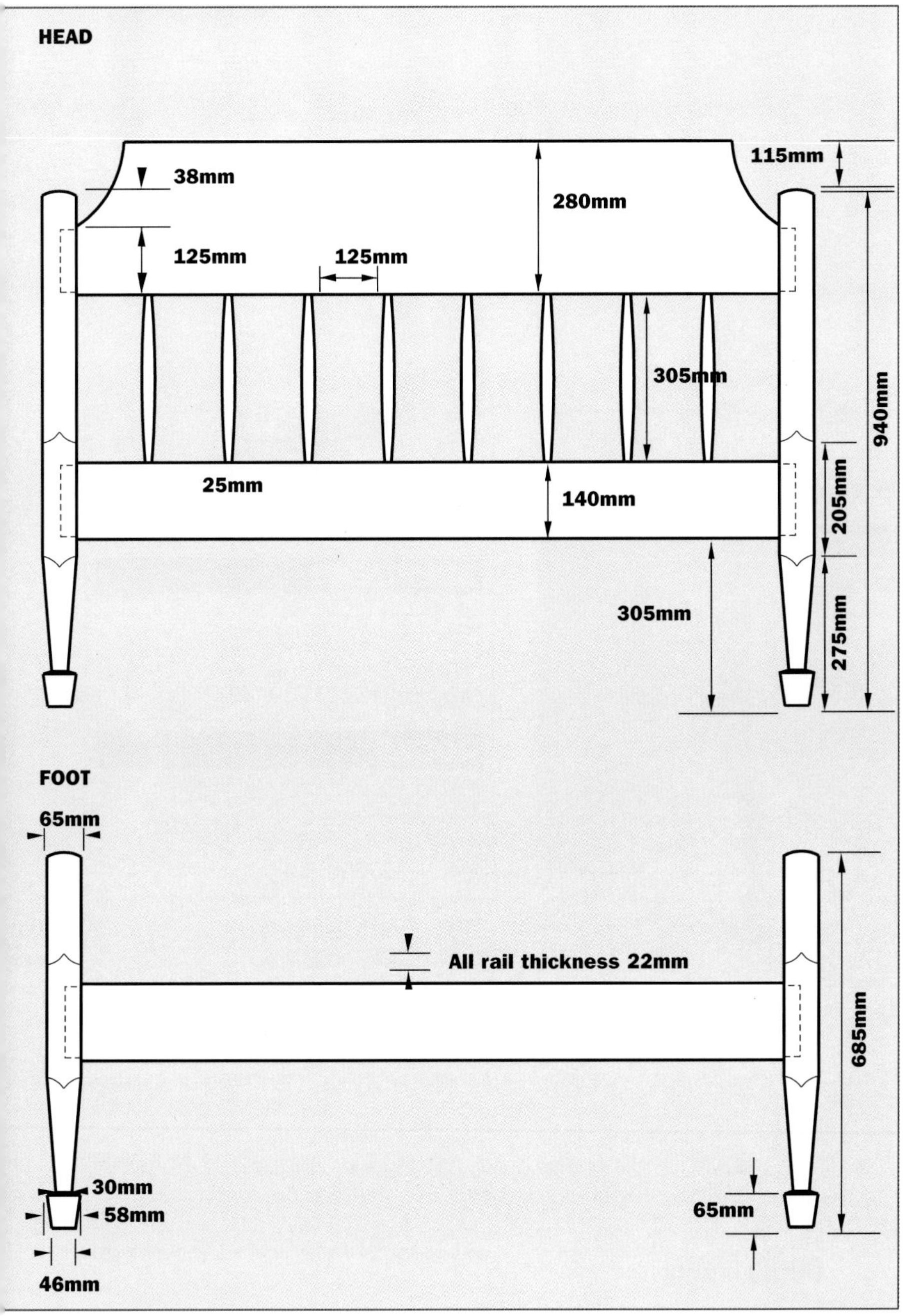

HEAD

38mm
125mm
125mm
280mm
115mm
305mm
940mm
25mm
140mm
205mm
305mm
275mm

FOOT

65mm
All rail thickness 22mm
685mm
30mm
58mm
46mm
65mm

Holes were drilled for the decorative oak dowel pegs which were glued and tapped into position and, once dry, sanded flush.

HEADBOARD

The top and bottom rails for the headboard were cut to size and tenons 22mm (⅞in) deep were made on the ends to fit the mortices in the legs. The shoulder on the top-rail tenon was undercut to fit over the curve of the leg. The top rail was shaped by cutting out a quadrant from each end. The top edge of this rail was rounded over to 6mm (¼in) radius using a rounding-over cutter with a bearing guide. Holes were then drilled in both rails to take the eight tapered spindles.

These spindles were cut to length, centred on each end and turned to shape. Again I used pre-set sizing tools to ensure that both the centre and end diameter fitted the pre-drilled holes in the rails.

All the pieces were belt-sanded to 150 grit and finished to 240 grit with a random orbital sander. Titebond glue was applied to the various joints and the headboard was clamped up, checked for square, and left to set.

FOOTBOARD

The footboard rail was cut to size and tenons were formed on the ends using the router mounted in its table. The top of the rail was rounded over in the same way as the top rail of the headboard. All the pieces were sanded to a finish. The footboard was glued and clamped up to the legs and left to set. A mortice was cut in the centre of the inside faces of the headboard's bottom rail and the footboard rail to take the ash centre-support rail for the slats.

SIDE RAILS

The side rails were cut to length and a 50mm (2in) deep tenon was formed on each end. The top edge was rounded over to match the head and foot rails. The side rails were slotted into the leg mortices and the frame was clamped up dry. It was all checked for square and the pilot holes for the fixing screws were drilled and countersunk on the inside of the legs. The screws were driven home and the clamps removed.

SLATS

The 22mm (⅞in) ash slats were cut to length, 3mm (⅛in) short, allowing for clearance between the slat ends and the side rails – to avoid any movement in the bed causing squeaks! A bearer rail of 50 x 22mm (2 x ⅞in) ash was glued and screwed to the inside of the bed frame, 50mm (2in) below the top of the rails, on the sides, head and foot, to screw the slats on to. This left a 29mm (1⅛in) recess below the top of the frame to the

"The wax on the **sycamore** gave a silky, very **'touchy-feely'** surface – appropriate to **bedroom furniture**"

The bare essentials of the bed

The head corner and leg

tops of the slats. This is where the mattress is dropped into. Loose spacers were cut to fit between the slats and glued and pinned into position on the bearer rail, as the slats were fixed.

FINISH

Once the bed was complete and I was sure everything fitted properly, it was taken to pieces for finishing – thus relinquishing a large proportion of my workshop's limited floor space!

Most of the sanding had been completed during the construction, so the pieces were finally checked over, marks and glue ooze removed, and the surfaces which would be visible hand-sanded down to 320 grit, prior to varnishing.

To maintain the pale creaminess of the sycamore, I chose a satin-finish, water-based acrylic floor varnish. I applied three coats with a paint pad, rubbing down with 320 grit between coats. The advantage of the acrylic finishes on pale woods is that they have a minimal initial yellowing effect and prevent long-term darkening by filtering out UV light.

Barford's Aqua Cote is my preferred water-based varnish. It dries quickly and it's possible to use up to four or five coats in a day. In a few days it cures to a very tough, durable surface. I also use the new matt finish extensively as it has a much lower sheen than the satin and is as tough and durable.

After the varnish had cured for a few days I cut it back with a Scotchbrite grey pad, applied a couple of coats of wax, and buffed it up to a nice sheen.

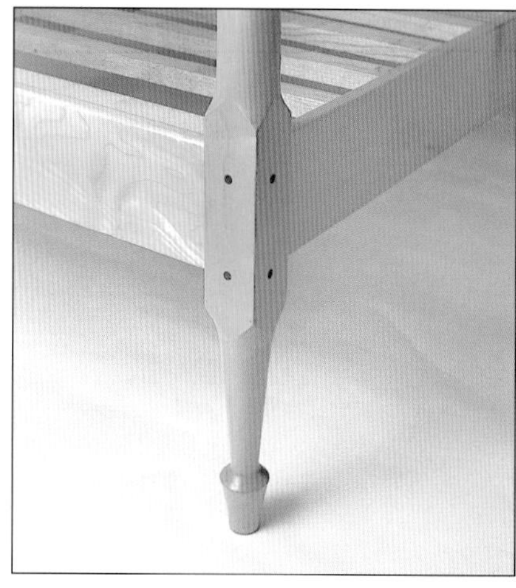

The foot corner and leg

The wax on the sycamore gave a silky, 'touchy-feely' surface that I felt was very appropriate for bedroom furniture.

The floor of the bedroom was bare wood, so I glued felt pads to the underside of the feet to enable the bed to slide without scuff marks.

CONCLUSION

The bed was assembled and positioned in my client's bedroom. I was a little nervous when I presented the finished piece to the client, but fortunately she thought it looked great. I was particularly pleased with the way it suited the room. As this was the first piece of this bedroom suite I had made, she was now very keen that I started on the bedside tables, utilising the same Shaker style. So, watch this space...

Below **The foot corner, showing the slat fixing**

SUPPLIERS

Aqua Cote acrylic varnish
Barford's - 01277 622050
Furniture buttons
Lakeland Ltd - 01539 488100

BOOKS

How to Build Shaker Furniture -
Thos. Moser
ISBN: 0-8069-8392-2
GMC: 01273 488005
Kevin Ley's Furniture Projects - Kevin Ley
ISBN: 1-86108-185-5
GMC: 01273 488005.

A pair of Shaker-style side tables provides a perfect accompaniment to the bed

A pair of tables

SHAKING SIDES

I had been wanting to make a pair of Shaker-style tables ever since I first saw them in Thos. Moser's book, *How to Build Shaker Furniture*. To my way of thinking they epitomise the delicacy and elegance of the Shaker design, with the added advantage of being relatively simple to make!

DESIGN

A pair of tables were required to go on each side of a Shaker bed that had already been made (see pages 100–4). My client wanted me to continue the uncluttered Shaker theme she was particularly fond of for the light, airy bedroom in her modernised cottage. The graceful taper on the legs, and the fielded, overhanging tops of these tables, gave just the look she wanted. In fact it was the bedside tables that had attracted her to the whole Shaker style in the first place. The other pieces of bedroom furniture – a bed, and a free-standing wardrobe – were selected to match.

The taper on the legs is only on the inside face, giving visual stability by making them appear to be spread slightly apart at the floor level. Tapering on all faces is acceptable but reduces this effect, while tapering on the outside face gives an ugly, 'pigeon-toed' look.

TIMBER SELECTION

In the past sycamore was a utilitarian wood used for a whole variety of things – draining and wash boards, butchers' blocks, kitchen tables, and a host of other utensils which came into contact with food. Its close grain allowed surfaces to be left unsealed, while the odd bleaching and scrubbing kept everything hygienic and looking good.

The first time I saw and touched finished sycamore, I was fascinated by its silky texture, gently understated figuring, and creamy colour. I was convinced that it would lend itself well to aesthetic and delicate work such as this.

The Georgians used both plain and figured sycamore as a decorative veneer on fine pieces, although it was usually stained grey and referred to as 'harewood'. The choice of sycamore for all the pieces in the room particularly suited the Shaker design, accentuating its lightness and delicacy.

Fumed oak was used in the form of the drawer pulls to give that small contrasting detail, as with the dowel pegs in the bed, and visually link the side tables to the other pieces in the room.

TIMBER PREPARATION

I had bought all the sycamore for all of the various Shaker-inspired projects at the same time. This gave a greater selection, and by cutting the larger pieces first, I was able to get the smaller pieces from the remainder – all very economical!

All of the pieces were cut slightly oversize, and stacked, with sticks placed between them, in my wood store with its dehumidifier. I left it there for a couple of weeks to settle. All the pieces for each individual project were dimensioned, as required, to final thickness, then stacked and sticked in the workshop.

My workshop is kept as close to end-use conditions as possible, with heaters and a dehumidifier, so that conditioning takes place all the time a piece is being worked on. It is no use spending a lot of money on quality kiln-dried wood, only to have it deteriorate in a cold, damp workshop. If you are not comfortable in your workshop, neither is your wood.

Photo 1 – **The finished table**

CONSTRUCTION

TOP

The tops were each made up from three widths of 22mm (⅞in) sycamore, the figure was carefully matched and the joints were strengthened with biscuits. Care was taken to stop the biscuit slots well short of the edge, so they would not be exposed when the edges were chamfered.

The chamfer on the underside of the top was then marked, and a strip of wood was clamped to the top to act as a fence. A sharp jack plane was used to remove the bulk of the waste. The plane was resharpened, set fine, and a final light finishing cut was made (**see Photo 5**). A light sanding finished the job, and the tops were placed on one side. If preferred, a router could be used to remove the bulk of the waste instead of a jack plane.

Photo 2 – **Close-up showing top overhang**

LEGS

Before tapering, the legs were morticed for the back, sides and front bottom drawer rail, using a 12mm (½in) cutter in my old MOF96 router. The taper was started 150mm (6in) down from the top of the legs and on the inside faces only. This could be achieved (using jigs) by a number of different methods – on the planer, thicknesser, or circular saw – but I found the simplest, safest, and most enjoyable way was to rough them out on the bandsaw and finish them by hand. The wood was a real joy to plane! To finish the legs off, the foot ends and edges were rounded over with a ¼in radius cutter on my small Trend router. The legs were carefully marked, to ensure that when it came to assembly, the taper on the legs would be on the correct faces.

FRAME

The back, sides, and front bottom drawer rail were now cut to size and tenons were formed on the ends to fit the mortices in the legs.

The top front drawer rails were cut to size and dovetails were marked and cut on the bandsaw. The sockets required in the tops of the front legs were marked from the tails, the bulk of the waste removed with a straight cutter on the router, and the sockets finished with a sharp bevelled-edged chisel. Countersunk holes to take the screws to fix the top were drilled in the top rail.

All these joints were dry-fitted to check that they measured up. In this project it was particularly important that they were a really good fit, because the joints needed to be as strong as possible. There would be no bottom rails to complete the square and brace the legs.

ASSEMBLY

All the individual pieces were finished as far as possible with both belt and random orbital sanders, down to 150 grit. The front drawer rails and backs were now glued and clamped to the relevant legs, checked for square and left to set, thus forming the frame fronts and backs.

The frames were completed by applying glue to the sides, mortices and tenons and clamping them into position (**see Photo 3**). Once again they were checked square and left to set.

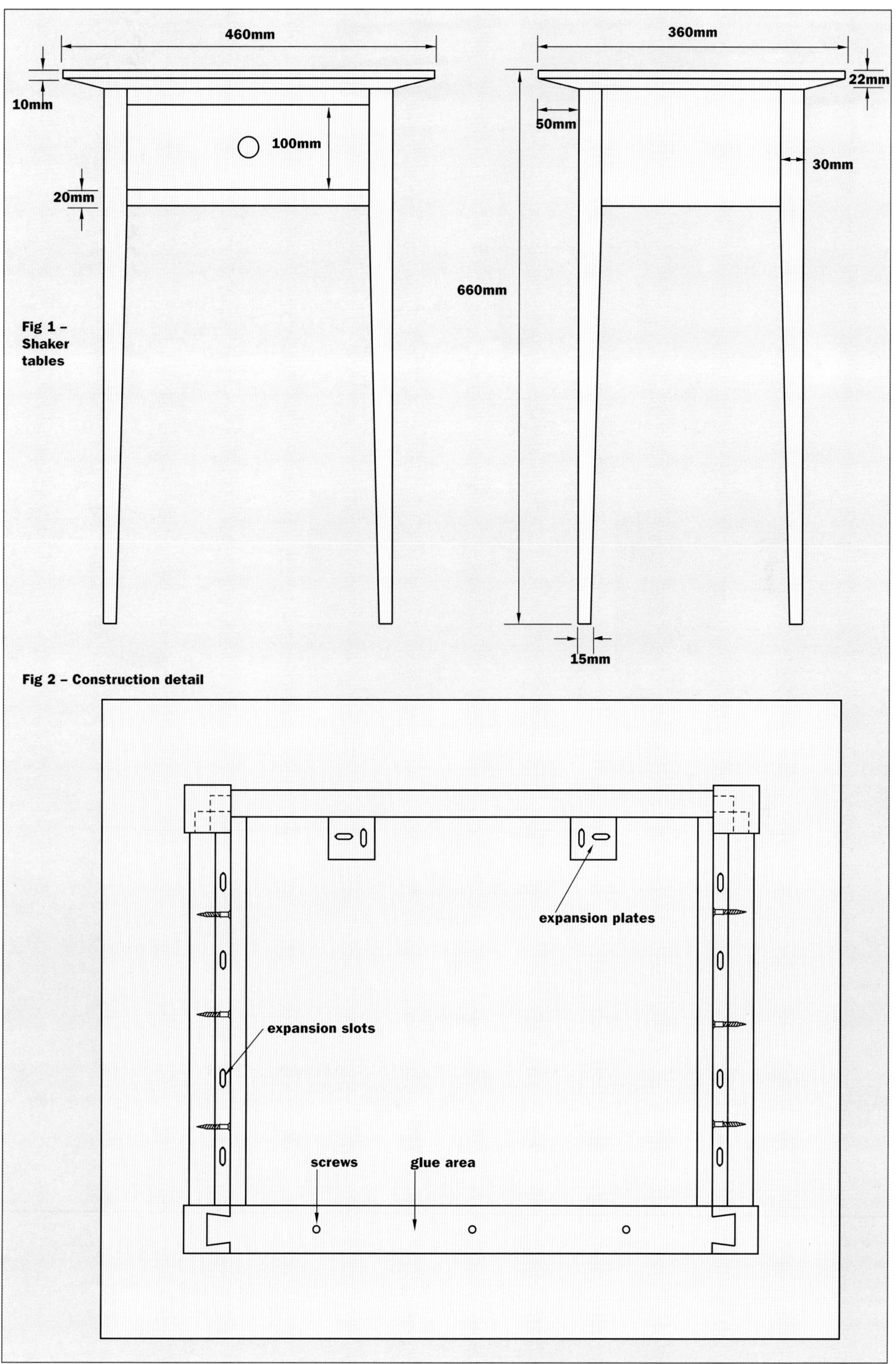
460mm
360mm
10mm
22mm
50mm
100mm
30mm
20mm
660mm
Fig 1 –
Shaker
tables
15mm
Fig 2 – Construction detail
expansion plates
expansion slots
screws
glue area

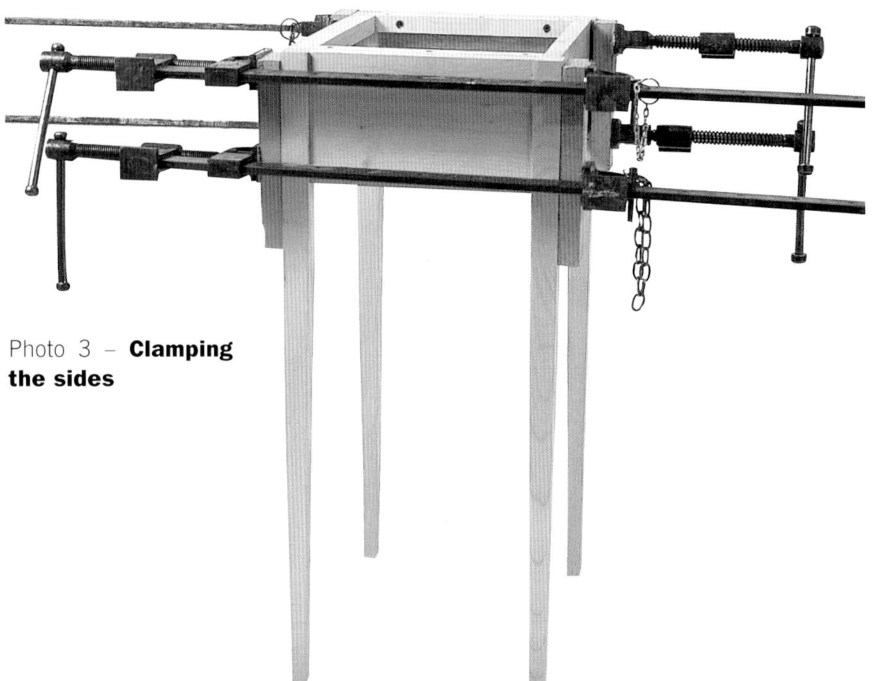

Photo 3 – **Clamping the sides**

Photo 4 (*above*) – **Finishing – acrylic varnish applied with a paint pad**

Photo 5 (*right*) – **Planing the top fielded overhang**

Drawer guides were fitted inside the frames at the top and bottom of the sides. The top guide had slots cut in it to take the screws to attach the top, while the bottom guide had a runner glued and screwed to it to carry the drawer.

FIXING THE TOP

Expansion brackets were fitted to the inside face of the backs of the frames, with the slots uppermost, set 1.5mm (1/16in) lower than the top edge of the backs to pull the top down onto the back and legs when screwed up.

The top was fixed at the front by gluing and screwing to the front top drawer rail, at the sides with screws through the expansion slots cut in the drawer guides, and at the backs with screws though the correct slot of the expansion brackets. Make sure the screws are the correct length and don't inadvertently go right through the top, which can happen – believe me!

DRAWERS

The drawer fronts and casings were cut to size. The fronts were made from sycamore 22mm (7/8in) thick, and cedar of Lebanon 10mm (3/8in) thick was used for the remainder of the casings. I chose the cedar because of its wonderful smell which tends to repel insects and attract clients!

The bases were made from cedar-faced MDF, which could be glued in all round to add strength. The sides were fitted and slotted with regard to the bases, taped together with the top one marked out, the pins cut on the bandsaw, and finished with a paring chisel.

The fronts and backs were marked one at a time from the pins, and the majority of the waste removed with a straight cutter on the router. Each joint was then individually finished with a sharp chisel. The drawers were assembled, with the MDF base glued in all round and pinned at the back, checked for square and wind, and left to set.

DRAWER PULLS

The oak pulls were turned on the lathe, sanded to a finish, placed in a small plastic container with some 890 ammonia, and left for 24 hours to darken. Sycamore reacts to the fuming process by going a greyish colour and I wanted to keep it as creamy-white as possible, so the fuming was done well away.

Great care is needed when handling ammonia as it burns the skin, especially open cuts, and has a particularly harmful effect on the eyes. Any contact can cause permanent damage. Always wear eye protection and rubber gloves and, if possible, do the whole thing outside so that any fumes disperse.

Once fumed, the drawer pulls were left for a few hours to ensure all the ammonia had dispersed, and then fitted to the drawer fronts. The drawers and stops were then fitted in the usual way, using a little wax on the guides and runners to ensure silky movement.

FINISH

Most of the sanding had been completed during construction so the pieces were finally checked over, marks and glue ooze removed, and the surfaces which would be visible were hand-sanded down to 320 grit prior to varnishing.

As with the bed, I wanted to keep the pale creaminess of the sycamore so I chose Barford's satin-finish, water-based acrylic floor varnish again. I applied three coats with a paint pad (**see Photo 4**), rubbing down with 320 grit between coats, to de-nib.

The advantage of the acrylic finishes on pale woods is that they have a minimal initial yellowing effect and prevent long-term darkening by filtering out UV light.

They dry quickly, enabling up to four or five coats in a day if necessary, and cure in a few days to a very tough, durable surface – ideal.

After the varnish had cured, I cut it back with a Scotchbrite grey pad, applied a couple of coats of wax, and buffed it up to a nice sheen with a silky feel.

CONCLUSION

These tables were a joy to make. They weren't complicated and act as proof, if it were needed, that making a quality piece of furniture doesn't have to be difficult. They complement the bed very well and fit nicely with the free-standing wardrobe which I will describe next. 

With the bed and side tables in place, the Shaker bedroom set is completed with a beautiful sycamore wardrobe

SHAKER MAKER

My client wanted a free-standing wardrobe to complete her Shaker bedroom set. Nowadays wardrobes tend to come in two forms – either built in or made from relatively cheap flat-pack units – but my client was adamantly opposed to either idea and wanted something that was consistent with the rest of her bedroom furniture.

Interestingly, the Shakers did tend to build floor-to-ceiling storage units in bedrooms, with various arrangements of drawers, shelves and hanging space. As they were obsessed with cleanliness, inaccessible tops tended to be regarded as dust traps.

DESIGN

With a piece of this size, handling and access are both limiting factors. Having determined the rough overall dimensions, I worked out that it would take at least two men to move the wardrobe into its final destination – the client's bedroom.

Another size-related aspect was rigidity – particularly considering it would have inset doors. Any 'diamonding' or 'ricking' of the carcass would cause problems. Internal shelving and a fixed, rigid back would help to brace the structure, and any unevenness in the floor would have to be addressed by wedging the wardrobe level *in situ* if necessary.

For the inside we decided on a full-length hanging space in one half of the wardrobe, and a shelf unit in the other. A high shelf over the hanging rail for occasional storage and carcass bracing was also included.

HANGING SPACE

In order to hang clothes sideways on to the door, a wardrobe needs an internal clearance depth of at least 510mm (20in) and a full-length hanging height of about 1230mm (48½in), although this depends on the required amount of shoe storage space under the hanging clothes.

Aesthetically, the piece was kept as clean and simple as possible. I included both an overhanging top to reflect the bedside table tops, and inset tapered feet to lighten the look of the wardrobe and to 'link' it with the tapered legs and posts of the side tables and bed. Fumed oak door pulls (to match those on the bedside tables, and the fumed oak pegs on the bed), together with traditional fielded panel doors, complete the picture. Now comes the tricky bit – the making!

TIMBER SELECTION

Sycamore (*Acer pseudoplatanus*) had been my client's choice of timber for the whole Shaker set, and it was particularly suitable for this piece. Its gently understated figure, creamy colour and silky texture is ideal for a lady's bedroom! The pale colour reduced the wardrobe's apparent size and prevented it from dominating the room. Strangely, it actually added brightness to the room by bouncing light in from an opposite window.

We decided upon cedar of Lebanon (*Cedrus libani*) for the internal shelves because of its wonderful smell and insect-repelling qualities. Apparently, my client loves the delicate scent it transfers to her clothes!

SYCAMORE

The Georgians used sycamore as a decorative veneer on fine furniture, although it was usually stained grey and referred to as 'harewood'. I have always found it baffling why anyone would change the natural colour of this wood – perhaps it was done more out of necessity than choice. A deep grey staining from the sap can result if the timber has not been correctly felled and seasoned. Sometimes this is only on the surface and comes off on the first pass over the planer. The point I'm trying to make is that if colour is an important consideration, test the wood with a plane before making a purchase.

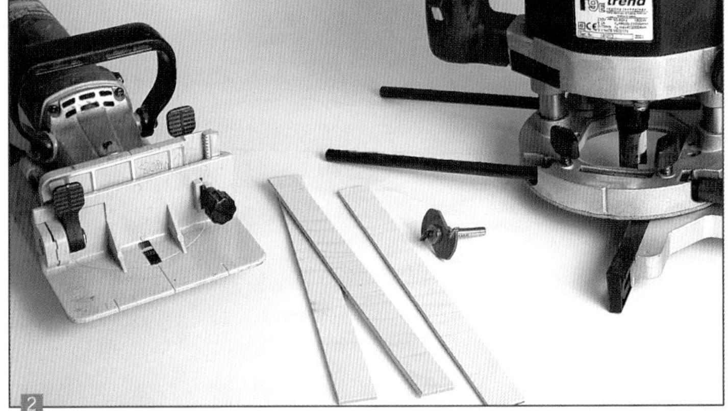

Photo 1 – **The wardrobe interior, showing the cedar back panel**
Photo 2 – **The Tanselli wafers, groove cutter, router and biscuit jointer**

TIMBER PREPARATION

The sycamore for the whole project was bought at the same time. The larger pieces were cut first, with the smaller pieces coming from what was left. They were all cut slightly oversize and stacked and sticked in my heated and dehumidified wood store, where they remained for a couple of weeks to settle.

At the beginning of the making process for each piece, the relevant cut timber was dimensioned to final size and moved into the workshop. This was kept as close to likely domestic temperature as possible – again with a heater and dehumidifier – so that conditioning took place during the making. Looking after the wood gave me the excuse I needed to work in a warm, dry place!

CONSTRUCTION

While there weren't too many components for this piece they were all large, so in order to manage them carefully I cleared the workshop to make as much space as possible. A remarkable amount of space is required when you are constantly turning round, armed with lengths of 600 x 2100mm (2 x 7ft) sycamore – particularly when you are inherently clumsy and blind in one eye!

Roller stands were used to support the longer lengths over the planer and tablesaw, and I made sure there was sufficient space to store the individual pieces during construction.

THE SIDES

The sides were made up first, each from three widths. The figure was matched carefully to run through and disguise the join, and the joint itself was strengthened with Tanselli wafers. These wafers are made from the same material as Tanselli biscuits, three-ply with the core grain running across the join. They come in 250mm (10in) lengths in the standard biscuit

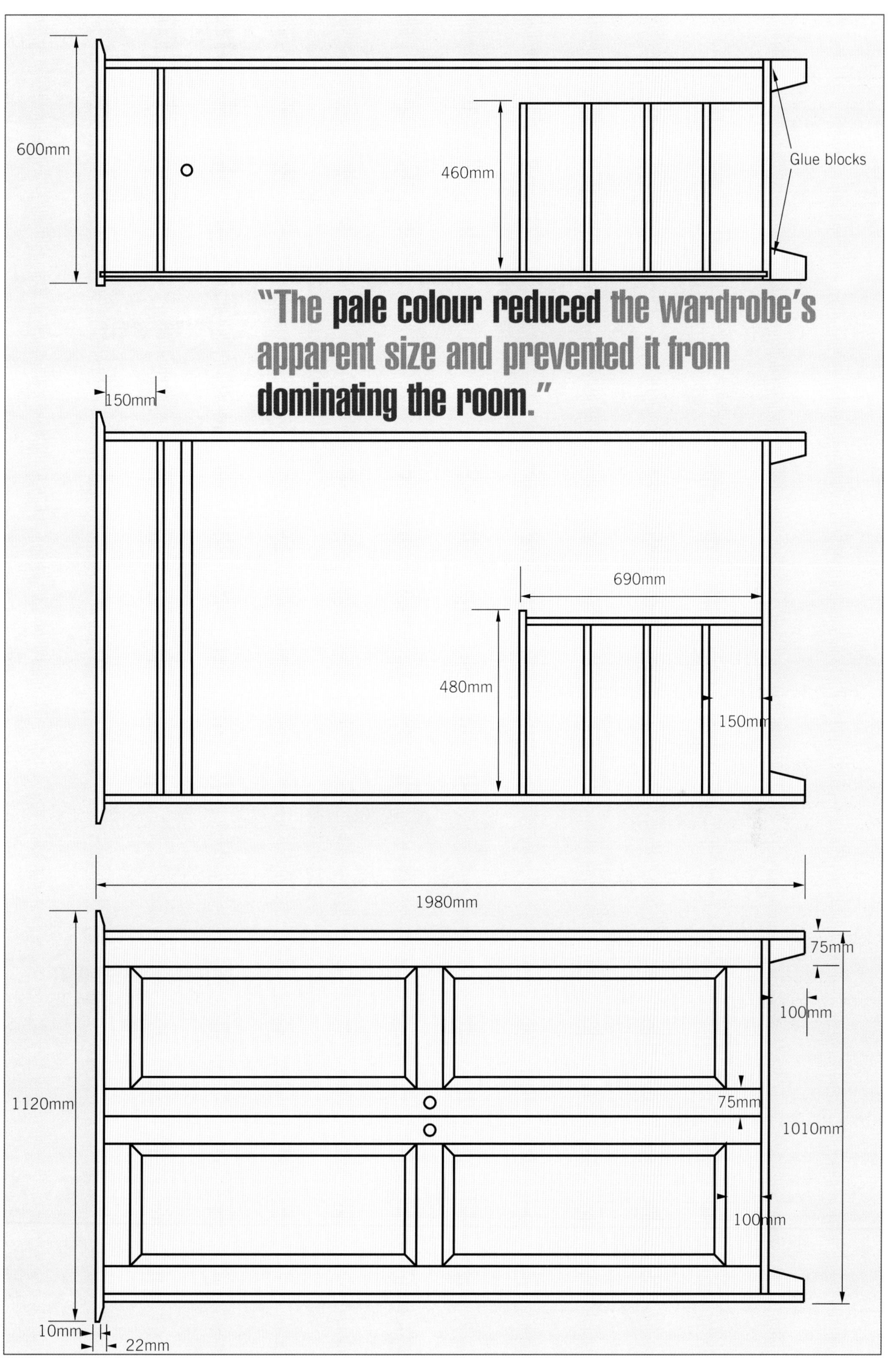

"The pale colour reduced the wardrobe's apparent size and prevented it from dominating the room."

Photo 3 – **The internal shelves and door catches**

Photo 4 – **Close-up of the foot insert**

widths and thicknesses. The cross grain gives great shear strength and I use them in most loose tenon applications. The groove can be cut either with a biscuit jointer or with a 4mm (5/32in) grooving cutter in the router; on this occasion I opted for the latter method.

The edges of the boards were planed on the surfacer, finished by hand to remove the ripples, and left slightly hollow in the middle so that when clamped, the ends would be under pressure. This allows for extra shrinkage at the ends, as the end grain loses water at a faster rate. A 4mm (5/32in) groove was cut the full length of the joint, glue applied in the usual way for a biscuit joint, and the sides clamped up.

Once the glue had set, the sides were cut to exact size, finished down to 120 grit on the belt sander, and a 10mm (3/8in) deep and 6mm (1/4in) wide slot cut to take the cedar of Lebanon-faced MDF back. Stopped housings were cut 22 x 6mm (7/8 x 1/4in) to take the shelf, base and shelving unit.

The housings to take the feet were cut in the front, set back 6mm (1/4in), and holes were drilled to take the hanging rail. The tops of the sides were shouldered to fit into the stopped housings in the top. Using the bandsaw, the shapes of the feet were cut in the bottom edges of the sides. Finishing was done by hand using a plane, chisel and scraper.

THE TOP

The top was made up in the same way as the sides, cut to size, and belt-sanded to 120 grit. The stopped housings for the sides were routed out, and the slot was cut for the MDF back, taking care to allow for the 50mm (2in) overhang on each side.

For the fielding on the underside of the front and sides, the bulk of the waste was removed using the surface planer, with both a support and the fence to hold the angle. The fieldings were finished with a hand plane, against a guiding batten-fence clamped to the top.

THE BASE

The base was made up, cut to size and finished in the same way. The stopped housings for the front feet and shelf unit were cut, and the ends were shouldered to fit the stopped housings in the sides.

THE SHELF

The internal top shelf was made up from cedar of Lebanon, cut to size and also finished in the same way. The front edges were rounded over with a 10mm (3/8in) radius cutter, and the ends shouldered to fit in the stopped housings in the sides.

HANGING RAIL

The hanging rail was made from a piece of 28 x 28mm (1 1/8 x 1 1/8in) ash (*Fraxinus excelsior*) with the top edges rounded over with a 12mm (1/2in) radius cutter. A dowell, 19mm in diameter and 13mm in length (3/4 x 1/2in), was formed on each end with a tenon saw and a paring chisel.

ASSEMBLY

All the pieces were finished with an orbital sander down to 120 grit, and the joints were dry-fitted and adjusted where necessary. The clamps were prepared and an area was cleared to assemble the carcass on its back. PVA glue was applied and the sides, shelf, base, and hanging rail were all clamped into position. The diagonals were measured and the carcass squared. The front feet were cut out of some scrap wood and glued into position with strengthening blocks (also from scrap) glued and screwed under the base to the sides.

INTERNAL SHELF UNIT

The shelves, top, and side of the cedar internal shelf unit were made up, cut to size and belt-sanded to 120 grit. The front edges of the shelves and the front and side edges of the top were rounded over with a 6mm (1/4in) radius cutter. Stopped housings were cut in the top and side. All the joints were dry-fitted and adjusted, the shelf unit was orbital-sanded to 120 grit and when the carcass had set, glued and clamped into position.

THE BACK

Once the shelf unit had set, the whole carcass was carefully stood up. After checking that it was still square, the cedar of Lebanon-faced 6mm MDF back was glued into the side slots and glued and screwed to the shelf, shelf unit, and base.

FINISHING THE TOP

This was finished with an orbital sander. Glue was applied to the housings and slot, after which the top was dropped on and clamped into position. When set, the carcass was levelled and checked for square before measuring for the doors.

DOORS

The stiles and rails of the doors were cut to size, and double biscuit joints were cut between them. The doors were dry-assembled and a note was taken of the measurements for the fielded panels, allowing them to recess 6mm (¼in) into the frame. The door panels were made up by deep-sawing some selected sycamore and match-jointing. Biscuits, positioned so they would not be exposed by the fielding, were used to strengthen the joint. The panels were cut to size and fielded using a vertical profile cutter, finished with a hand plane and then sanded. The panel faces were finished, a slot was cut on the inside edges of both the rails and stiles, and the inside edges of the frames were finished. The doors were assembled, glued and clamped, checked for square and left to set.

FITTING THE DOORS

Once set, the faces of the door frames were sanded, and the completed doors fitted to the opening, leaving about 1mm (3⁄64in) clearance all round, which would be adjusted to 2mm (5⁄64in) on the final fitting. Full-length piano hinges were used on these doors as they give extra strength, leave a neat line, and even out the load. The hinges did not need to be recessed and a self-centring hinge pilot drill, along with my excellent power screwdriver, made short work of fitting them. The positions for the hinges were marked on the inside face of the cupboard, and a cutting gauge was used to scribe the line for the screws. The doors were held at the correct height by a metal rule, wedged as a spacer underneath them.

The line for the screws was centred in the hinge screw hole and the self-centring pilot drill was used to drill a pilot hole at the top, middle, and bottom of each hinge. The screws were driven home and the door was checked for fit, some adjustments were made and the remaining holes were drilled. Brass double-ball catches were fitted to the top and bottom, and the springs were adjusted to give a satisfying 'clunk-click'.

FINISH

This piece was a classic case for power sanding. Without the belt and orbital sanders the preparation of these large surfaces would have been an expensive and boring chore. Virtually all the sanding was done on the individual components before assembly. The final sanding was done using a palm sander and hand blocks.

As with all the other Shaker furniture I had made, Barford's Aqua Cote satin finish was used to maintain the pale creaminess of the sycamore. It is a water-based acrylic floor varnish which dries quickly and hardens to a tough satin finish. I applied three coats with a paint pad, rubbing down between coats to de-nib.

In order to allow its scent to permeate freely, the cedar of Lebanon was not sealed. Masking tape was used to protect the edges when the varnish was applied to the sycamore.

Photo 5 – **Deep-sawing the panels for the doors**

Photo 6 – **Fielding the panels with a vertical cutter in a router table**

DRAWER PULLS – FUMED OAK

The oak pulls had been made at the same time as the pulls and pegs for the other items in the set (see pages 102 and 108). They were all turned on the lathe, sanded to a finish, placed in a plastic tub with some 890 ammonia, and left for 24 hours to darken. As I have stated in previous articles and will again re-emphasise, great care is needed when handling ammonia as it stings the skin, especially open cuts, and has a particularly harmful effect on the eyes – even the slightest contact is capable of causing permanent damage, so wear eye protection and rubber gloves, and, if possible, do the whole process outside so that any fumes disperse into the atmosphere.

Once fumed, the drawer pulls were left for a few hours to ensure all the ammonia had dispersed.

The fuming kit

CONCLUSION

All in all, the wardrobe was a fairly simple but very rewarding piece to make and complemented my client's now completed Shaker bedroom set delightfully. However, I would not like to have attempted it without my trusty power tools and, having said that, another pair of hands would have been useful at times! If only...

ROUTER USEFUL SUPPLIERS

●Tanselli wafers:
The Woodcut Trading Company
80 Ninfield Road
Bexhill-on-Sea
East Sussex TN39 5BB
Tel: 0800 378027

●Aqua Cote Acrylic Varnish:
Ardley Works
London Road
Billericay
Essex CM12 9HP
Barford's - 01277 622050

ROUTER RECOMMENDED READING

Making Shaker Furniture, Barry Jackson, GMC
In the Shaker Style, Best of Fine Woodworking Magazine, Taunton
The Shaker Legacy, Christian Becksvoort, Taunton
Kevin Ley's Furniture Projects, Kevin Ley, GMC

●All the above titles are available from GMC Publications Ltd, 166 High Street, Lewes, East Sussex BN7 1XU
Tel: 01273 488005

METRIC/IMPERIAL CONVERSION TABLE

MILLIMETRES TO INCHES

mm	in	mm	in	mm	in	mm	in
1	0.03937	26	1.02362	60	2.36221	310	12.2047
2	0.07874	27	1.06299	70	2.75591	320	12.5984
3	0.11811	28	1.10236	80	3.14961	330	12.9921
4	0.15748	29	1.14173	90	3.54331	340	13.3858
5	0.19685	30	1.18110	100	3.93701	350	13.7795
6	0.23622					360	14.1732
7	0.27559	31	1.22047	110	4.33071	370	14.5669
8	0.31496	32	1.25984	120	4.72441	380	14.9606
9	0.35433	33	1.29921	130	5.11811	390	15.3543
10	0.39370	34	1.33858	140	5.51181	400	15.7480
		35	1.37795	150	5.90552		
11	0.43307	36	1.41732	160	6.29922	410	16.1417
12	0.47244	37	1.45669	170	6.69292	420	16.5354
13	0.51181	38	1.49606	180	7.08662	430	16.9291
14	0.55118	39	1.53543	190	7.48032	440	17.3228
15	0.59055	40	1.57480	200	7.87402	450	17.7165
16	0.62992					460	18.1103
17	0.66929	41	1.61417	210	8.26772	470	18.5040
18	0.70866	42	1.65354	220	8.66142	480	18.8977
19	0.74803	43	1.69291	230	9.05513	490	19.2914
20	0.78740	44	1.73228	240	9.44883	500	19.6851
		45	1.77165	250	9.84252		
21	0.82677	46	1.81103	260	10.2362	600	23.6221
22	0.86614	47	1.85040	270	10.6299	700	27.5591
23	0.90551	48	1.88977	280	11.0236	800	31.4961
24	0.94488	49	1.92914	290	11.4173	900	35.4331
25	0.98425	50	1.96851	300	11.8110	1000	39.3701

IMPERIAL/METRIC CONVERSION TABLE

INCHES TO MILLIMETRES

in	mm	in	mm	in	mm	in	mm
1/64	0.3969	5/8	15.8750	2¾	69.8501	33	838.202
1/32	0.7937			2⅞	73.0251	34	863.602
3/64	1.1906	41/64	16.2719	3	76.2002	35	889.002
1/16	1.5875	21/32	16.6687			36 (3ft)	914.402
5/64	1.9844	43/64	17.0656	3⅛	79.3752		
3/32	2.3812	11/16	17.4625	3¼	82.5502	37	939.802
7/64	2.7781	45/64	17.8594	3⅜	85.7252	38	965.202
1/8	3.1750	23/32	18.2562	3½	88.9002	39	990.602
		47/64	18.6531	3⅝	92.0752	40	1016.00
9/64	3.5719	3/4	19.0500	3¾	95.2502	41	1041.40
5/32	3.9687			3⅞	98.4252	42	1066.80
11/64	4.3656	49/64	19.4469	4	101.500	43	1092.20
3/16	4.7625	25/32	19.8437			44	1117.60
13/64	5.1594	51/64	20.2406	5	127.000	45	1143.00
7/32	5.5562	13/16	20.6375	6	152.400	46	1158.40
15/64	5.9531	53/64	21.0344	7	177.800	47	1193.80
1/4	6.3500	27/32	21.4312	8	203.200	48 (4ft)	1219.20
		55/64	21.8281	9	228.600		
17/64	6.7469	7/8	22.2250	10	254.001	49	1244.60
9/32	7.1437			11	279.401	50	1270.00
19/64	7.5406	57/64	22.6219	12 (1ft)	304.801	51	1295.40
5/16	7.9375	29/32	23.0187			52	1320.80
21/64	8.3344	59/64	23.4156	13	330.201	53	1346.20
11/32	8.7312	15/16	23.8125	14	355.601	54	1371.60
23/64	9.1281	61/64	24.2094	15	381.001	55	1397.00
3/8	9.5250	31/32	24.6062	16	406.401	56	1422.20
		63/64	25.0031	17	431.801	57	1447.80
25/64	9.9219	1	25.4001	18	457.201	58	1473.20
13/32	10.3187			19	482.601	59	1498.60
27/64	10.7156	1⅛	28.5751	20	508.001	60 (5ft)	1524.00
7/16	11.1125	1¼	31.7501	21	533.401		
29/64	11.5094	1⅜	34.9251	22	558.801	61	1549.40
15/32	11.9062	1½	38.1001	23	584.201	62	1574.80
31/64	12.3031	1⅝	41.2751	24 (2ft)	609.601	63	1600.20
1/2	12.7000	1¾	44.4501			64	1625.60
		1⅞	47.6251	25	635.001	65	1651.00
33/64	13.0969	2	50.8001	26	660.401	66	1676.40
17/32	13.4937			27	685.801	67	1701.80
35/64	13.8906	2⅛	53.9751	28	711.201	68	1727.20
9/16	14.2875	2¼	57.1501	29	736.601	69	1752.60
37/64	14.6844	2⅜	60.3251	30	762.002	70	1778.00
19/32	15.0812	2½	63.5001	31	787.402	71	1803.40
39/64	15.4781	2⅝	66.6751	32	812.802	72 (6ft)	1828.80

ACKNOWLEDGEMENTS

It still amazes me that I enjoy writing for GMC so much – after all, I left the RAF because I didn't like staff work. Everyone is so friendly, helpful, and hospitable, from Jill with her unfailing cheerfulness and pleasant greetings whenever I call GMC, to Sule who sends the cheques.

I would like to thank particularly Stuart Lawson, editor of *The Router* and *New Woodworking*, and Colin Eden-Eadon, editor of *Furniture & Cabinetmaking*, for their ability to turn my raw material into the superbly produced articles that make the GMC woodworking magazines market leaders, and from which this book has come. Also Ian Hall and Simon Rodway for their brilliant illustrations, which make the construction so clear.

For turning the articles into a book, thanks to April McCroskie for her planning and organisation, Stephen Haynes for his editing, and both for their advice.

My thanks also go to Paul Richardson for getting me writing in the first place, for his sound advice and cheerful patience in our negotiations; to Jonathan Phillips for selling the first book, and hopefully this one; and to Alan Phillips for financing the whole show.

Most of all, my thanks to my wife Yvonne for her advice and constructive criticism, help and encouragement. Her assistance with the photography is invaluable, and her patience in putting up with me, and all the sawdust, remarkable!

ABOUT THE AUTHOR

Kevin Ley retired from the Royal Air Force in 1987 and developed his hobby of furniture making into a successful business, designing and making bespoke pieces in North Yorkshire. He has been writing for GMC for several years, and now lives with his artist and teacher wife, Yvonne, in their picturesque cottage in a South Shropshire wooded nature reserve.

Kevin divides his time between making furniture in his workshop next to the house, writing and photography for the GMC woodworking magazines, and working with Yvonne on the improvements to their cottage, and maintenance of their large garden. Both enjoy fast cars, reading, talking, music, sampling the delights of the local eating and watering holes, keeping fit, and being in charge.

INDEX

TITLES AVAILABLE FROM
GMC PUBLICATIONS
BOOKS

Woodcarving

Beginning Woodcarving — *GMC Publications*
Carving Architectural Detail in Wood: The Classical Tradition — *Frederick Wilbur*
Carving Birds & Beasts — *GMC Publications*
Carving the Human Figure: Studies in Wood and Stone — *Dick Onians*
Carving Nature: Wildlife Studies in Wood — *Frank Fox-Wilson*
Carving on Turning — *Chris Pye*
Celtic Carved Lovespoons: 30 Patterns — *Sharon Littley & Clive Griffin*
Decorative Woodcarving (New Edition) — *Jeremy Williams*
Elements of Woodcarving — *Chris Pye*
Essential Woodcarving Techniques — *Dick Onians*
Lettercarving in Wood: A Practical Course — *Chris Pye*
Making & Using Working Drawings for Realistic Model Animals — *Basil F. Fordham*
Power Tools for Woodcarving — *David Tippey*
Relief Carving in Wood: A Practical Introduction — *Chris Pye*
Understanding Woodcarving in the Round — *GMC Publications*
Woodcarving: A Foundation Course — *Zoë Gertner*
Woodcarving for Beginners — *GMC Publications*
Woodcarving Tools, Materials & Equipment (New Edition in 2 vols.) — *Chris Pye*

Woodturning

Adventures in Woodturning — *David Springett*
Bowl Turning Techniques Masterclass — *Tony Boase*
Chris Child's Projects for Woodturners — *Chris Child*
Colouring Techniques for Woodturners — *Jan Sanders*
Contemporary Turned Wood: New Perspectives in a Rich Tradition — *Ray Leier, Jan Peters & Kevin Wallace*
The Craftsman Woodturner — *Peter Child*
Decorating Turned Wood: The Maker's Eye — *Liz & Michael O'Donnell*
Decorative Techniques for Woodturners — *Hilary Bowen*
Green Woodwork — *Mike Abbott*
Illustrated Woodturning Techniques — *John Hunnex*
Intermediate Woodturning Projects — *GMC Publications*
Keith Rowley's Woodturning Projects — *Keith Rowley*
Making Screw Threads in Wood — *Fred Holder*
Turned Boxes: 50 Designs — *Chris Stott*
Turning Green Wood — *Michael O'Donnell*
Turning Pens and Pencils — *Kip Christensen & Rex Burningham*
Useful Woodturning Projects — *GMC Publications*
Woodturning: Bowls, Platters, Hollow Forms, Vases, Vessels, Bottles, Flasks, Tankards, Plates — *GMC Publications*
Woodturning: A Foundation Course (New Edition) — *Keith Rowley*
Woodturning: A Fresh Approach — *Robert Chapman*
Woodturning: An Individual Approach — *Dave Regester*
Woodturning: A Source Book of Shapes — *John Hunnex*
Woodturning Masterclass — *Tony Boase*
Woodturning Techniques — *GMC Publications*

Woodworking

Advanced Scrollsaw Projects — *GMC Publications*
Beginning Picture Marquetry — *Lawrence Threadgold*
Bird Boxes and Feeders for the Garden — *Dave Mackenzie*
Celtic Carved Lovespoons: 30 Patterns — *Sharon Littley & Clive Griffin*
Celtic Woodcraft — *Glenda Bennett*
Complete Woodfinishing (Revised Edition) — *Ian Hosker*
David Charlesworth's Furniture-Making Techniques — *David Charlesworth*
David Charlesworth's Furniture-Making Techniques – Volume 2 — *David Charlesworth*
The Encyclopedia of Joint Making — *Terrie Noll*
Furniture-Making Projects for the Wood Craftsman — *GMC Publications*
Furniture-Making Techniques for the Wood Craftsman — *GMC Publications*
Furniture Projects with the Router — *Kevin Ley*
Furniture Restoration (Practical Crafts) — *Kevin Jan Bonner*
Furniture Restoration: A Professional at Work — *John Lloyd*
Furniture Restoration and Repair for Beginners — *Kevin Jan Bonner*
Furniture Restoration Workshop — *Kevin Jan Bonner*
Green Woodwork — *Mike Abbott*
Intarsia: 30 Patterns for the Scrollsaw — *John Everett*
Kevin Ley's Furniture Projects — *Kevin Ley*
Making Chairs and Tables — *GMC Publications*
Making Chairs and Tables – Volume 2 — *GMC Publications*
Making Classic English Furniture — *Paul Richardson*
Making Heirloom Boxes — *Peter Lloyd*
Making Screw Threads in Wood — *Fred Holder*
Making Shaker Furniture — *Barry Jackson*
Making Woodwork Aids and Devices — *Robert Wearing*
Mastering the Router — *Ron Fox*
Pine Furniture Projects for the Home — *Dave Mackenzie*
Practical Scrollsaw Patterns — *John Everett*
Router Magic: Jigs, Fixtures and Tricks to Unleash your Router's Full Potential — *Bill Hylton*
Router Tips & Techniques — *Robert Wearing*
Routing: A Workshop Handbook — *Anthony Bailey*
Routing for Beginners — *Anthony Bailey*
Sharpening: The Complete Guide — *Jim Kingshott*
Sharpening Pocket Reference Book — *Jim Kingshott*
Simple Scrollsaw Projects — *GMC Publications*
Space-Saving Furniture Projects — *Dave Mackenzie*
Stickmaking: A Complete Course — *Andrew Jones & Clive George*
Stickmaking Handbook — *Andrew Jones & Clive George*
Storage Projects for the Router — *GMC Publications*
Test Reports: *The Router* and *Furniture & Cabinetmaking* — *GMC Publications*
Veneering: A Complete Course — *Ian Hosker*
Veneering Handbook — *Ian Hosker*
Woodfinishing Handbook (Practical Crafts) — *Ian Hosker*
Woodworking with the Router: Professional Router Techniques any Woodworker can Use — *Bill Hylton & Fred Matlack*

Upholstery

The Upholsterer's Pocket Reference Book — *David James*
Upholstery: A Complete Course (Revised Edition) — *David James*
Upholstery Restoration — *David James*
Upholstery Techniques & Projects — *David James*
Upholstery Tips and Hints — *David James*

Toymaking

Scrollsaw Toy Projects — *Ivor Carlyle*
Scrollsaw Toys for All Ages — *Ivor Carlyle*

Dolls' Houses and Miniatures

1/12 Scale Character Figures for the Dolls' House — *James Carrington*
Americana in 1/12 Scale: 50 Authentic Projects — *Joanne Ogreenc & Mary Lou Santovec*